Praise for *The Philosophy of Dark Paganism*

"Frater Tenebris sheds fresh light (yes, pun intended) into Dark Paganism. This book is both a comparative work of the early influencers of the Dark Paganism movement as well as a well-crafted personal exploration into the subject, making this an ideal modern reference guide for those struggling to find their own unique balance." —**John J. Coughlin, author of *Out of the Shadows***

"Before embarking on any spiritual path, a seeker must understand the foundation upon which their practice is built. *The Philosophy of Dark Paganism* draws upon the wisdom of experts past and present to create an extensively researched exploration into the why and how of Dark Paganism. Frater Tenebris dissects this controversial and mostly secret philosophy layer by layer, providing a solid framework for beginner and seasoned Pagans. A lifetime of deep study and experience is condensed into this work, making it a valuable source of knowledge and a useful learning resource." —**Kate Freuler, author of *Of Blood and Bones***

"Differing from 'black' magick or baneful sorcery, this deeply intelligent and honest book explores darker magickal elements through a lens of Neopaganism. Focused on self-development by way of shadow, the reader is given an opportunity to cohesively improve themselves and search for life's greater purpose. I have never experienced a book like this. It is packed to the brim with educational references and citations, all of which boil down to a metaphysical perspective. The author's refreshing approach encompasses solid academic history and philosophy alongside practical theory aimed toward self-empowerment. The shroud of darkness is enchanting… Why not take a peek?" —**Raven Digitalis, author of *Esoteric Empathy***

T0274833

THE PHiLOSOPHY OF
DARK
PAGANiSM

About the Author

Frater Tenebris is a public speaker, blogger, philosopher, and practitioner of Dark Paganism. He's a member of the Covenant of Unitarian Universalist Pagans (CUUPS) and the Tsubaki Grand Shrine of America. He lives in a quiet neighborhood in a Texas suburb with his wife and two dogs.

THE PHILOSOPHY OF
DARK
PAGANISM

WISDOM & MAGICK TO CULTIVATE THE SELF

FRATER TENEBRIS

LLEWELLYN PUBLICATIONS
WOODBURY, MINNESOTA

FIRST EDITION
First Printing, 2022

Book design by Christine Ha
Cover design by Shannon McKuhen
Interior art (pages 18, 19, 22, 23, 205 & 208) by the Llewellyn Art Department
Tarot card illustrations (pages 28, 36, 37 & 201) are based on those contained in *The Pictorial Key to the Tarot* by Arthur Edward Waite, published by William Rider & Son Ltd., London 1911.

Llewellyn Publications is a registered trademark of Llewellyn Worldwide Ltd.

Library of Congress Cataloging-in-Publication Data
Names: Tenebris, Frater, author. | Storm, Marysa, editor.
Title: The philosophy of dark paganism : wisdom & magick to cultivate the self / Frater Tenebris.
Description: First edition. | Woodbury, Minnesota : Llewellyn Worldwide, Ltd, 2022. | Includes bibliographical references. | Summary: "Discover a life-changing spiritual paradigm that honors the divine Self and strives to elevate it to a higher state of being"—Provided by publisher.
Identifiers: LCCN 2022024111 (print) | LCCN 2022024112 (ebook) | ISBN 9780738772608 | ISBN 9780738772653 (ebook)
Subjects: LCSH: Spiritual life--Miscellanea. | Self—Religious aspects—Miscellanea. | Paganism. | Light and darkness—Miscellanea. | Magic.
Classification: LCC BF1999 .T366 2022 (print) | LCC BF1999 (ebook) | DDC 133.9—dc23/eng/20220729
LC record available at https://lccn.loc.gov/2022024111
LC ebook record available at https://lccn.loc.gov/2022024112

Llewellyn Publications
A Division of Llewellyn Worldwide Ltd.
2143 Wooddale Drive
Woodbury, MN 55125-2989
www.llewellyn.com

Printed in the United States of America

This book is dedicated to my father, who would take me to the library every weekend and taught me a love of learning and living virtuously.

CONTENTS

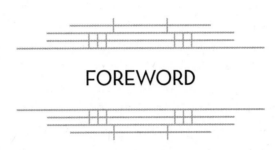

FOREWORD

Back in the late '90s, when I was struggling to find my own spiritual balance in Paganism, I had no idea I was about to start something that would take on a life of its own. At the time I felt very much alone and out of place. There seemed to be a phobia toward anything that hinted of darkness or (gasp) the dreaded Left Hand Path. In hindsight, I am sure the "satanic panic" of the '80s and early '90s set the stage for very defensive Pagans battling with that stigma and led to a bit of overcompensation, to say the least! But as a young man just coming into his own spiritually, I felt all the more isolated and confused. Somewhere I seemed to have taken a bit of a detour. Was I still a Pagan? Did it even matter? In my youth I was still so fixated on labels and conditioned from my Christian upbringing to think I had to follow something "official." But if I had questioned the faith I was raised in, why could I not question the faith I was drawn to?

It was from this confusion that I began to write small essays, purely for myself to better organize and articulate my thoughts. Those essays eventually took the form of chapters, and thus *Out of the Shadows* came into being. When the book was released, I was expecting the worst. I envisioned angry emails, bad reviews, and generally becoming an outcast in the local Pagan community. But that was not what happened. Suddenly I began to get emails and written letters of thanks. I had put into words something that others lurking in the shadows of Paganism had been feeling. As it turned out, none of us were as alone as we had believed.

As I began to tour and speak at various gatherings (not an easy task for an introvert like myself), I had the opportunity to meet these kindred spirits.

What intrigued me was how diverse we could be when it came to details of belief and practice, and yet we were still able to relate on a deeper level. Dark Paganism is very much more a mindset than a specific path or tradition, and I was always careful not to share the details of my personal practices in fear of influencing how others would express themselves.

That was a long time ago (like "before iPhone" long time ago), and thanks to the internet, Paganism has become extremely diverse and Dark Pagans abound in various forms and names. Others have since shared their perspectives on the subject—some I feel aligned to, and some that make me cringe, and both have their place. Each perspective offers the reader an opportunity to explore how it applies to THEM. After all, I did not write *Out of the Shadows* to tell readers what to do. I threw out a lot of ideas to see how it landed and to encourage others to explore for themselves.

Over the years many have written to me asking for advice on how to get started in Dark Paganism, and I am sure most found my response a bit…unexpected. I had no "dark spells" (whatever those are) to share or mysterious rites and practices to offer. Instead, I suggested a few books I personally found useful (such as the works of Jung and Ouspensky) and said the best thing they could do is learn critical thinking skills and embrace a consistent meditation practice. Independent thinking and self-reflection, to me, are the greatest skills for anyone who walks a dark path. I dare say they are essential for any practitioner of magic. Are you walking your path, or buying into someone else's approach? Are you changing the world to conform to your will, or are you conforming to the will of others? Why do you do what you do and believe what you believe? It is that journey of self-exploration and expression that is the hallmark of those who walk the darker paths. It is what unites us despite our varied outward appearances and practices. We have all embarked on a journey of self-discovery and self-transformation and have come into our own in the process.

This is why, ultimately, I have always been more interested in what YOU were doing with these ideas. How do they reflect in your magic and life? I did not care how gothic you looked, or how cool your tools were, or how spooky your rites could get. I wanted to know about your journey and struggles. Some may argue this had made me a good mentor, but in all honesty, it was just as much for selfish reasons. You see, I am painfully aware as humans our perception will always be limited. We are all wearing blinders of some form, and while

I have spent decades learning to recognize and see past my blind spots, I will never be fully free of them. So it is from hearing of your journeys that I often find inspiration and fresh insights to keep me out of boxed-in thinking. I may not always agree with it all, but it has never failed to make me think. Besides, who am I to judge your path? While some have dubbed me the father of Dark Paganism, I only refer to myself as that in jest. As I quickly found out, I was never alone—I just helped to get the conversation going.

So here we are, twenty-two years or so since I first released *Out of the Shadows*, and it excites me to see what Frater Tenebris is doing here. This is exactly what I like to see—others sharing their own insights, learnings, and practices. My advice to the reader, which may sound heretical for an author, is not to take any of us too seriously. Play with these ideas. Question them. Take nothing at face value. My challenge to you is to not base your findings on assumption. Get your hands dirty. I have found myself humbled many times in my life by stepping out of my armchair and actually doing the work only to find my assumptions and opinions wrong. How glorious it is that the universe is far more interesting and expansive than we give it credit for! The greatest trapping on a dark path is the ego. As great and profound as we can be, we are still human, and always growing. It is when you feel you know it all, or have reached some pinnacle of perfection above others, that you can be sure you took a wrong turn along the way. My parting advice is this: Get over yourself, stay curious, and, most importantly, have fun!

—John J. Coughlin
New York
February 2022

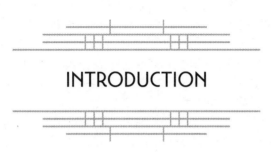

INTRODUCTION

The Western world has been fertile ground for alternative spiritual movements for a long time. For example, America saw new spiritualities appear during the first Great Awakening and later in the two subsequent Great Awakenings, which stretched into the early twentieth century. After the Second World War, the Western world saw the birth of other new spiritual movements, which exploded in numbers during the counterculture of the 1960s.

New spiritual movements didn't cease to appear after the 1960s. This book is an introduction to a recent spiritual movement called Dark Paganism. Dark Paganism is a positive, life-affirming spiritual philosophy centered on honoring and cultivating the Self.

For forty-plus years, ever since my early teen years in the 1970s, I had bounced around from various spiritual traditions, some Pagan while others not. Never did I find one that was a good fit. Then I learned of Dark Paganism in John J. Coughlin's landmark book *Out of the Shadows: An Exploration of Dark Paganism*. Something about his book resonated with me. Then, through years of meditation, magick, and applying his philosophy to my life, I gradually understood the truth of his dark spiritual philosophy.

It's because of Dark Paganism that I learned to trust myself. Years of indoctrination by anti-Self traditions had left me with self-doubt and anxiety. I began to accept my True Self and to live accordingly. As a result, my confidence increased, and the day-to-day anxiety I suffered significantly reduced. These improvements in my life drove me to write this book.

Dark Paganism is a spiritual philosophy and not a religion. While there are historical wisdom traditions that incorporate Dark Pagan philosophical elements, Dark Paganism is a philosophy as understood by the ancient Greeks. The centrality of reason and rational analysis, rather than faith and revelation, was the distinguishing feature of ancient Greek philosophy.[1] Dark Paganism is a philosophy because reason, not revelation, rests at its core. Even when a Dark Pagan incorporates spiritual exercises and beliefs of otherworldly matters, as the Neoplatonists did, Dark Pagans accept these matters based on rational judgment rather than blind faith.

Philosophy to the ancient Greeks was a way of life.[2] Dark Pagan philosophy shares this attribute with philosophy in that it's more than theory. Dark Paganism is a way of life.

While Dark Paganism is a philosophy in the Greek's spirit, it's not a descendant of any known classical school. Dark Paganism isn't Stoicism, skepticism, or even Neoplatonism. One will not find Dark Paganism among the various philosophical schools. The nearest one might say that Dark Paganism is an eclectic school of philosophy in the same spirit as the third-century-CE philosopher Potamo of Alexandria, who was known to adopt ideas from multiple philosophical schools.

Dark Paganism draws upon more than Greek philosophy. It also includes contemporary philosophy, such as existentialism and absurdism. As part of contemporary Paganism, Dark Paganism, as presented here, incorporates concepts from the great Eastern wisdom traditions, including Hinduism, Buddhism, Shinto, Taoism, and Confucianism. European thought, such as pre-Christian Paganism, medieval alchemy, and esotericism, also provides insight. Dark Paganism is highly eclectic and syncretic.

Because of its emphasis on the Self, Dark Paganism is a deeply personal and individualized philosophy. While there are common elements found among the various Dark Pagan writers and practitioners, each person has a unique take on Dark Paganism and emphasizes specific details more than others. Those familiar with the topic, or those exploring other similar writings, will recognize my work as being in the same family as other Dark Pagan writers. However, you will also notice the differences in my understanding of it.

1. Cooper, *Pursuits of Wisdom*, 17.
2. Cooper, *Pursuits of Wisdom*, 7.

Syncretism, Modernity, and Risk

Syncretism and eclecticism come with inherent risks. Specifically, there is a severe risk of cultural appropriation. Blogger Courtney Weber defines cultural appropriation as "the misuse, and/or profiting off the culture of another, particularly of a colonizing culture taking practices from an indigenous culture."[3] Eclectics, like myself, have to take special care to avoid this misstep. One method is to remember that principles are universal, while tools are culturally specific. For example, burning incense is an ancient method found in numerous cultures and is used to cleanse and purify, making it universal. However, the current popularity of using white sage in smudging is cultural appropriation. The solution for the eclectic Pagan is to use an alternative, such as myrrh or frankincense, to cleanse a space or object.

Cultural appropriation isn't the only challenge. Living in Western society, one tends to look to science to justify spiritual matters. This practice arose as part of modernity in which any form of legitimacy for a concept demanded a scientific explanation. Modernity is a totalitarian belief system in that it tries to dominate all aspects of a person. Any idea without a materialistic explanation is considered a primitive superstition and subject to ridicule. Therefore, it's common to find writers attempting to explain metaphysical concepts using scientific language.

The practice of explaining metaphysics with science isn't new. Éliphas Lévi's *Transcendental Magic* is full of explanations of the occult by misapplying late nineteenth-century science. This practice of explaining esoterica and the occult away as being a yet undiscovered science is termed *positive occultism*.[4]

Indeed, some scientific theories and observations are exciting from a Pagan perspective. Quantum physics and the theories explaining laboratory results are especially intriguing. One can't help but begin to wonder as they read the latest theory or observation. Might this theory prove our beliefs?

This tendency to be drawn into using cutting-edge science as proof of metaphysical belief is a modern-day error. Druid priest and author John Beckett said it best: "Claiming scientific backing or proof for spiritual ideas where none

---

3. Weber, "The Nightmare Before Christmas and Lessons on Cultural Appropriation."
4. Webb, *Energy Magick of the Vampyre*, 196.

exists isn't just bad science, it's also bad religion."[5] While the scientific method is very efficient in understanding the physical world, it's woefully ill-equipped to study metaphysical topics. Possibly someday in the far future, science and technology will have advanced to a degree where scientists can systematically study esoteric matters in the same way they currently examine bacteria under a microscope.

The fact that science is limited concerning metaphysics doesn't mean that scientific knowledge and theories can't be helpful. Certain esoteric principles, which I will explore later, teach us that understanding the physical world provides us with an indirect picture of grand Cosmic matters. Another way science can be helpful is that many scientific theories can serve as metaphors in describing esoteric phenomena.

The fact that the scientific method cannot currently explain metaphysical matters doesn't contradict Dark Pagans' use of reason and rational thought. The scientific method, or natural philosophy in classical Greek philosophical terminology, is only one tool in the philosopher's toolbox. Reason, or philosophical reflection, is well suited for studying metaphysical issues even though they're still outside the reach of contemporary scientific methods.

While we discuss the use of reason, we need to remember the importance of mystery. As I present the various beliefs about Dark Paganism and related metaphysical ideas, I must acknowledge that more is unknown than known. Any legitimate philosophy should recognize that some questions currently have no answers. It's the height of hubris for anyone to claim that they have sufficient wisdom and knowledge to answer all questions. Though Dark Paganism as a worldview provides answers to many existential and esoteric questions, it cannot explain everything, nor does it claim to do so. As Albert Einstein wrote, "The more I learn, the more I realize how much I don't know."[6]

Mystery is a good thing. It reminds us of the wonder of our brief time as embodied beings. While we shouldn't shrug off every difficult question as a mystery, neither should we believe that every question has an answer. This book aims to embrace what we cannot answer without hubris and acknowledge the limitations of what I think I can answer.

---

5. Beckett, *The Path of Paganism*, 33.
6. Kenny, *Ahead of the Curve*, 108.

About This Book

Niccolò Machiavelli, in his infamous how-to manual for aspiring tyrants, *The Prince*, wrote, "There is nothing more difficult to take in hand, more perilous to conduct, or more uncertain in its success than to take the lead in the introduction of a new order of things."[7] That's true for more than just political power. It also applies to presenting new philosophies.

Self-help and self-care have become commodified and cliché. There are mountains of books and programs about self-care available to you. This book is not one of them. Instead, this book is about a philosophical reorientation concerning the individual and their relationship with others.

You will notice that I provide many sources. I do so even at the risk of reducing my authority. I reference these resources because I'm deeply in debt to many great minds. I could never have written this book without their works, and they deserve credit. As Isaac Newton wrote, "If I have seen further [than you and Descartes], it is by standing on the shoulders of Giants."[8]

However, all of these great minds are very human with flaws. Sometimes these flaws are dramatic. For example, the work of H. P. Lovecraft has inspired numerous writers over the years. However, Lovecraft was such an extreme racist and anti-Semite that he went beyond even many others of his time.[9] As vulgar as Lovecraft was, I will still reference him and his work when appropriate.

We live in an age when the character of every individual in the public eye is under scrutiny. There's some good in this. At times, we have gone so far as to ignore the humanity of some individuals and deify them. A good example is the US Founding Fathers, to whom we have built monuments on the same scale as ancient Rome. Recognizing the flaws of our public individuals helps us not elevate them to unrealistic heights. However, many still slide through life without consequences for their actions.

Unfortunately, some have gone to the extreme of throwing the baby out with the bathwater. Some want to declare anyone *persona non grata* when their flaws become public. I disagree with this practice. Former president Barack Obama said, "The world is messy, there are ambiguities. People who do really

---

7. de Jager, "The Tarde Challenge," 31.
8. Bartlett, *Bartlett's Familiar Quotations*, 313.
9. Guran, *The Mammoth Book of Cthulhu*, xv–xvii.

good stuff have flaws."[10] He's correct. There will always be writers with serious flaws, but their works are so valuable that we must not ignore their contributions. Therefore, I sometimes reference or quote someone despite the severe character flaws they may have.

As I write this, the academic world is debating the use of trigger warnings. A trigger warning is an up-front statement that a subject of study may contain distressing content. Trigger warnings arose from therapeutic settings to aid those with PTSD. Today these appear in a variety of nontherapeutic settings. It's not my intention to address the usefulness of trigger warnings outside therapeutic settings. But I will say, out of courtesy to those readers who consider trigger warnings helpful, that hopefully the last few paragraphs about references and quotes from individuals with severe character flaws are sufficient to constitute a trigger warning.

I use gender-neutral language throughout this book. This style of writing is extremely new. Historically, most English authors wrote with a masculine gender bias. Unfortunately, many of the quotes used in this book will reflect this historical bias. I don't change their words, nor do I avoid them. I quote them as written.

In part 1, *Dwelling in the Dark,* I review Paganism's basics and the various definitions of the movement. To understand Dark Paganism, we must first understand the larger movement of which it is a part. Therefore, this book begins with a general look at modern Paganism. This part also provides chapters about the basics of Dark Paganism and the source for the nine Dark Pagan principles.

Part 2 is titled *The Dark Shall Be Light.* This part covers each of the nine philosophical principles of Dark Paganism with a brief essay on each.

The third and final part is *Dark Enough.* This part explores Dark Paganism's insights into aesthetics, esoterica, gods, magick theory, and reincarnation. I also explore whether Dark Paganism is part of the Left-Hand Path. This part includes my last comments, along with an appendix and recommended reading section.

Dear reader, I now invite you to enter into the mysterious and fantastic world of Dark Paganism.

---

10. Cillizza, "What Barack Obama Gets Exactly Right about Our Toxic 'Cancel' Culture."

PART I
DWELLING IN THE DARK

"The moon will guide you through the night with her brightness, but she will always dwell in the darkness, in order to be seen." [11]

—SHANNON L. ALDER

11. Ahlquist, *Moon Spells*, 97.

I

UNDERSTANDING PAGANISM

The philosophy of Dark Paganism exists with a broader community of contemporary Paganism. To understand Dark Paganism, we must first have a good understanding of Paganism itself.

According to scholar of religious studies Huston Smith, if one strips away the various tropes of different religions, such as Hinduism, Buddhism, Christianity, or Islam, their underlying beliefs are revealed. What's left is a collection of core beliefs that, when taken together, make up what he calls a "wisdom tradition."[12] Therefore, we begin our study by looking behind the tropes to understand the wisdom tradition of Paganism.

The Pagan Wisdom Tradition

The origin of the very word *pagan* is controversial. Historically, the term *pagan* was derogatory, used primarily by Christian missionaries about Indigenous religions, and it is still used by many to carry the same meaning.[13] The most widely referenced origin is that the English word is from the Latin *paganus*, which meant one who was a "peasant" or "rustic."[14] However, according to historian Ronald Hutton, *paganus* meant "civilian" rather than "peasant."[15] Pierre Chuvin, Hellenist and historian, provides an alternative source to the origin. According to Chuvin, *pagan* is from an older word than *paganus*. He states that

---

12. Smith, *The World's Religions*, 5.
13. York, *Pagan Theology*, 12.
14. Bonewits, *Neopagan Rites*, 201.
15. York, *Pagan Theology*, 6.

the Latin root was *pagani*, which means "people of the place" and someone who preserved local traditions.[16]

According to Brendan Myers, author of *The Earth, the Gods, and the Soul*, the modern application of *Pagan* describes "a person whose religion is not Abrahamic; that is a person whose religion is not Judaism, Christian, or Islam."[17] Myers limits Paganism to the West, including Europe, the Mediterranean, and the Near East. On the other hand, Michael York, author of *Pagan Theology: Paganism as a World Religion*, asserts that Western Paganism, both classic and contemporary, is part of a larger global Pagan religion that includes Chinese folk religions, Shinto, and various Indigenous religions.[18]

A lesser-used term for Paganism is neopaganism, which wizard Isaac Bonewits coined. Bonewits begins his definition by limiting Neopaganism's origins to no further back than roughly 1940. According to Bonewits, Neopaganism blends elements of various Indigenous religions, historical and living, with modern Western, or Aquarian, ideas minus monotheism and dualism.[19] In many ways, Bonewits's definition of Neopaganism resembles the description of the contemporary retropunk movements, such as dieselpunk, which blend modern ideas with the tropes of the past.

Wouter J. Hanegraaff, professor of history of Hermetic philosophy and related currents at the University of Amsterdam, describes Neopaganism as a product of the counterculture of the 1960s. According to Hanegraaff, Neopaganism "exists in many countries as a vital subculture that celebrates diversity and emphasizes natural ecological lifestyles." Hanegraaff also labels Neopaganism as being part of esotericism.[20]

The term *esotericism* is also controversial among many scholars because, according to Hanegraaff, the word is retroactively applied to categorize various cultural trends and currents without a solid definition. *Esoteric* (*eso* meaning "inside") is from the eighteenth-century German word *esoterik*.[21] The French

---

16. York, *Pagan Theology*, 12.
17. Myers, *The Earth, the Gods, and the Soul*, 2.
18. York, *Pagan Theology*, 8.
19. Bonewits, *Neopagan Rites*, 5.
20. Hanegraaff, *Western Esotericism*, 44.
21. Faivre, *Access to Western Esotericism*, 4.

later picked the word up during the early nineteenth century as *l'esoterisme*, and it finally became English in the late nineteenth century.[22]

The scholar Antoine Faivre provides the most widely referenced definition of *esotericism*, though some scholars, such as Hanegraaff, are critical of his description. According to Faivre, the word *esotericism* has two connotations. One is a form of secret knowledge, while the other is being from a spiritual source that enables transcendence.[23]

Faivre describes esotericism as having four fundamental elements. Esotericism includes a belief called correspondences, in which all parts of the universe interconnect. According to esoteric thought, the world is alive and exists in an intricate hierarchical design. Esoteric thought holds that imagination can influence reality through mediating symbols, rites, and spirits. Finally, esotericism holds that the transformation of the individual is possible through dedication to esoteric practices.[24]

Dennis D. Carpenter, who wrote, "Contemporary Paganism represents a synthesis of historical inspiration and present-day creativity," goes on to note that Paganism is a "new religion that involves a revision of pre-modern truths and values." Carpenter points out that this doesn't mean Pagans reject modern science for a pre-modern lifestyle. He says that research done by others supports that Pagans advocate a synthesis of pre-modern with the contemporary.[25]

Christine Hoff Kraemer of the Theology and Religious History department at Cherry Hill Seminary has provided an excellent list of defining characteristics of contemporary Neopaganism. According to Kraemer, Pagans find the Divine within the natural world and this divinity manifests as multiplicity (i.e., polytheism). Paganism includes reverence to nature and the human body, focusing on pre-Christian mythology and religions. Pagan rituals and festivals center around the seasons and life events. Paganism relies on a personal understanding of the Divine and the belief that an alternation of consciousness can change reality. While there is no orthodox Pagan ethical system, many Pagans prefer ethics

---

22. Hanegraaff, *Western Esotericism*, 3.
23. Faivre, *Access to Western Esotericism*, 5.
24. Faivre, *Access to Western Esotericism*, 10–13.
25. Carpenter, "Emergent Nature Spirituality," 47.

based on virtues. Finally, in Paganism, there is an acceptance of multiple traditions and understandings rather than a strict orthodoxy.[26]

The previously listed insights by scholars inspire the definition of Paganism as used in this book. The working definition used here is this: Paganism is an umbrella term for various contemporary spiritual paths of Western esotericism inspired by pre-Abrahamic concepts, tropes, and mythology. A review of the various elements of this definition is needed.

Paganism is contemporary in that it's classified as a New Religion Movement (NRM) by most sociologists. It's derived primarily from modern writers, including Charles Godfrey Leland, Éliphas Lévi, Helena Blavatsky, Margaret Murray, Aleister Crowley, and Gerald Gardner. Paganism draws on many ancient practices and beliefs, but Paganism itself is modern. Hence, Paganism is "contemporary" to differentiate it from the many Indigenous religions, some of which date back thousands of years.

As mentioned, Hanegraaff classifies contemporary Paganism as a modern form of esotericism. While his definition differs from Faivre's, contemporary Paganism contains the same elements identified by Faivre. Paganism includes the use of correspondences, including astrology and divination; a belief that nature itself is divine and conscious (e.g., animism and pantheism); and practices that incorporate imagination and meditation (i.e., ritual) as a means with the goal of transcendence to higher states of being.

Finally, the reference to "pre-Abrahamic concepts, tropes, and mythology" is standard within the Pagan community. As mentioned, Myers defines this as being "not Judaism, Christian, or Islam."[27] Paganism's non-Abrahamic nature doesn't mean that Pagans deny the existence of Yahweh or are opposed to Him. It merely means that Paganism isn't part of the same literary, cultural, or philosophical thread that unites the big three Abrahamic religions.

Mythology: The Penultimate Truth

There have been many theories about myths over the ages. Plato considered them falsehoods. Early Christian theologians claimed they were stories given by demons. Some nineteenth-century anthropologists such as Sir James Frazer

---

26. Kraemer, *Seeking the Mystery*, xi–xii.
27. Myers, *The Earth, the Gods, and the Soul*, 2.

considered myths prescientific explanations by "primitive" people. Today there is a movement to better understand myths as complex and multifaceted phenomena without Western scorn or bias.

One of the most influential modern mythologists was Joseph Campbell. He believed that myths served the function of aiding in individuation. Campbell combined various fields of study to create a theory of a "mono-myth" that he thought underlined all myths. While some recent scholars have questioned the details of his mono-myth theory, his work is still highly valued and influential in studying myths.

In his landmark interview with Bill Moyers, Campbell stated that the Ultimate is beyond any words or images we can create. According to Campbell, mythology is, therefore, the "penultimate truth" because it takes the mind into the realm of the Ultimate in a way that nothing else can.[28] Thus, myths aren't just stories. They're means by which we explore great truths of ourselves and the Cosmos.

People make a common mistake believing that myths are locked in stone. However, that's far from the truth. Myths have always been fluid, and we are continually reimagining them. The reimagining of myths is especially true when society ceases serving people and social institutions. As the need arises, we create new myths.

According to Campbell, mythology has four functions. One function is mystical. It explores the wonder and mystery of life and the Cosmos. The second function is to understand the Cosmos's shape and function without taking away its mystery or claiming to be science. The third function is when the social order is supported while not claiming to be history. Finally, there is the fourth function in which mythology teaches us how to live regardless of the age in which we live.[29] These four functions exist in mythologies of various world religions, including the myths of Paganism.

The mystical function in myth exists in the Pagan festivals. One example is the springtime festival of Beltane. The most notable element of this is the Maypole ritual. Beltane, which occurs on the first day of May, celebrates the marriage of the deities the Red Man and the Green Maid.[30]

---

28. Campbell and Moyers, *The Power of Myth*, 206.
29. Campbell and Moyers, *The Power of Myth*, 38–39.
30. Zell-Ravenheart, *Grimoire for the Apprentice Wizard*, 189.

We find the second function in the faery creation myth. In this myth, the Mother Goddess creates the Cosmos when She sees Herself reflected from space and not only falls in love but makes love to Herself. In doing so, She creates the Cosmos and all of its inhabitants.[31] This myth aids in exploring the sacred mystery of the Cosmos and of life itself.

Mythology's third function is in Paganism's historically based myths. A historically based myth reimagines the past in a counterfactual manner. Kraemer describes three Pagan historically based myths. One myth is the myth of Paganism as a root religion, which is that Paganism, as it exists today, was the original religion from which all modern religions are derived. Another Pagan myth is the myth of matriarchal prehistory, in which Goddess worship was a universal ancient religion dating back to prehistory and replaced by a patriarchal system. A third Pagan myth is the myth of the Burning Times, which ties into the other two myths by holding that the witch trials' victims were practitioners of the ancient root Goddess religion that had survived underground and that the victims were the ancestors of contemporary Paganism.[32]

The fourth function of mythology is in the popularity of the Mesopotamian myth of the Descent of Inanna. In this ancient myth, the goddess Inanna travels to the underworld, is killed, hung on a stake for three days, resurrected, and ascends to glory. There are several Pagan books in which Inanna's descent to the underworld helps those struggling with depression and aids in making it through the dark night of the Soul.

In addition to the four functions of mythology, Campbell points out that mythology can serve as a metaphor. Through metaphor, mythology presents higher truths.[33] Using the aforementioned Descent of Inanna for therapy presents it as a metaphor, for example. Metaphor is also how the subconscious speaks to us.

Pagan Religions

With this background, we're now able to understand Paganism as a religion. Back in the 1950s, contemporary Pagan religion was largely monolithic. Gradually this changed. Over time Paganism developed subgroups and divisions,

---

31. Starhawk, *The Spiral Dance*, 41–42.
32. Kraemer, *Seeking the Mystery*, 52–56.
33. Campbell and Moyers, *The Power of Myth*, 67.

much like other religions have over the ages. These Pagan divisions are far from static. New ones appear while the older ones evolve.

The first step in understanding the structure of Paganism as a religion is to understand its four centers. In his book *The Path of Paganism*, John Beckett presents the "Big Tent of Paganism."[34] Beckett's model describes Paganism's various traditions in four overlapping centers.

The Four Centers

A brief note about terminology: Beckett uses *centered* for each structure found within Paganism. For example, he describes one center as "nature-centered." In this book, the word *centric* replaces the term *centered*. Otherwise, the primary source of Big Tent Paganism, as presented here, comes from Beckett's book.

Nature-Centric

What Shinto calls "Great Nature" is the focus of nature-centric Paganism, which not only sees the Divine within the natural world but believes that it is worthy of worship. According to Beckett, animism plays a prominent role in nature-centric Paganism. Nature-centric Pagans tend to be ardent environmentalists inspired by the sacred that they find within Nature Herself.

Deity-Centric

Deity-centric Pagans emphasize the worship of gods and goddesses and forming reciprocal relationships with divine beings. Often their focus is on devotionals, offerings, sacrifices, prayers, and meditations.

Self-Centric

In the model I present, Dark Paganism is part of the Self-centric circle. Self-centric Paganism focuses on self-improvement and finding the Divine within one's Self. According to Beckett, a Self-centric Pagan dedicates themselves to myth, mysticism, self-knowledge, practice, and self-change. Self-centric is not to be confused with self-centered or selfish. It's because of the negative meaning of the word *self-centered* that I use *centric* rather than *centered*.

---

34. Beckett, *The Path of Paganism*, 35–53.

Community-Centric

Community-centric Pagans focus on their family, ancestors, and tribe. A good illustration of this is a quote Beckett includes from a follower of the Heathen tradition of Paganism: "If you feel a tap on your shoulder, it's probably your grandfather, not the Allfather."[35]

The Traditions

It's important to emphasize that few Pagans fall exclusively in any one center. It's safe to say that most Pagan traditions fall where the deity-centric and nature-centric overlap. While various traditions focus on family and ancestors, which would place them as community-centric, many still worship multiple gods and goddesses. Plus, while some traditions focus exclusively on the development of the Self and would be considered Self-centric, they may also place belief in the divinity of nature and hence be nature-centric.

With an understanding of the four Pagan centers, we can better understand the different traditions within Paganism. Most of these traditions have a founder or influential person, and a brief review of the prominent traditions is needed. What follows does not include any Dark Pagan traditions. Those appear in a later chapter.

Wicca

The Pagan tradition of Wicca might be the most influential of all the traditions. Some describe Wiccans as being dualists or soft polytheistic in that they honor a god and goddess whom they believe manifest as the multitudes of gods and goddesses across the globe.

There are several branches of Wicca, such as Gardnerian and Alexandrian. As mentioned by Hanegraaff, Aleister Crowley heavily influenced Gerald Gardner, the founder of Gardnerian Wicca.[36] Gardner stated that he had received Wicca from a coven of witches in 1939 who had practiced witchcraft from ancient times. Once the United Kingdom repealed the Witchcraft Act, Gardner went public with Wicca and published several books during the 1950s. Alex and Maxine Sanders founded Alexandrian Wicca. It bears a significant similarity to Gardnerian Wicca; however, its practices are much more eclectic.

---

35. Beckett, *The Path of Paganism*, 48.
36. Hanegraaff, *Western Esotericism*, 44.

Feri

A growing Pagan tradition is the Feri tradition, which Cora and Victor Anderson founded. Sensual experience and awareness play an essential role in this tradition. A prominent person in the Feri tradition is Starhawk, who founded the Reclaiming tradition.

Stregheria

Stregheria is a Pagan tradition originating in southern Italy that, like Wicca, claims ancient roots. Its primary text is Charles G. Leland's *Aradia or the Gospel of the Witches* from 1899. The most prominent person of this modern Pagan tradition was Raven Grimassi, who died March 10, 2019.

Ethnic Reconstructionism

Ethnic reconstructionism is a growing trend within Paganism to attempt to reconstruct various ancient Pagan religions. Examples of such traditions include Hellenists, Druidism, Sumerians, and Heathens.

Traditional Witchcraft

Traditional witchcraft is an umbrella term for various paths and traditions that self-identify as not Gardnerian or Alexandrian. One of the most referenced is British traditional witchcraft.

Eclecticism

Although one couldn't call eclecticism a tradition per se, it is one of Paganism's fastest-growing trends. An eclectic Pagan strives to take the best within and outside Paganism to form the individual's beliefs and practices.

The Symbols of Paganism

While the different Pagan traditions have their symbols, the pentagram is most commonly associated with Paganism as a whole. Its origins are lost in the mists of time. The earliest pentagram is on Mesopotamia artifacts dated to 2750 BCE.[37] In the West, the pentagram is most famously associated with the Greek philosopher Pythagoras around 500 BCE and was a symbol of purity and

---

37. Zell-Ravenheart, *Grimoire for the Apprentice Wizard*, 146.

magick. Members of his magickal order wore a ring with a pentagram. The Celts knew of the pentagram, and the Druids would wear it on their sandals.[38]

In Japanese, the pentagram is called the *seiman* and is a symbol of protection.[39] Its name comes from the sorcerer Abe no Seimei, who used it as his symbol. Seimei is still revered in Japan and has become a popular character in anime. The Seimei-jinja Shrine in Kyoto is dedicated to Seimei.[40]

Pentagram

In 1510, Heinrich Cornelius Agrippa von Nettesheim wrote —and finally published in 1533—*De occulta philosophia libri tres (Three Books on Occult Philosophy)*, which is considered an occult classic. In his book, Agrippa argued for a magickal framework built on Neoplatonism and Hermeticism. His book includes an illustration of a pentagram placed over a man and surrounded by five planetary astrological symbols.

One cannot overstate the influence of the occultist and magician Éliphas Lévi in modern esoteric thought, especially concerning the pentagram, which he considered to be a symbol of the microcosm or human.[41] Lévi, in his book *Transcendental Magic: Its Doctrine and Ritual*, was the first to write that an inverted pentagram symbolizes evil.[42]

The debate over orientation continues today among Pagans. According to Corvis Nocturnum, many Pagans view the upright pentagram as representing "positive intent," while the inverted pentagram represents "negative intent." He points out that an alternative opinion exists in the Pagan community in that the upright pentagram represents the release of power. The inverted pentagram then represents the drawing in of power.[43] Wiccans and other Right-Hand Path Pagans are commonly critics of the inverted pentagram. In contrast, Left-Hand Path Pagans often adopt the inverted pentagram as a positive symbol.

Dark Paganism doesn't have a preference for whether the pentagram should be vertical or inverted. I primarily use the vertical pentagram in my practice, although I will, at times, use the inverted pentagram. One will also find the

38. Digitalis, *Goth Craft*, 239.
39. Cummins, *The Dark Side of Japan*, 52.
40. Foster, *The Book of Yōkai*, 41.
41. Lévi, *Transcendental Magic*, 70.
42. Lévi, *Transcendental Magic*, 237.
43. Nocturnum, *Embracing the Darkness*, 58.

vertical pentagram illustrated on books by Dark Pagan authors John J. Cough-lin, Raven Digitalis, and Konstantinos.

While the pentagram is the most commonly recognized symbol of Paganism, it's not the only one. Many Wiccans use the triple moon symbol, consisting of a circle flanked by a cres-cent moon on each side. Often

Triple Moon

the pentagram is shown in the circle. The Wiccan triple moon is symbolic of the three masks of the Goddess: the Maiden, Mother, and Crone.

Awen

Druids often use the awen, which consists of a vertical bar flanked by another bar leaning into it on each side. Where the three bars meet at the top are three dots. Another popular symbol for Druids is the triskele, a triple spiral radiating from a single source.

Heathens and Asatru commonly use Thor's hammer, also known as *Mjölnir*. Thor's ham-mer appears as an inverted T decorated with Celtic or Nordic knots. Another symbol of Nordic Paganism is the *valknut*, which appears as three interlocking triangles. Unfortunately, both Thor's hammer and the valknut have been co-opted by some neo-Nazis and other racist groups. With this information, we're now ready to explore Dark Paganism itself.

Thor's Hammer

Reviewing the Concepts

While there are a variety of definitions of Paganism, the working definition that I use is this: Paganism is an umbrella term for various contemporary spiritual paths of Western esotericism inspired by pre-Abrahamic concepts, tropes, and mythology.

Paganism as a religion is structured around four centers: nature-centric, deity-centric, Self-centric, and community-centric. In practice, these four cen-ters often overlap. Dark Paganism is primarily a form of Self-centric Paganism, although it can include elements of the other centers.

There are different Pagan traditions. The most common are Wicca, Feri, Stregheria, ethnic reconstructionism, and eclecticism. Paganism uses different symbols to represent itself. Just as the cross represents Christianity and the dharma wheel represents Buddhism, the pentagram is the most common symbol of Paganism. Each Pagan tradition has its symbols, such as the triple moon, awen, and Thor's hammer.

Questions to Consider

- * What does Paganism mean to you?
- * Do you believe that contemporary Paganism is the Old Religion descended from an ancient matriarchal faith?
- * Of the four Pagan centers, which one appeals to you most and why?

II

DARK PAGAN PRIMER

The roots of Dark Paganism are in the works of three authors: John J. Coughlin, Konstantinos, and Raven Digitalis. Each writer presents a unique vision of Dark Paganism and what it means to be a Dark Pagan.

As presented in this book, the primary source for Dark Paganism is Coughlin's work. Coughlin is the author of the book *Out of the Shadows: An Exploration of Dark Paganism and Magick*. He's also the author of *Ethics and the Craft: The History, Evolution, and Practice of Wiccan Ethics*. As a highly private individual, he refers to himself as an "obscure occult author." Coughlin was also the founder and editor of the NYC Pagan Resource Guide and is active in the goth scene.[44]

According to the tradition's website, Digitalis is a priest of the tradition Opus Aima Obscurae, which provides a "ceremonial space and resource center for the study of global earth-based spirituality."[45] Digitalis has a degree in anthropology and is active in the goth community, EBM, and industrial music culture. He's the author of the *Goth Craft: The Magickal Side of Dark Culture*, *Shadow Magick Compendium: Exploring Darker Aspects of Magickal Spirituality*, *Planetary Spells & Rituals: Practicing Dark & Light Magick Aligned with the Cosmic Bodies*, and *Esoteric Empathy: A Magickal & Metaphysical Guide to Emotional Sensitivity*.

44. Coughlin, "About."
45. "About OAO."

Konstantinos is a prolific author and public speaker. His published work includes *Gothic Grimoire, Summoning Spirits: The Art of Magical Evocation, Nocturnicon: Calling Dark Forces and Powers, Speak with the Dead: Seven Methods for Spirit Communication, Nocturnal Witchcraft: Magick after Dark, Vampire: The Occult Truth,* and *Werewolves: The Occult Truth.* Konstantinos is also a trained stage mentalist who uses his training to debunk frauds.[46]

The Two Sides of Spirituality

According to Coughlin, spirituality exists as two schools of thought. Each school shares the same emphasis, which is an exploration of existential matters. However, the two schools each address this exploration from different directions.

The most common school of thought is the external approach. This school seeks meaning and purpose outside the individual. The primary existential question in the external approach, according to Coughlin, concerns the meaning of the universe. In the external approach, reality is viewed as One. Any alternative to the One is evil. This viewpoint often results in a dualistic worldview where good struggles against evil. According to the external approach, life's meaning is in uniting oneself and actions with this great Unity.[47]

In the internal approach, reality is a complex mix of interactions and relationships. Because of this complexity, there is no underlying Unity or dualistic battle between good and evil. The primary existential question for the internal approach isn't about the meaning of the universe but about searching for personal meaning and learning how the individual fits into this complex reality. Therefore, the emphasis of the internal approach is on the Self and the search for personal identity.[48]

To represent the two approaches to spirituality, Coughlin uses the yin-yang symbol of Taoism. For Coughlin, the yin (black or dark side) represents the internal approach, while the yang (white or light side) represents the external.[49] Neither side of the symbol is good or evil. Each side also has a dot of the opposite color, for life is more complicated than just one or the other.

Yin-Yang
Symbol

46. Konstantinos, *Nocturnal Witchcraft,* inside cover.
47. Coughlin, *Out of the Shadows,* 125.
48. Coughlin, *Out of the Shadows,* 126.
49. Coughlin, *Out of the Shadows,* 125.

While Konstantinos's Dark Paganism differs from Coughlin's, he provides a model of spirituality that includes both dark and light aspects. Rather than the Taoist yin-yang symbol, he uses a Cartesian grid divided into four equal parts with a horizontal line, or x-axis, and a vertical line, or y-axis, that intersects in the middle of the graph. The two upper quarters above the x-axis represent good, while the lower two represent evil. The two quarters on the left-hand side of the y-axis (negative of the intersection) make up the dark approach, while the two on the right (positive of the intersection) are part of the light approach.[50] Since the dark side is negative of the intersection, it, too, is internal rather than external.

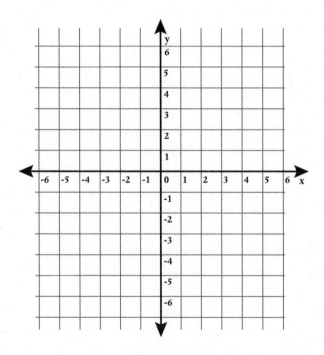

Cartesian Grid

Digitalis considers Dark Paganism as a recovery of the balance between light and dark, which he terms the "middle path." In his book *Goth Craft*, he wrote, "To practice dark Witchcraft is to walk a light path in a dark skin, balancing lightness with darkness for the sake of balance." The goth subculture

---

50. Konstantinos, *Nocturnal Witchcraft*, 5.

represents the dark by Digitalis. Also, for Digitalis, Dark Paganism focuses on the person's dark aspects, such as understanding one's own Shadow.[51]

According to Socrates, most phenomena have a dual trait in the same way all animals have bilateral symmetry.[52] However, bilateral symmetry doesn't mean that the traits are the same for both sides. Most people have a dominant hand, which tends to be stronger and more dexterous than the other. Spirituality shares this dual-trait characteristic, and, as we shall see later, the concept of left-handedness and right-handedness plays a symbolic role.

In addition to the Socratic dual trait, according to Neoplatonism, all phenomena have an inner and outer activity.[53] For example, a rosebush's internal activity would be photosynthesis, while its external activity would be the leaves and flowers that it produces. We also see this same Neoplatonic principle in internal and external approaches to spirituality.

As indicated, *light* is often applied to the external approach to spirituality. In contrast, the internal approach to spirituality is *dark*. To understand this terminology, imagine a cave. During the daytime, the outside of the cave is light, while the cave inside is dark. Dark and light are metaphors for internal and external.

When we apply these metaphors to the person, we find that the dark represents the Self, while the light represents the world external to the Self. The Self is dark because, like the cave's interior, it's hidden from sight. Each person's psyche, or internal behavior, is, in a sense, a black box. No one else can directly observe our private thoughts and feelings, making them "dark." The psyche's privacy differs from a person's actions, or external behavior. Because others can observe the world outside a person, it's "light."

So what does the interior/dark and exterior/light approach to spirituality translate into practice? According to Coughlin, the lightside approach aligns with the "active/masculine/yang/logical aspects of the universe and human nature."[54] Such approaches tend toward varying degrees of dogma and focus on the behaviors of their followers.

---

51. Digitalis, *Goth Craft*, 83–84.
52. Ustinova, *Divine Mania*, 1.
53. Wildberg, "Neoplatonism."
54. Coughlin, *Out of the Shadows*, 131.

The darkside practice, according to Coughlin, aligns with the "passive/feminine/yin/intuitive aspects of the universe and human nature."[55] These practices are usually less structured and are profoundly individualistic. Dark Pagans are unlikely to blame a devil or karma for the adverse events in their lives. And while a Dark Pagan may have a relationship with a deity, that relationship will be undoubtedly less critical than the Self and its development. Dark Pagans tend to be solitary and eclectic practitioners and are often not members of an organized religion or Pagan tradition.

A Few Words about "Reason"

In the introduction, I wrote that Dark Paganism is a philosophy in that it's a way of life based on human reasoning. In this sense, Dark Paganism is in the same spirit as ancient Greek philosophy, which valued reason above all else. Rational thought or reason has been the subject of discussion and study since Plato.

Most ancient Greek philosophers viewed human passions as secondary to rational thought. While they didn't believe that it was possible or desirable to eliminate passion, they thought it was possible to train one's desire to follow reason. Reason, they believed, could master passion.[56]

After the end of the Classical Age, Western philosophers started to question the centrality of rational thought. David Hume, for example, dramatically limited the power of reason. He went so far as to write, "Reason is the slave of passions, and can aspire to no other office than to serve and obey them."[57]

While accepting nonrationality as valid might seem to contradict the classic Greek philosophers, we now understand that they did accept nonrational answers derived from divine sources. According to Yulia Ustinova of Ben-Gurion University of the Negev, ecstatic knowledge, labeled *mania*, when divine in origin was considered more significant than human reasoning by Socrates and others.[58]

Dark Paganism is a rational philosophy in the sense that it's human centered. Dark Paganism claims no divine revelation or gnosis. Human discernment is the ultimate judge for Dark Paganism rather than blind faith. It's in the

---

55. Coughlin, *Out of the Shadows*, 132.
56. Cooper, *Pursuits of Wisdom*, 86.
57. Blackburn, *The Oxford Dictionary of Philosophy*, 319.
58. Ustinova, *Divine Mania*, 1.

same spirit as the ancient Greek philosopher Protagoras who wrote, "Man is the measure of all things."[59]

The use of reason or rational thought doesn't make Dark Paganism scientism or logical positivism. Dark Paganism understands that there are sources of knowledge other than the senses or logical deduction. We know that there are, as the Bard wrote, more things in heaven and earth than are dreamt of in our philosophy. However, the validity of information from these esoteric sources and the conclusions aren't taken at face value. In Dark Paganism, esoteric knowledge is subject to rational thought and debate.

Though Dark Paganism is built on reason, we're realistic about the limits of rational thought. As we shall see later, the human mind isn't unitary. The ego, or conscious mind, which is the seat of reason, is just the tip of the iceberg. The majority of the mind is hidden in the unconscious. The result is that the unconscious often yanks about the ego like a puppet on a string. The influence of the unconscious doesn't negate the power of reason. It does, however, set limits on what's genuinely rational and what's not.

Just as rational thought is often subject to unconscious whims, we understand that passion isn't secondary to reason. We might like to think that rational thought guides everything we do, but the reality is that passion has a constructive role to play as well. Today we call this constructive role of passion "emotional intelligence." Emotional intelligence knows the emotions of oneself and others. The result is someone who can manage their feelings and properly respond to the emotions around them. Emotional intelligence then provides support for the efficacy of rational knowledge.

With this understanding of rational thought and reason, we see that the reason central to Dark Paganism is a realistic one. It acknowledges that there are sources of knowledge beyond the five senses and logical deduction. It also recognizes the reality of the unconscious mind and the importance of emotional intelligence.

Going Deep into the Dark

Humans have mixed feelings about dark and darkness. The close association of the color black with darkness is that they're usually interchangeable. Rudolf

---

59. Bartlett, *Bartlett's Familiar Quotations*, 78.

Steiner, esoterist and social reformer, summed up the fear of darkness and the color black when he wrote that black is "hostile to life."[60] However, darkness and the color black have also represented power and sophistication throughout the centuries.

The negative reputation of the dark and its cousin, the color black, originates in prehistory. The night was once a hazardous time. Predators roamed the night, hidden in the darkness. Not only was there a threat from predators, but the risk of falling and being injured from hidden obstacles increased in the dark. Daylight, though, was different. It was more difficult for predators, human and otherwise, to hide, giving us more opportunities to escape. Plus, we could see the path before us and avoid any potential obstacles.

Therefore, darkness, night, and the color black became associated with fear, evil, and death. We see examples of this association in the Greek pantheon with Hades, the underworld god, who sits on a throne made of black ebony. The doors to the Greek underworld were also black, and black poplars grew there. The underworld rivers of Styx, Lethe, and Acheron are either dark or black in color.[61] We know that the ancient Greeks wore black to funerals. In the Greek play *Libation Bearers,* the character Orestes asks, "What's this crowd of women coming here / All wearing black?"[62]

The color black and darkness aren't just negative in meaning. Both are associated with divinity. The ancient Celts had a god named Ogmios, who was the color black. According to Lucian, a Celtic translator explained that Ogmios was black in color because he was the god of eloquence.[63] In Sumo, a black tassel is hung in the *dhojo* to represent winter and the tortoise god named Genbu.[64] Other deities with the color black include the Egyptian god of reproduction, Min; the Navajo fire god called Black God, who spread the stars across the Milky Way; and the Aztec medicine god Ixtilton. Also, the Hindu goddess Kali isn't always the color blue but is sometimes the color black. These are just a few of the deities associated with the color black found in pantheons worldwide.[65]

---

60. Harvey, *The Story of Black*, 14.
61. Harvey, *The Story of Black*, 45.
62. Harvey, *The Story of Black*, 42.
63. Harvey, *The Story of Black*, 64.
64. Bargwanna, "Religious Symbolism in Sumo Today."
65. Harvey, *The Story of Black*, 31–32.

The color black can represent
infinite possibilities. Rachel Pollack points out that the black staff
appears in the Fool and the Six of
Swords in the Rider-Waite tarot
deck. According to Pollack, the
color black represents life's infinite
possibilities and energy before
being constrained by consciousness rather than a symbol of evil.
Fearing the darkness is a sign of
fearing life itself.[66]

The Fool   Six of Swords

The color black has long had mixed political messages. The powerful have
always used fear as a weapon. As a result, the color black has become the color
for representatives of the state in many countries. In Europe, it became the
color of clergy, academics, and merchants. Judicial robes in many countries
are black.[67]

On a positive note, black is a symbol of democracy. Johann Wolfgang
von Goethe wrote that "black was intended to remind the Venetian noble-
man of republican equality."[68] Black clothing was a democratic color worn
by both men and women in the young American republic shortly after the
Revolutionary War.[69]

One cannot avoid the racist roots in certain uses of the color black. Its racist roots date back to the Talmudic that associated the "curse of Ham" and his
descendants to be Africans. The British further emphasized the racist association of "black" with evil and "white" with good as their slave trade expanded.[70]

With its association with darkness by its nature, the color black carries a
connotation of secrecy. Modern covert military units are "black ops." The phrase
"going dark" is a military term for terminating communication to avoid the
enemy's detection.

66. Pollack, *Seventy-Eight Degrees of Wisdom*, 28.
67. Harvey, *The Story of Black*, 97.
68. Harvey, *The Story of Black*, 243.
69. Harvey, *The Story of Black*, 243.
70. Harvey, *The Story of Black*, 168.

Black and darkness can also symbolize rebellion. The musician Johnny Cash once said that his style of always wearing black was a symbol that represented a rebellion against the status quo, "hypocritical houses of God," and closed-mindedness to the ideas of others.[71] The black flag has long been a symbol of political anarchism.

The color black is also associated with elegance and wealth. Gifts of black ebony are on the walls of the tomb of Rehmir, who was the vizier to fifteenth-century-BCE Pharaoh Tuthmose III. In ancient Egypt, men and women wore lush black wigs and black eyeliner. Artifacts, such as obelisks, were sometimes made of black limestone.[72]

Black has gone in and out of men's fashion. A significant boost to black in men's fashion occurred when Beau Brummell adopted it in the early nineteenth century. Brummell's friend Prince Regent then picked it up, which spread its popularity. As a result, black became no longer limited to clergy, academics, and law.[73]

With the electrification of cities, the night and its darkness have lost their fearfulness. Individuals can now go out and enjoy entertainment late into the evening safely. Terms such as "after dark" are now used in conjunction with sophisticated, as well as adult, entertainment.[74]

In 1926, women's fashion forever changed when Coco Chanel created the "little black dress." In the latter half of the nineteenth century, simple dark or black clothing had been domestic servants' style. Chanel flipped around cultural norms into a new status symbol by declaring the color black fashionable.[75]

The color black has been the color of choice for youth culture over the centuries. Late eighteenth-century European youth preferred black. The black leather jacket was the wardrobe of choice for young men in the 1950s. The mods during the 1960s wore dark black suits. And since the 1980s, black has been the preferred color in the goth subculture.[76]

---

71. Johnny Cash Trail, "Why Did Johnny Cash Always Wear Black?"
72. Harvey, *The Story of Black*, 27–28.
73. Harvey, *The Story of Black*, 209.
74. Zeitz, *Flapper*, 30–31.
75. Fred, *Fashion, Culture, and Identity*, 64–75.
76. Harvey, *The Story of Black*, 271.

The color black continues to be a common symbol of evil in pop culture, with bad guys in Westerns wearing black hats, while the good guys wear white. The villain Darth Vader wears all-black armor. Horror movies are full of vampires and other "creatures of the night" who come out in the dark to attack and kill the innocent.

In recent years the cinematic good guys are sometimes dressed in black. In *The Matrix*, the heroes Neo, Trinity, and Morpheus wear all-black suits. The movie version of the comic book hero Batman often wears black and is known as the "Dark Knight."[77] In *Star Wars: Episode VI—Return of the Jedi*, the character Luke Skywalker redeemed the color black when he donned it.

With this history, we see that the "dark" in Dark Paganism has numerous meanings:

* Dark is about coming to terms with our inner demons. Understanding and accepting the Self often involves facing Carl Jung's "Shadow," which can be terrifying.

* Dark is about individuality because of the privacy it gives. It's a type of humanism that recognizes that, though we are social beings living embedded in the community, each individual has the right to live their life as they deem fit as long as it harms no one else.

* Dark is about rebelling against those forces that attempt to crush our individuality. Socio-economic forces strive every day to control us and make us part of the herd.

* Dark is about empowerment. Empowerment to be true to one's Self and the power to achieve personal sovereignty.

* Dark is about infinite possibilities. It represents the potential that resides in the unconscious before the conscious places roadblocks in its path.

* Dark is about birth and rebirth. We each spend the beginning of our lives in the darkness of the womb.

---

77. Harvey, *The Story of Black*, 290.

* Dark is about divinity. The color dark represents not just the divinity of gods and spirits but of our Divine Self. It's a black fire that burns within each of us.

* Dark is about personal growth, materially and spiritually. Black soil is fertile soil.

* Dark is about mystery. It's about the mystery found in the existential questions of being and becoming.

* Dark is about the emptiness of existence. At the heart of our existence is a void. Therefore, we each must create our meaning.

* Dark is about the hidden or occult. Just as most of the Cosmos is dark (i.e., unknown), the spiritual aspects of existence are hidden from our day-to-day lives.

* Dark is about the intimacy of the Self. No matter how many people we are around, we are each alone. Dark is about acknowledging this isolation and learning to love the Self.

* Dark is about coming to terms with the truth of our mortality. Death comes for us all. Remembering the inevitability of our future deaths reminds us of the need to enjoy living today.

Reviewing the Concepts

Spirituality exists as two schools of thought: external and internal. The external school seeks meaning and purpose outside the individual. External spirituality views reality as One, which often leads to a dualistic worldview in which there is an ongoing battle between good and evil. In the internal approach, reality is a complex mix of interactions and relationships. Because of this complexity, there is no underlying Unity or dualistic battle between good and evil. The primary existential question for the internal approach isn't about the meaning of the universe but about searching for personal meaning and learning how the individual fits into this complex reality.

Dark Paganism is an internal spiritual philosophy based on human reasoning. Dark Paganism is a rational philosophy in the sense that it's human centered. Dark Paganism claims no divine revelation or gnosis. Human discernment is the ultimate judge for Dark Paganism rather than "blind faith." It's in the same spirit as the ancient Greek philosopher Protagoras who wrote, "Man is the measure of all things."

Questions to Consider

* For you, what is the focus of spirituality? Is it to find the meaning of the Cosmos, or is it to find personal meaning?

* Do you see darkness and the color black as negative or positive?

* Is human discernment sufficient, or is divine revelation necessary?

III
PRINCIPLES OF DARK PAGANISM

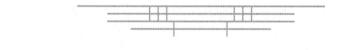

For Dark Paganism to be a philosophy, as I claim it to be, it needs philosophical principles upon which to build. The place to begin searching for these is classic Greek philosophy.

Living in the fourth century BCE, Aristotle is one of the most influential philosophers of the Western world. Aristotle was born in Stagira, Macedonia, and his father was Nicomachus, who was the royal court physician. At 17, Aristotle entered Plato's Academy, where he stayed for the rest of his life. Aristotle wrote volumes of books on numerous subjects, including philosophy and the natural world, during his lifetime.[78]

In his book *Nicomachean Ethics*, Aristotle presented his concept of eudaimonia, which translates as "good spirit." *Eudaimonia* is variously interpreted as "happiness," "success," or "well-being."[79] It can best be understood as a state of living at its best or the most optimal. In modern terms, I'm reminded of the recruitment slogan by the US Army from the early 1980s claiming that, through joining, one could "be all that you could be."

For Aristotle, eudaimonia was more than just a slogan. He described it as the "best, noblest, and most pleasant thing in the world." For Aristotle, it was living a life of virtue guided by reason.

Eudaimonia has been described as a placeholder term awaiting a definition. Many different philosophers have provided what they considered to be a

---

78. Blackburn, *The Oxford Dictionary of Philosophy*, 24.
79. Blackburn, *The Oxford Dictionary of Philosophy*, 127.

life of eudaimonia.[80] Studies in eudaimonia continue today. One of the leaders in the modern-day study of eudaimonia is psychologist Carol Ryff, the director of the Institute on Aging and professor of psychology at the University of Wisconsin–Madison.

Ryff developed the six-factor model of psychological well-being. Research performed by numerous researchers over the years plays a factor in Ryff's measurement of well-being. According to Ryff, research has indicated that the higher one scored on six factors, the greater the sense of well-being or eudaimonia one felt.[81] Those six factors are:

1. Self-acceptance

2. Personal growth

3. Autonomy

4. Environmental mastery

5. Satisfying relationships

6. Purpose in life

For my vision of Dark Paganism, I incorporate these six factors into Dark Paganism's philosophical principles. However, the Dark Pagan principles aren't identical to Ryff's six factors. Therefore, changes were necessary.

One change was that I renamed Ryff's "personal growth" element to "magnum opus," since personal growth in Dark Paganism consists of much more than Ryff had in mind. Another change, since Dark Paganism is a spiritual philosophy, is that the principles needed elements found in the Pagan wisdom tradition. So, in addition to Ryff's six principles, Dark Paganism has three more:

7. Self-knowledge

8. Magick

9. Corpospirituality

---

80. Blackburn, *The Oxford Dictionary of Philosophy*, 127.
81. Ryff, "Happiness Is Everything, or Is It?" 1069–81.

These elements add up to a total of nine philosophical principles: self-knowledge, self-acceptance, autonomy, magick, corpospirituality, environmental mastery, purpose in life, satisfying relationships, and magnum opus. These nine principles make up the core of Dark Paganism presented here.

The Magick of Nine

Nine is an auspicious number. A brief review of the number reveals it as intriguing in many ways.

In nature, the most obvious is that nine is the number of months for human pregnancy. In about nine months, a human develops from a zygote to personhood. The fact that the nine principles are essential elements of personal growth is an interesting similarity with fetal development.

In classical Greek Paganism, there were nine Muses. The Muses bestowed divine inspiration and talent upon people. Sometimes a writer or artist describes something or someone as "their muse." This is the statement's origin. The classic nine Muses of Greece are Clio (history), Euterpe (music), Thalia (comedy), Melpomene (tragedy), Terpsichore (dance), Erato (love poetry), Polymnia (sacred poetry), Urania (astronomy), and Calliope (heroic poetry).[82]

The number nine was significant to the ancient Greeks beyond the number of Muses. In the arithmological symbolism of Pythagoras of Samos, the number nine, or *ennead*, represented humanity, likely because of the gestation period mentioned earlier. The ennead also represented infinity, for it was the last number before the perfect *decad*, or number ten.[83]

The number nine is important to the Left-Hand Path. The highly controversial Anton LaVey, founder of the Church of Satan, believed the number nine to be the most magickal of numbers and that there is a historical cycle based on the number.[84] He incorporated the number nine in his Nine Satanic Statements.[85] Michael Aquino developed the ritual the Ceremony of the Nine Angles based on the number nine. Advocates of the ritual say that it's a helpful model for obtaining self-knowledge and self-transformation.[86]

---

82. Illes, *Encyclopedia of Spirits*, 731.
83. Chappell, *Infernal Geometry and the Left-Hand Path*, 39–41.
84. Chappell, *Infernal Geometry and the Left-Hand Path*, 2.
85. LaVey, *The Satanic Bible*, 25.
86. Chappell, *Infernal Geometry and the Left-Hand Path*, 1–2.

The tarot provides some fascinating insight into the number nine as well. A man named Bonifacio Bembo designed the tarot for the Visconti family of Milan in the fifteenth century.[87] The cards were originally used for gambling, but, since the early nineteenth century, occultists and other esoterics have found the tarot rich in symbolism and valuable for spiritual practices, such as divination and exploring deeper esoteric meanings of a person.[88]

THE HERMIT.

The Hermit

The number nine applies to two cards of the major arcana of the tarot. The Hermit card, which is number nine in the deck, represents turning inward toward the unconscious mind.[89]

If we double the number nine, which is a common practice in numerology, the number is eighteen. In the major arcana, the eighteenth card is the Moon. If we go beyond its obvious connection to darkness, we find that the Moon card has a significant meaning in Dark Paganism. The Moon is an introspective card, just like its predecessor card, the Star. However, while the Star represents inner calm, the Moon card represents fear of the unconscious.[90] The Moon card is the opposite of the wise hermit. It's the animal side of humans. As we shall see later, exploring the deeper aspects of the Self, such as the Shadow Self, can indeed be most frightening.

THE MOON.

The Moon

87. Pollack, *Seventy-Eight Degrees of Wisdom*, 3.
88. Pollack, *Seventy-Eight Degrees of Wisdom*, 6.
89. Pollack, *Seventy-Eight Degrees of Wisdom*, 77.
90. Pollack, *Seventy-Eight Degrees of Wisdom*, 125–29.

When one looks at the minor arcana, one finds the number nine appearing as both bad and good. According to Pollack, in the minor arcana, cards with the nine represent struggle and compromise.[91] The Nine of Wands represents a strong defense arising out of conflict, resulting in someone ready to go on the offensive.[92] In contrast, the Nine of Cups rep-

Nine of Wands   Nine of Cups

resents using physical indulgences as a defense mechanism to avoid conflict.[93]

We might think of these cards as the fight or flight responses. Even constructive solutions have their duality. The Nine of Swords represents extreme pain and worry, while the Nine of Pentacles represents the enjoyment of the fruits of our labor.[94] These two cards represent the fear of failure and the hope of success. Both of which are in any endeavor.

Nine of Swords   Nine of Pentacles

Celtic legends associate the number nine with Morgan le Fay. Rather than being a villain, early legends portrayed Morgan le Fay as a healer who ruled over the Celtic afterlife known as Avalon. Under her charge were the Nine Holy Women of Avalon who, along with Morgan, tended to King Arthur's wounds after the Battle of Camlann.[95]

---

91. Pollack, *Seventy-Eight Degrees of Wisdom*, 158.
92. Pollack, *Seventy-Eight Degrees of Wisdom*, 172.
93. Pollack, *Seventy-Eight Degrees of Wisdom*, 195.
94. Pollack, *Seventy-Eight Degrees of Wisdom*, 218, 243–44.
95. Illes, *Encyclopedia of Spirits*, 724.

The number nine was also important to classic Germanic Pagans. A tenth-century Old English charm is the Nine Herbs Charm. The Nine Herbs Charm included nine herbs for healing and references to the god Odin. In traditional Germanic Pagan cosmology, the Cosmos is organized into nine worlds connected to a world tree named *Yggdrasil*. Yggdrasil is the same tree that Odin hung upside down for nine nights to receive runic wisdom.[96]

Applying the Nine Principles of Dark Paganism

The goal of these nine principles, which build upon the work of Ryff, helps us develop a picture of a Self that's flourishing. We can compare this to medical research, identifying optimal blood glucose levels for good health. Just as the blood sugar levels provide us a goal to strive for concerning good health, the nine principles provide us goals to strive for the well-being of the Self.

Matters become more complex when it comes to applying the nine principles. I encourage you to consider the questions to explore. One might want to maintain a journal while reading this book to record one's thoughts. Ultimately, each individual will have to decide how best to incorporate the nine principles into their daily lives and personalize this to meet their own needs.

Reviewing the Concepts

Ryff developed the six-factor model of psychological well-being. Her work forms the basis of the nine principles of Dark Paganism. The goal of these nine principles is to help us develop a picture of a Self that's flourishing, or eudaimonia. The nine philosophical principles are self-knowledge, self-acceptance, autonomy, magick, corpospirituality, environmental mastery, purpose in life, satisfying relationships, and magnum opus.

Questions to Consider

* What do you consider the characteristics of a flourishing life?

* Is it possible to determine eudaimonia through human reason, or are we dependent upon divine revelation?

* Are the nine principles sufficient, or are additional principles needed to determine well-being?

---

96. Chappell, *Infernal Geometry and the Left-Hand Path*, 35–36.

PART II

THE DARK
SHALL BE LIGHT

"I said to my soul, be still, and wait…So the darkness shall be the light, and the stillness the dancing."[97]

—T. S. ELIOT

97. Heaven and Buxton, *Darkness Visible*, 77.

IV
PRINCIPLE 1: SELF-KNOWLEDGE

First principle: Dark Pagans understand that
the highest knowledge is that of oneself.

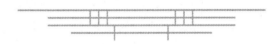

I f Dark Paganism is honoring and cultivating the Self, then we must know what we mean by the *Self*. This need to understand the Self isn't limited to Dark Paganism, and it's not new. Classic Pagans understood the need for self-knowledge. As early as the fourth century BCE, the Greek aphorism "know thyself" was carved into the walls at the Oracle of Delphi. It was Aristotle who wrote that "knowing yourself is the beginning of all wisdom."[98]

Self-knowledge is the most important of all the Dark Pagan principles. It was Sun Tzu who wrote, "If ignorant both of your enemy and yourself, you are certain to be in peril."[99] Without knowledge of yourself, you are doomed to failure. Self-knowledge is, therefore, where we start.

Before exploring the Self, it's important to point out that it's a complex phenomenon with many different aspects. Philosophers, psychologists, sociologists, mystics, and more have spent lifetimes trying to understand the Self. Therefore, this chapter can only scratch the surface of the topic.

Before examining the five characteristics of the Self, we have to answer a fundamental question: What is the Self? For our purpose, we will use the definition provided by Carl Jung. Jung defined the Self as "not only the centre, but also the whole circumference which embraces both conscious and unconscious;

---

98. Hillol and Sanyal, "The Status of Subjective Well-Being."
99. Tipton and Nozaki, *Information Security Management Handbook*, 981.

it is the centre of this totality, just as the ego is the centre of consciousness." Roger Brooke, author of *Jung and Phenomenology*, explains that, according to Jung, the Self as a "centre" does not mean that it's a thing or entity. The Self is the "totality to structure social life around a centre."[100]

Five Characteristics of the Self

What follows are brief descriptions of five of the characteristics of the Self specifically as they apply to Dark Paganism.

The Self Is Divine

The first characteristic of the Self is that it is powerful yet also misunderstood by many people. If you, dear reader, find it shocking or offensive, I encourage you to continue reading.

To put it bluntly: *You are a god.*

This idea, known as self-deification, or apotheosis, has been commonly credited to Anton LaVey since he declared it.[101] Others claim that it's a fluffy New Age concept created by individuals such as Shirley MacLain.[102] However, the idea of the Divine Self didn't originate with LaVey, nor is the belief the product of MacLain and other New Age writers.

The ancient Greek philosophical concept of the Self changed dramatically around the start of the first century CE. Greek philosophy had focused on the embodied Self. To the ancient Greek philosophers, the key to a good life was how one lived in the here and now rather than worrying about achieving a good afterlife.

This view of the Self changed with the Neoplatonists (also known as Late Platonists). Plotinus, considered Neoplatonism's father, moved from looking at our nature as human animals to looking at us as pure intellectual minds.[103] To the Neoplatonists, each soul was derived from the world-soul and, therefore, was

---

100. Roger, *Jung and Phenomenology*, 100.
101. LaVey, *The Satanic Bible*, 96.
102. Sire, *The Universe Next Door*, 178.
103. Cooper, *Pursuits of Wisdom*, 306–7.

itself divine.[104] Plotinus considered the soul to be "a god, owing little more than a passing nod to its 'noble brethren' in the heavens."[105]

We see similar thoughts in Hermeticism. Marsilio Ficino, during the Renaissance, was the first person to translate the *Corpus Hermeticum*, which is one of the core Hermetic texts. According to the book, the concept of the soul as having a divine nature is central to Hermeticism.[106]

Shinto refers to humans as *waketama*. *Waketama* can be translated as "separated individual soul," referring to the human soul being a sliver or piece of the Divine. It's often translated as "children of the kami," which carries the same meaning.[107]

According to Hindu thought, the soul, which it calls *atman*, is one with godhead, referred to as *Brahman*. And it considers the soul to be the True Self. Therefore, the Self is, by default, divine.[108] Note: The Hindu True Self should not be confused with developmental psychologist Donald Winnicott's "true self."

Dark Paganism focuses not on the soul but the Self. The soul is a component of the Self, just as the heart is an organ of the body. However, the principle of the Divine Self in Dark Paganism is very similar to the classics' divine soul. With consciousness being divinity, the Self is, therefore, as the Gnostics called it, a "divine spark."[109]

When they learn of their divinity, some jump to unrealistic conclusions about themselves. For some, their ego becomes inflated as they believe themselves superior to others and lack responsibility to anyone but themselves. These individuals see their divinity as freeing them from social obligations and don't consider themselves under others' constraints.

The reality is that, while each of us is a god, we are each very minor gods. Iamblichus believed that the human soul was the "lowest of the divine beings."[110] The Gnostic phrase "divine spark" used to describe humans is fitting. We might imagine the Self as a tiny spark popping out of a much larger burning log. Also, if each person is a god, there are billions of other gods on

---

104. Wildberg, "Neoplatonism."
105. Moore, "Neo-Platonism."
106. Bartlett, *The Afterlife Bible*, 153.
107. Yamamoto, *Kami No Michi*, Appendix C.
108. Smith, *The World's Religions*, 21.
109. Giversen, Petersen, and Sørensen, *The Nag Hammadi Texts in the History of Religions*, 157.
110. Shaw, *Theurgy and the Soul*, 50.

this little planet with whom we must interact. We'll return to the subject of the relations later.

The Self Is Real

The second characteristic of the Self is that it's real and not an illusion. The belief that the Self is real is one of the essential items that sets Dark Paganism apart from several non-Abrahamic religions. It also distinguishes it from several Western philosophers and psychologists, such as Hume.

The Buddhists say that there is no such thing as an immutable, permanent Self. If we limit the conversation to the corporeal Self, Dark Paganism agrees with Buddhism. The corporeal Self is perpetually changing. Our thoughts and feelings change from moment to moment. No one can grasp and take hold of the Self. The moment one thinks one has found the Self, it disappears like a shadow person out of the corner of your eye.

However, the fact that the corporeal Self is continuously changing doesn't prove its nonexistence. Nor does our failure to capture it. The corporeal Self exists according to the nature of the corporeal world. And everything in the corporeal world is in perpetual change. Heraclitus captured this when he wrote, "All is in flux, nothing stays still."[111] Any attempt to hold on to the material life is doomed to failure. Everything turns to dust.

Though fluid and temporary, the corporeal Self is still functionally real. As a functional reality, the corporeal Self is real in the same sense that a river is real as a topography feature. Like the Self, a river is constantly flowing and changing. No one can hold a river. The best one can do is to scoop up the river water. But that water will gradually disappear due to either evaporation or absorption.

What about the spiritual Self? Plato described the classic view when he described the soul, saying, "The soul of man is immortal and imperishable."[112] This view continues to be the gold standard today. While Plato referenced the soul, Dark Paganism understands that the soul and the Self are the same. Plato's "soul" is but one component of the Self.

The fact that the corporeal Self is fluid and transient doesn't contradict the classic view that the spiritual Self is "immortal and imperishable." Components

---

111. Bartlett, *The Afterlife Bible*, 69.
112. Bartlett, *The Afterlife Bible*, 85.

of the human body, for example, function differently at the same time. While I enter a state of unconsciousness every night, my heart never stops beating. It's not unreasonable that the corporeal Self differs from the spiritual Self in the same way. The nature of the spiritual Self, and its relation to the corporeal, will be addressed later.

The fact that one can't see the spiritual Self fails to disprove its existence. The absence of evidence as a disproof is a logical fallacy. For example, in the fifth century BCE, Democritus proposed atoms as the smallest components of matter. However, empirical proof of atoms didn't appear until the early nineteenth century CE. Those living between the fifth century BCE and nineteenth century CE would have been wrong to have used the lack of evidence to disprove the atomic theory. Before we go too far with this criticism, we must remember that this street runs both ways. If we're seeking proof of the soul, we must not forget that the burden of proof is on us and not the critic. We can't use the fact that the soul's existence cannot be disproven as proof that it exists.

So why is the spiritual Self part of Dark Paganism if we can't prove it? There are many reasons, some of which we explore later, but one is instinct. I instinctively sense that something about myself fits Plato's description of the soul. Even some Buddhists admit that, while humans might intellectually deny the immortal and imperishable aspect of the Self, they feel as though it exists.[113] Reason includes input from instinct, which is part of the unconscious, and instinct tells us that the Self's spiritual aspect is real.

The Self Is Eternal

The third characteristic of the Self is that you are an eternal being. As mentioned, Plato described the soul as being "immortal and imperishable." You existed before your birth and will continue to exist afterward.

There are those in various wisdom traditions that hold that even if the Self isn't an illusion, it must be temporary. For them, the eternal True Self is a spirit or soul existing outside the corporeal body. Many that hold this view believe that when the corporeal body dies, the True Self retains the memories of life on earth, but the corporeal personality or ego dies. Some refer to the ego's end during the body's death as "ego death."

---

113. Batchelor, *Buddhism without Beliefs*, 78.

This belief isn't limited to lightside traditions. The idea of ego death is present in some Dark Pagan traditions. One example is the *Strigoi Vii* tradition, which teaches that, unless one follows certain rituals, when the physical body dies, the consciousness undergoes a "second death" as the etheric body dissolves.[114]

In Dark Paganism, while the corporeal Self's existence is temporary, for everything corporeal is, the Self as a total entity is eternal. A common metaphor is of a snake. A snake sheds its skin, yet the snake continues. The Self will shed its corporeal body, but the Self will continue. The ego doesn't end at the death of the corporeal body either. While it changes, it doesn't end. Instead, as part of the Self, the ego wakes up at death. To understand this, let us look at an analogy from entertainment.

A common trope found in classic film noir is amnesia. The storyline would often involve the protagonist waking up in a seedy motel. He (there was a misogynist bias in that the protagonist in these movies was usually male) doesn't know where he is or how he got there. He doesn't even know his name, nor does he remember his past, and he sure doesn't know the identity of the person lying dead at his feet or why he's holding a bloody knife. By the film's dramatic conclusion, the protagonist has regained his memory, solved the mystery, and brought the villain to justice, even if it means the protagonist's death.

Like the protagonist, we begin our corporeal existence with a loss of memory. With a few exceptions, people are born with no recollection of their previous lives. We then go through our time on earth, trying to solve the mystery of the miracle of life. After our deaths, which are comparable to the protagonist at the conclusion of the film noir, we each recover our memories of who we were before birth.

While the Self doesn't die when the corporeal body dies, it's also true that the Self changes in the afterlife. Some think they will be just the same in the afterlife, but that's not the case. It may seem simple to say, but death changes us. While the ego doesn't end at death, it does change. Like the film noir character remembering his life, we each wake up after our death and remember all of the prior lives that we have lived. Part of our existence in the afterlife is the process

---

114. Sebastiaan, *Vampyre Sanguinomicon*, 22.

of making ourselves whole and reconciling the many lives we've lived with the most recent.

There's precedence for the idea of reassociation of past lives at death. In the book *Lifecycles*, Christopher M. Bache, PhD, wrote of an out-of-body (OOB) experience by Robert Monroe. While discussing his OOB event, Monroe described traveling down the long tunnel that many others encounter during near-death experiences. As he flew, his tunnel merged with other lives he had lived. Each time it joined another, he felt his past lives returning to him in a joyous reunion.[115]

The Self Is Empty

The fourth characteristic is that, at its core, the Self is nothing or empty. Nothingness or emptiness, in this case, means a void. According to Greek cosmology, while the Chaos from which the Cosmos perpetually originates can mean undifferentiated, primordial material, it also means a void or emptiness, as used here.[116] And while Dark Paganism differs from Buddhism in the Self's ultimate nature, the idea that the Self is empty or nothing is similar.

This characteristic may seem paradoxical at best and contradictory at worst when one considers the previous attributes of the Self. How can the Self be real and yet still be nothing? Let's look at the cyclone.

The cyclone is a dynamic phenomenon. It's in constant motion as waves of wind and rain rotate like a spin wheel around a center known as the eye. This spinning feature is one of the defining aspects of a cyclone, such as a hurricane or a typhoon. The US agency NOAA has several aircraft that fly through cyclones to collect data. Strong winds and rain rock the planes as they fly through the hurricane. Then, suddenly, they reach the eye of the storm with its peaceful winds and blue skies. As they emerge from the other side of the eye, they're rocked again by the wind and rain.

The cyclone is a terrifying phenomenon; however, its center is no different than the atmosphere surrounding it. There is no wind, no rain, and no clouds in the eye. One might say that the cyclone's center is empty because it lacks the characteristics, such as wind and rain, that we identify as making up a cyclone.

---

115. Bache, *Lifecycles*, 110–11.
116. Fry, *Mythos*, 3.

In comparison to the rest of the cyclone's atmosphere, the eye of the cyclone is nothing.

After examining the cyclone, we can see how the Self can be both real and nothing. The Self is real and can dramatically impact the world around it. We observe the collective effect of billions of real Selves in the destruction of the environment. However, like the cyclone, nothing exists at the core of each Self.

The Self Is a Mystery

The fifth Dark Pagan characteristic of the Self acknowledges that the Self is a mystery. After all of our theorizing, there is still so much that we don't understand about the Self. To paraphrase Winston Churchill, the Self is a riddle, wrapped in a mystery, inside an enigma. No one, including myself, can claim to have all of the answers about the Self. To do so would be the height of hubris.

Possibly the biggest mystery is the origin of the Self. Many traditions across the globe have presented a variety of ideas. Is the Self the result of the interaction of Cosmic substances of forms and soul? Or might it have appeared spontaneously like the Egyptian god Osiris?

A theme found in some myths is that the Self is the result of the gods mixing divine elements with the physical. In one Greek myth, the Titan Prometheus molded humans from mud while the goddess Athena breathed in life. In another, Zeus formed humans from the heart of the murdered god Dionysus and the ashes of Titans. In the Babylonian creation story, Marduk took the blood of the slain demon Kingu, son and betrothed of the primordial dragon Tiamat, and mixed it with soil to make the mud that He used to mold humans.

The Neoplatonists used less mythological language for the origins of the Self. To them, the human soul was a divine creation that descended from the divine substance of the soul to become embodied in this world. This descent wasn't negative but more like descending a staircase. The descent and the resulting embodiment were to bring the gods' will to the physical world. The physical realm is a pivot point where the soul returns to the heavens.[117]

It's not possible to say what the origin of the Self is. However, there is one thing that we can say with certainty. Whatever its origins, the Self makes us, as Shakespeare wrote, the paragon of animals.

---

117. Shaw, *Theurgy and the Soul*, 94.

Existentialism and Dark Paganism

While Dark Paganism, as presented, is not an existentialist philosophy—it's closer to the absurdism of Albert Camus—the works of great existentialists such as Friedrich Nietzsche and Jean-Paul Sartre have left a lasting impact on it. Therefore, to further understand the Self, we need to review a few of the concepts that Dark Paganism shares with existentialism.

The Single Individual

Dark Paganism and existentialism share a focus on the single individual above the crowd, or what Nietzsche referred to as the "herd." Studies have shown that people act differently in groups rather than when alone. People who usually might not harm anyone are known to commit terrible atrocities in a group. Dark Paganism, like existentialism, emphasizes the single individual over the group.

For some, this emphasis on the individual becomes an aversion by some to any obligatory activity set by groups of people. Some become absolute antinomminalists, declaring any limits or rules as unacceptable, while others become radical individualists and condemn any group activity as collectivism. Others sink into social Darwinism.

Such conclusions result from an inaccurate understanding of individuality. I disagree that recognizing the individual over the "herd" is somehow incompatible with compassion. There is not some form of duality with individuality on one side and collectivism on the other. Individuality fits well within mutual aid, cooperation, and obligation among persons.

Facticity and Transcendence

What creates the identity of the Self? What is the origin of the "I"? Existential philosophers believe that our identity is primarily generated by facticity and transcendence. Facticity is the characteristics that third parties discern about each of us. These features include how much someone weighs, skin color, social class, and character traits. However, there is an alternative to being defined by facticity. One can choose to define oneself, which existentialists call transcendence. Transcendence in existentialism, which is different from the esoteric meaning of transcendence, defines oneself from the first-person perspective. I am more than facticity. I chose who I am.

The fact that I choose what I'm to be doesn't mean that the individual is self-made and solely responsible for who they are. We are still social creatures and are the products of our personal histories, both environmental and genetic. Our personal histories influence who we become.

Embodiment

Cartesian thought dominated philosophy for thousands of years. Descartes is one of the most famous of the advocates. Cartesian belief is that the locus of the Self exists in the soul rather than the body. In a parable, Plato described the soul as a charioteer with the body as the chariot.

In existential thought, the Self is embodied within the world. Many of the classic existentialist philosophers were secularists who denied the existence of a soul. Death was simply the end. Thus, the belief in the finality of death is a significant element in much of existentialist thought.

Dark Paganism shares the existentialist belief in the embodiment. We are very much part of this world. We differ from existentialists in that we believe in a continuation after death and the soul's existence. While we will explore the Soul's function later, it's sufficient to say that the Self's locus is corporeal rather than spiritual during our physical life.

Anxiety, Abandonment, and Despair

The existentialists felt their secularism was liberating. Being free of a constrictive and punitive god, they experienced freedom as few had felt before. However, the existentialists understood that there was a price to pay for this freedom. With freedom comes responsibility. No savior is coming down from the heavens to save us. The actual work, the heavy lifting, belongs to the individual.

The absence of god can be a heavy burden. For some, a loss of faith is like being a child who suddenly finds themselves orphaned. Existentialists referred to this by various terms, such as *anxiety* or *anguish*.

While the ancient Greek philosophers weren't as publicly open to atheism as the existentialists—that would have brought a death sentence in ancient Greece—some felt that it was a waste of time to turn to the gods for aid. For example, Epicurus believed in the existence of gods; however, he also thought that the gods had no interest in human affairs. Like the existentialists, he also found this liberating.[118]

Regardless of the nature of the gods, a god or other divine spirit must honor the individual's autonomy. Even if one accepts the reality of gods as independent agents, assistance from a divine entity requires the human's active participation. As the Pagan fabulist Aesop wrote, "The gods help those who help themselves."[119] The person must decide and take responsibility for whether to obey. Existentialists refer to this weight of being responsible for one's own life as "abandonment."

The samurai and philosopher Miyamoto Musashi captured this concept when he wrote, "Respect the gods and Buddhas but do not depend on them."[120] Therefore, pray to your gods, practice your rituals, and cast your spells; however, understand that we can't turn over the responsibility for our lives. Our salvation rests individually with each of us and with no one else. Not even the gods.

Authenticity

Existentialists ask the question of authenticity. Am I acting true to myself, or am I acting according to what others dictate? To be authentic, one must acknowledge the reality of existence and choose to live by it. Hence, freely responding to anxiety can lead to authenticity.

Authenticity is also important in Dark Paganism. We know that authentically acting isn't easy. It's sometimes hard to tell if one is successful at authenticity. French author Simone de Beauvoir explained that while we are each born free, society imposes certain standards upon us. She pointed out that this is especially true for the effects of patriarchy and other socio-economic factors.[121]

The existentialist concept of authenticity is very similar to the idea of the True Self. Once again, we use the term *True Self* in a manner that differs from the esoteric concept of the higher Self. The pediatrician and psychoanalyst Donald Winnicott developed the idea of the True Self and the False Self. Over

---

118. Cooper, *Pursuits of Wisdom*, 227.
119. Barlett, *The Afterlife Bible*, 66.
120. Miyamoto, *The Book of Five Rings*, xxxiii.
121. Rooney, *The Story of Philosophy*, 77.

the years, others fleshed out this concept. Essentially, the True Self is spontaneous and authentic, while the False Self is superficial and empty.

The psychotherapist Carl Rogers was a pioneer in the study of the authentic Self. According to psychologist Stephen Joseph, Rogers believed that "authenticity meant being the author of one's own life."[122] Unless a person understands oneself, then the person would not be able to live an authentic life. Once a person gained such an understanding and accepted themselves, they could drop the False Self's facade.[123]

Freedom and Justice

Freedom is important to existentialism. For existentialists, they not only have the freedom from what they perceive as an oppressive god but, more importantly, the freedom to make their own choices. We have to own our identities and our actions. We can't give credit to a god or blame the devil for our decisions. Sartre describes blaming others for our behavior as acting in "bad faith."[124] Our freedom is defined by our responsibility for our actions and autonomy. However, freedom can be a heavy burden. Hence, existentialists referred to the knowledge of this obligation of personal choice as being "condemned to be free."[125]

Camus also included freedom as an essential element in his philosophy of absurdism. However, he believed that freedom must be balanced with justice. Absolute freedom results in oppression of the weak by the strong, while absolute justice suppresses freedom.

Individual freedom is the foundation of Dark Paganism. The Self as a divine being is free. Individuals create themself through the choices they make. Yet, we must not allow our rush to freedom by our Divine Self to run over the freedom of another Divine Self. Therefore, Dark Pagans understand the need for justice alongside freedom, just as Camus did.

122. Joseph, *Authentic*, 1.
123. Joseph, *Authentic*, 1–2.
124. Rooney, *The Story of Philosophy*, 77.
125. Rooney, *The Story of Philosophy*, 76.

Alienation

Finally, the embodied Self is alienated. According to existentialism, this means that the Self is estranged from both the world and from itself. This problem, which is a central existentialist and Dark Pagan theme, is more an issue for modern humans than it was for most people over the eons of human existence. Moreover, postmodernism is enhancing this alienation even further.

As a Dark Pagan's awareness of freedom grows along with their feelings of anguish and abandonment, so grows their sense of alienation. The world seems alien to them. The Dark Pagan may begin to see themself as a "stranger in a strange land." While this can be disturbing at first, it's an essential step in their growth and the cultivation of the Self.

Eastern Insight of the Self

We've covered the Self from a Western standpoint until this point. However, a Western bias ignores the important understanding of the Self found in Eastern thought. Also, Eastern thought has played an integral role in developing contemporary Paganism. The Eastern view of the Self isn't a unified viewpoint but varies greatly. A review of some of the Eastern views of the Self would be helpful.

Hinduism

As mentioned, the Hindu term for the individual soul is *atman*. In Hinduism, atman, or the individual soul, is one with the universal soul called Brahman.[126] According to Hindu thought, liberation consists of realizing that the universal soul (Brahman) is within the Self's identity (atman).[127]

There is no denying that the stuff of the Self is the same as the greater world. Animism holds that a universal consciousness is in all things. There is an unbroken connection between me and the rest of the world.

Hinduism and Dark Paganism differ in the importance of the form. Hinduism holds that the form is meaningless, while the substance has real meaning. As mentioned earlier, Dark Paganism views the Self as "functionally real" and

---

126. Renou, *Hinduism*, 24.
127. Renou, *Hinduism*, 42.

this function is what gives the cup meaning. Without form, the cup loses its value. The Self may be a form, but that form makes the Self precious.

Buddhism

While Gautama Buddha was raised in a Hindu family, his views of the Self were dramatically different from those in Hinduism. The Buddhist term for the soul or Self is *anatta*, which means "no-Self" or "no-soul." In Buddhist thought, there is no eternal and unchanging soul at the heart of the Self. The Self is a transient phenomenon arising from an interaction of physical and environmental forces. No one has ever been able to prove an eternal, unchanging soul, and people get along just fine without such proof. While most people believe in the soul, believing doesn't make something so.[128]

It's undoubtedly true that the manifested Self in the corporeal world is a transient phenomenon arising primarily from many internal and external forces. Descartes was wrong. Our bodies aren't driven around by a soul like someone remotely operating a drone.

We shouldn't assume that the lack of proof of the soul's existence supports the claim that the soul doesn't exist. As mentioned previously, absence of proof isn't proof of absence. This error falls under the logical fallacy *argumentum ad ignorantiam*, or argument from ignorance.

The soul isn't an unchanging bedrock of the person. It is dynamic and constantly changing. Some have theorized that a significant reason for corporeal existence is the perfect venue for the soul to grow and progress. We will explore the relation between the soul and the corporeal Self later.

Confucian

In Confucianism, the Self is defined by its relation to others. Known as "relational identity," the Confucian view of the Self is that significant social relationships define the person. Rather than looking inside to understand the Self, the Confucian looks outside to the person's relationships with others, such as authority figures and family members.[129]

---

128. Dhammananda, *What Buddhists Believe*, 115–17.
129. Ho, "Selfhood and Identity," 115–39.

Although Confucianism defines the Self by its relations, it doesn't deny the existence of the Self's inner world. However, it doesn't see the interior Self as stable and unified. Many different internal desires and forces pull the Self to and fro, causing the Self to change over time.[130]

This flexibility of the Self means that it's possible to improve it. Cultivation of the Self is the ultimate goal in Confucian thought. Self-cultivation may seem inconsistent with the Confucian emphasis on relationships, but it's not. Confucianism holds that relationships are a means rather than a goal. Confucianism acknowledges the Self's reality but sees it as a social product rather than an independent entity.[131]

There is no disagreement that relationships are essential to the Self. The Self does not exist in a vacuum. However, while positive social relationships are essential for a healthy Self, they don't make up the total of a person.

Dark Paganism also agrees that the Self isn't unified and stable but divided and flexible. Psychologists, such as Sigmund Freud and Jung, have long known that the mind isn't unified but consists of different psychic apparatus. The Self is a dynamic phenomenon that's always in flux and changes as we age. Long-term studies confirm that the personality traits of someone sixty-nine years old differ from nineteen years of age.[132]

Dark Paganism shares the Confucian belief in the importance of Self-cultivation. Not only does Dark Paganism honor the Self, but it believes that the Self can and should be cultivated. We can be better.

However, Confucianist Self-cultivation differs from the Dark Pagan concept. In Confucian thought, Self-cultivation requires one to "subdue one's self." According to Confucianism, subduing oneself means impulse control and harmonizing relationships to the point of submission.[133] Dark Pagan Self-cultivation aids the flourishing of the Self rather than submission to others.

Taoism

Taoism doesn't focus on family and social relations. The heart of Taoism is individuality and personal freedom. According to Taoist thought, the inner Self is

---

130. Pruett and Gross-Loh, *The Path*, 11–13.
131. Ho, "Selfhood and Identity," 115–39.
132. Harris, Johnson, and Deary, "Personality Stability from Age 14 to Age 77 Years."
133. Ho, "Selfhood and Identity," 115–39.

a manifestation of the Tao, and therefore, there is no need for Self-cultivation. Also, because the Self is a manifestation of the Tao, there is no need to look to society. The key is to look inside, let go of control, and learn to live in the universe's natural flow.[134]

John J. Coughlin describes Taoism as the only major world wisdom tradition that follows a "dark path."[135] I agree with Coughlin about Taoism. Dark Paganism champions individuality and personal freedom, just as Taoism does. Also, like Taoism, Dark Paganism looks inside to the Self rather than to society.

However, Dark Paganism understands that we're highly social creatures. Who we are is shaped by our social interactions, starting from the moment we're born. Also, as mentioned, Self-cultivation is central to Dark Paganism.

The Importance of Desire

It's impossible to understand the Self without understanding the role of desire. Is desire good or bad? Should we give in to our desires or try to snuff them out?

In his acceptance speech of the 1950 Nobel, Bertrand Russell said, "All human activity is prompted by desire." He lists what he saw to be the four infinite desires of humans. These four infinite desires, Russell believed, were unique to humans and not found in other animals. The four infinite desires are acquisitiveness, rivalry, vanity, and love of power.[136]

According to Russell, the least powerful of these infinite desires is acquisitiveness. No matter how much we acquire, we always seem to want more. We see this in lottery winners who suddenly have everything they need and end up going bankrupt because, although they're millionaires, they spend beyond their means. I see this in myself; I love books to the degree that I have many that I've never read or finished, yet I'm sure I'll buy more soon.

Acquisitiveness, although powerful, ranks below rivalry, according to Russell. The most famous example of rivalry was the space race between the United States and the USSR. Shortly after the Americans landed a man on the moon, they abandoned future moon missions. They had beat the "Reds" to the moon and therefore saw no reason to keep returning.

---

134. Ho, "Selfhood and Identity," 115–39.
135. Coughlin, *Out of the Shadows*, 138.
136. Russell, "What Desires Are Politically Important?"

W. L. George wrote that "Vanity is as old as the mammoth."[137] Russell certainly agreed and made vanity the next powerful desire. Many will sacrifice everything they've built over a lifetime if it means fame. In the musical *Chicago*, one of my favorite plays, Roxy expresses frustration after her acquittal when the attention of the press shifts from her to another murderer. Her vanity was so extreme that she couldn't rejoice that the jury spared her life. Instead, she sulked because she was no longer the center of attention.

Russell believed that the love of power was the most significant motive of these desires. Everything, including the acquisition of wealth, is a means to power. Power is a desire for its own sake. George Orwell captured this understanding in his novel *1984* when he wrote that "The object of power is power." A person will live in abject poverty if it means that they have a sense of power. In John Milton's *Paradise Lost*, Satan says, "It's better to rule in Hell than to serve in Heaven." Even the pursuit of scientific knowledge, according to Russell, is a pursuit of power.

Dark Pagans understand that these infinite desires reside in all of us, and we do not condemn them. Our desires drive us toward greatness. Desire is the motivation behind every great inventor. Olympians are driven to athletic excellence by desire. It is the drive behind the Great Work and the cultivation of the Self. James Hollis, PhD, former executive director of the Jung Educational Center in Houston, wrote, "We are *ipso facto* creatures of desire, or we would have no skyscrapers, no symphonies, no space travel, no sons and daughters."[138] Therefore, Dark Pagans have no interest in eliminating desire but wish to channel it to our benefit.

Some may question how the love of power can be beneficial. The power to do good, such as altruism, is still power. The will and the desire to achieve a virtuous aim are frustrating and meaningless if one lacks the power to make it a reality.

I grant that it's possible to twist desire into something destructive to both the Self and others. It happens all of the time. History is replete with tales of people who destroy themselves and those around them in their drive to satisfy their desire. Madison Avenue and politicians have long understood that they

---

137. George, *The Intelligence of Woman*, 29.
138. Hollis, *Why Good People Do Bad Things*, 74.

could manipulate us by tapping into these four infinite desires. The result is that these desires become our Achilles' heel.

However, we should not confuse the abuse of something with the thing itself. The consumption of food is necessary for a healthy body. Yet, overeating, even nutritious food, is harmful. Healthy desire, like a healthy diet, is essential to a healthy Self. And just because someone else attempts to use our desires to control us doesn't make our desires wrong. We must not assign blame to the victim. As part of the Self's cultivation, Dark Pagans strive not to eliminate desire but to cultivate it for our betterment. Also, because we understand that our enemies seek to use our desires against us, we are on guard for their manipulation.

Reviewing the Concepts

Dark Pagans understand that the highest knowledge is that of one's Self. Jung defined the Self as the whole circumference, which embraces both the conscious and unconscious. While the Self is multifaceted, we focus on five characteristics: the Self is divine, the Self is real, the Self is eternal, the Self is empty, and the Self is a mystery.

Dark Paganism focuses on the individual above the crowd and emphasizes authenticity. To be authentic, one must acknowledge the reality of existence and choose to live by it. While liberating, realizing one's freedom can also create a sense of abandonment and anxiety.

Dark Paganism doesn't strive to eliminate desires. Instead, it recognizes that desire is an integral part of being human. Russell identified what he saw as the four infinite desires of humans. The four infinite desires are acquisitiveness, rivalry, vanity, and love of power. While these four desires can be twisted into something evil, they're not themselves evil. Instead, they are driving forces for greatness.

Questions to Consider

* How do you define the Self?
* Is the Self truly divine, or is divinity reserved for the gods?
* Can the individual define themselves, as the existentialists believe, or are we solely the product of outside forces, such as the environment or genetics?

* Are Russell's four infinite desires inherent or culturally determined?

* Is desire benign, evil, or neutral?

V
PRINCIPLE 2: SELF-ACCEPTANCE

Second principle: Dark Pagans embrace all aspects of the Self.

The second principle of Dark Paganism is self-acceptance, which is the first of Carol Ryff's well-being factors. According to Ryff, a high scorer on self-acceptance "possesses a positive attitude toward the self; acknowledges and accepts multiple aspects of the self including good and bad qualities; feels positive about past life."[139] The aspect of the Self that may be the most difficult to accept is the Shadow Self.

The Shadow Self

Stephen King wrote, "That truth is that monsters are real. Ghosts are real, too. They live inside us, and sometimes they win."[140] These monsters exist within the Shadow. Working with the Shadow is essential in accepting the Self; it's a core element of who we are. Therefore, it's also an important part of Dark Paganism. Konstantinos and John J. Coughlin have written about the Shadow in their books on Dark Paganism. Raven Digitalis wrote an entire Dark Pagan book about it.

Shadow work has gained popularity outside Dark Paganism as well. Whenever something like this happens, the concept is often corrupted into something that it's not. However, the current fad of Shadow work doesn't change the fact that the integration of the Shadow with the Self is essential for healthy

---

139. Ryff, "Happiness Is Everything, or Is It?" 1069–81.
140. King, *The Shining*, xvii.

self-acceptance. According to Carl Jung, "Everyone carries a Shadow, and the less it is embodied in the individual's life, the blacker and denser it is."[141]

What is this Shadow that Jung speaks of with such dramatic language? According to Coughlin, the Shadow Self is the repressed element of our psyche.[142] Digitalis provided a similar description of the Shadow Self.[143] And according to James Hollis, PhD, "Expressed in its most functional way, the Shadow is composed of all those aspects of ourselves that tend to make us uncomfortable with ourselves."[144]

The Shadow Self is the product of our nature as social animals. Hollis points out that humans, compared to other animals, are one of the most dependent for survival. This dependency is especially true during childhood. Therefore, to survive, we must adapt to others. In adapting to others, our true Selves become alienated and pushed down into the unconscious. This process results in the unconscious collection of repressed desires, feelings, and thoughts that Jung termed the "Shadow."

The psyche isn't a unified thing. The sense of having a unified mind is an illusion created by the ego. Hollis explains that the psyche "is diverse, multiplicitous, and divided … always divided."[145] The Shadow is part of that divided mind. It's the unconscious portion that's pushed down and repressed. By the nature of its existence, the Shadow is often frightening and repulsive to the individual's consciousness. However, there is a paradox because the Shadow is also attractive. It becomes the forbidden fruit.

The Shadow is a natural and essential part of the Self. Therefore, Dark Paganism doesn't shy away from or fear the Shadow. Instead, it accepts and embraces it. We do not consider the Shadow evil. How can the Shadow be evil if it's an integral part of the Self, which itself is divine? That's not to say that there aren't characteristics of the Shadow Self that aren't disturbing and difficult to face, for there certainly are. We should avoid confusing what might be difficult or unpleasant with evil.

---

141. Digitalis, *Shadow Magick Compendium*, 2.
142. Coughlin, *Out of the Shadows*, 67.
143. Digitalis, *Shadow Magick Compendium*, 2.
144. Hollis, *Why Good People Do Bad Things*, 9.
145. Hollis, *Why Good People Do Bad Things*, xi.

Not only is the Shadow not evil, it's also not always wrong. Because the Shadow is a product of one's life events, sometimes healthy behaviors and feelings also get shoved down. In these cases, acting upon these positive hidden drives can improve a person's life.

Accepting the Shadow doesn't mean voluntarily acting on every whim buried within the Shadow. Acceptance isn't the same as acting. Exhibiting certain behaviors can be destructive to oneself and others. The classic Pagan virtue of practical wisdom, usually referred to as prudence, is needed to discern when, how, or if the Shadow's drives should be allowed to manifest.

The Shadow Self has long been a part of literature. Dr. Jekyll and Mr. Hyde was a tale of a scientist whose experiments manifested his Shadow Self into an alternate personality. In contemporary pop culture, we see the Shadow Self portrayed in the comic book character the Hulk, in which a scientist transforms into a monster when angered. And the subject of the song "The Stranger" by the musician Billy Joel closely resembles Jung's Shadow.

Pop culture has, at times, acknowledged the Shadow Self as necessary. *Star Trek* fans will recognize the Shadow Self in the episode "The Enemy Within." In this classic episode, Kirk was split into two by a transporter accident. One Kirk was kind, gentle, and brave, while the other was violent, cruel, and frightened. At the end of the episode, the crew realized that the gentle Kirk needed his brutal half. Without it, he was weak and unable to function as a leader.

Each individual's Shadow Self is as unique as their fingerprint. Sometimes we can learn to see our Shadow Self, while sometimes only others can see it. Understanding one's Shadow Self is not easy and requires effort. At times the process can be terrifying and exhausting.

One might ask why we should go through such an effort. A person might argue that while self-knowledge from integrating the Shadow Self is good, the price of pain and effort is too high. Shouldn't we just accept that the Shadow Self exists and move on? Isn't it better for those feelings and thoughts to be left buried?

The answer is that we don't have the luxury of avoiding the Shadow Self. The Shadow Self will always make itself known, and sometimes not in a healthy manner. It's like a B-movie vampire who rises from the grave because there's always some idiot who comes along and pulls out the damn stake.

This unconscious influence of the Shadow has wide-reaching consequences. Lives are torn apart and shattered by the Shadow. The Shadow influences our daily lives, whether we're aware of it or not. Many of our decisions are rationalizations of deeper motivations bubbling up from the Shadow. The unconscious motivations of the Shadow can have profound influences on relationships.

Pathologies can have many origins, including biological, environmental, or a combination of the two. According to Jungian psychology, the Shadow is one of the causes in some cases. Depression, bigotry, fundamentalism, addiction, and an unhealthy manifestation of sexual desires (known as paraphilia) can result from the Shadow's unconscious influence.[146]

We can't run from the Shadow. Therefore, we must continually work to bring the Shadow into our conscious Self. We must strive to make the unconscious part of the conscious. Jung wrote about the integration of the Shadow, saying that "This act is the essential condition for any kind of self-knowledge."[147] Dark Paganism works to understand the Shadow Self in ourselves and integrate it into our conscious mind.

Self-Acceptance and Dark Emotions

Not all of our darkness is hidden in the Shadow. Everyone consciously feels anger, lust, greed, sadness, and more. These feelings are as much a part of the human experience as joy and happiness.

Some have stigmatized these dark emotions. We're told that we have to be positive all of the time and that negative emotions only bring pain. Like Charlie Chaplin, we're told to smile even though deep inside we're hurting.

There's a growing body of evidence that this insistence on positive thinking isn't healthy. In fact, the evidence is that it's perilous. The repression of dark emotions is harmful to the person and reduces their quality of life. In 2018 the *Journal of Personality and Social Psychology* published findings about the effects of the acceptance of dark feelings. They found that those individuals who accepted their dark feelings were more likely to have higher life satisfaction levels.[148]

---

146. Hollis, *Why Good People Do Bad Things*, 62–72.
147. Digitalis, *Shadow Magick Compendium*, 2.
148. MacLellan, "Accepting Your Darkest Emotions."

Catholic priest and historian Bede Jarrett wrote that "The world needs anger. The world often continues to allow evil because it isn't angry enough."[149] Feeling anger or sadness isn't wrong. It's called being human.

The Goodness of the Ego

An essential aspect of Dark Paganism is that it celebrates the ego. By ego, I'm referring to the sense of Self, including self-esteem and self-identity. The ego could be thought of as the psychoanalytical name for Ipseity. Ipseity, or selfhood, is the natural state of being for the Self. The acorn isn't meant to rot and mix into the soil. Instead, an acorn aims to plant roots deep into the earth and draw nutrients to grow into a singular majestic oak. The Cosmos is the soil for the Self. The Self doesn't blend into the Cosmos. Instead, it draws upon it as a resource to grow and develop.

It's not uncommon to read New Age material that expresses disdain for the ego and strives to destroy it. On the website *Hack Spirit*, Lachlan Brown wrote that the ego is something that we create, holds us back, and establishes duality in the world. He advocates "ego death," in which a person "transcends" the ego and lives their life "without its influence."[150]

Ego death may not even be possible. While Plotinus believed that ascension would result in a merger with the One, Iamblichus did not think we could achieve a union with either the gods or the One. Instead, he believed that ascension would elevate us to a higher divine state of being and allow us to become participants with the gods in the act of Creation while remaining individual souls.[151]

We should not condemn the ego but strive to understand it, accept it, and learn how to tap into its potential. Management consultant Dave Logan wrote in a commentary for *CBS Moneywatch* that while the ego can be selfish and destructive, it's also the driving force behind significant advances. He points to technological developments, such as advances in computers, as being products of strong egos.[152] I would point to the strong egos that influential persons of

149. Sams, *I WANT TO BE A.L.I.V.E.*, 30.
150. Brown, "Ego Death."
151. Shaw, *Theurgy and the Soul*, 89.
152. Logan, "In Praise of Ego."

modern Paganism certainly would have had. Many of these founders, such as Gerald Gardner, would have had strong egos to achieve what they did.

According to Logan, the ego loses power over time. He believes that its role diminishes as we age, and the ego becomes less focused on the personality. The person starts to focus more on others. Community and future generations take on greater importance. While Logan is correct that the ego's focus changes with age, I disagree that the ego loses power. Instead, its strength grows so great that it expands beyond the Self. To understand this growth, we need to understand the role of self-love.

Self-Love

An essential element of self-acceptance is self-love. The debate over whether self-love is good or bad has gone on for ages. The topic exists in both Western and Eastern non-Abrahamic traditions.

Jainism, Hinduism, and Buddhism view self-love as a negative and one of the rebirth causes. Confucius believed that self-love conflicted with the love of the state. However, both Lao Tzu and Yang Zhu saw self-love as a virtue. In classical Europe, Aristotle held a more nuanced view of self-love. He believed that the goal determined whether self-love was good or bad. For Aristotle, self-love for personal gain was bad, while self-love to achieve a virtuous goal was good.[153]

As modern Europe awoke from the Middle Ages' limiting mindset, it saw new philosophical discussions about self-love. Dutch philosopher Baruch Spinoza considered self-preservation to be the highest good. The eighteenth-century French philosopher Jean-Jacques Rousseau, like Aristotle, thought that self-love could be either good or bad. However, Rousseau believed that the key was the source. If it's determined by the opinions of others about you, then it's negative. However, when it arises naturally from the individual, self-love is healthy.

In the 1950s, the psychologist and philosopher Erich Fromm saw self-love in a positive sense. Rather than being arrogant and selfish, Fromm considered self-love good and necessary for healthy relationships. According to Fromm, one could not truly love another unless one loved oneself. Similar ideas were

---

153. Lokke, "Nichomachean Ethics," 57.

presented in the 1960s by the psychologists Erik H. Erikson and Carl Rogers. Such views are echoed today by celebrities. As RuPaul says, "If you don't love yourself, how in the hell are you gonna love somebody else?"[154]

Earlier I indicated that with age, the ego changes. As we age, the sphere of our ego often expands outward; so does self-love. The "I" becomes more than the individual Self and engulfs others. The result is that the ego starts to consider others' welfare the same as its own. M. Scott Peck, a psychiatrist, wrote that self-love and the love of others are so closely connected that one can't distinguish one from the other.[155]

Self-love rests at the heart of the Golden Rule, which is the core principle of practical ethics. Should you harm another? No. Because of self-love, you would not want someone else to hurt you. Should you give aid to another person? Yes. Because of self-love, you would desire assistance from someone else. Without self-love, the Golden Rule would collapse, for it would no longer have a foundation.

Most Westerners associate the Golden Rule with Jesus of Nazareth. This association is due mainly to the strong influence of Christianity over thousands of years upon our culture. Few modern Westerners realize that the Golden Rule isn't original to Jesus. Jesus most likely adopted his version of the Golden Rule from Hillel.

The Golden Rule is not unique to Judeo-Christian thought. Several versions of the Golden Rule are in the writings of the ancient Greeks. In the sixth century BCE, Pittacus wrote, "Do not do to your neighbor what you would take ill from him." During the fourth century, Isocrates wrote, "Do not do to others what would anger you if done to you by others."[156]

The Golden Rule is in nearly all contemporary non-Abrahamic wisdom traditions. Confucius wrote, "What you do not wish for yourself, do not do to others."[157] According to Taoism, "Regard your neighbor's gain as your own gain, and your neighbor's loss as your own loss."[158] In Hinduism, "Do not do to

---

154. Brown, *The Pretty One*, 219.
155. Peck, *The Road Less Traveled*, 83.
156. de Biasi, *Rediscover the Magick of the Gods and Goddesses*, 83.
157. Gildenhuys, *Ethics and Professionalism*, 75.
158. Mann, *Science and Spirituality*, 143.

others what if done to you, would cause you pain."[159] While in Buddhism one finds, "Consider others as yourself."[160]

Self-love creates the Golden Rule. The Golden Rule supports self-love.

Achieving Authenticity

Earlier, I wrote that existentialists include authenticity as an essential part of a healthy Self. Living an authentic life is also a necessary part of self-acceptance. Psychologist Stephen Joseph wrote, "Being true to yourself is about what you do, think, feel, right now at this moment."[161] If you are not true to yourself, then you're saying that your True Self lacks value. The result is that you let the others replace it for a False Self that someone else created.

Living an authentic life sounds great. However, the reality is that it's often easier said than done. We're under constant pressure from many directions to live according to their standards. Television, movies, music, social media, family, friends, and others are continually trying to create us in their image.

Joseph writes that there are three steps to achieving authenticity: know yourself, own yourself, and be yourself. Each step allows one to gain knowledge of the Self and enables one to incorporate and apply this knowledge so that the Self can grow.[162]

As mentioned, the Dark Pagan principle of self-knowledge is built upon the ancient Pagan virtue of "know thyself," which is inscribed on the walls of the Oracle at Delphi. Without knowing the Self, the other two steps of authenticity are impossible. Self-knowledge must be the basis of self-acceptance.

The step of owning oneself ties into the second Dark Pagan principle of self-acceptance. Ownership means accepting the Self, warts and all. Ownership of the Self requires unconditional acceptance of the Self. Acceptance must be of those aspects considered "good" and those labeled "bad."

Finally, there's the third step of being yourself. Jung wrote, "The privilege of a lifetime is to become who you truly are."[163] Because one knows the Self and accepts ownership, one can now decide what aspects of the Self one wants

---

159. Mann, *Science and Spirituality*, 143.
160. Borg, *Jesus and Buddha*, 15.
161. Joseph, *Authentic*, 10.
162. Joseph, *Authentic*, 143.
163. Okun, *The Sun, the Moon, the Stars, and Maya*, 39.

to manifest and what aspects one doesn't. In doing so, one's self-acceptance becomes more than just internal. It also becomes external, thus including the whole person.

There is no easy process to authenticity. Claims that there's an easy path are part of toxic positivity. Authenticity is never fully achieved and is a lifelong process.

Reviewing the Concepts

Dark Pagans embrace all aspects of the Self, including the Shadow. Not only is the Shadow not evil, but it's also not always wrong. We don't have the luxury of avoiding the Shadow Self. While pathologies can have different origins, depression, bigotry, fundamentalism, addiction, and paraphilia can result from the Shadow's unconscious influence. Therefore, Dark Pagans work to become aware of their Shadow and accept it as a normal part of themself.

We all feel dark emotions, such as anger, greed, and sadness. These feelings are as much a part of the human experience as love, joy, and happiness, and they shouldn't be condemned. Plus, we shouldn't condemn the ego but strive to understand it, accept it, and learn how to tap into its potential. Self-love is necessary for the person to accept all of these elements of the Self.

Dark Paganism celebrates the ego and the sense of Self, including self-esteem and self-identity. The ego isn't something bad that we should strive to discard. The ego allows us to achieve greatness in this life and the next.

Living an authentic life sounds great. However, the reality is that it's often easier said than done. There exist numerous forces in society that work against us living authentic lives. You can take three steps to achieve authenticity: know yourself, own yourself, and be yourself.

Questions to Consider

* Not all psychologists accept Jungian psychology as valid. Do you think the Shadow or something similar exists as a psychological phenomenon?

* Dark emotions are part of everyday life. Should we strive to limit our dark emotions? If so, how do we accomplish this? If not, how should we handle these dark emotions when they arise?

* Whether the ego is natural or a product of socialization, is it a good thing? Or should we strive for ego death?

* Three steps to achieving authenticity are knowing yourself, owning yourself, and being yourself. What additional steps can you take to live an authentic life?

VI
PRINCIPLE 3: AUTONOMY

Third principle: Dark Pagans set our standards,
are independent, and act for ourselves.

Autonomy is complex and challenging to define. Philosophers have debated the definition of autonomy and its very existence for ages. Returning to Carol Ryff's well-being scale, a higher score in autonomy would be "self-determining and independent; able to resist social pressures to think and act in certain ways; regulates behavior from within; evaluates self by personal standards."[164] To better understand Ryff's inclusion of autonomy, we need to explore its philosophical history.

The philosopher Immanuel Kant placed autonomy at the heart of his moral theory. Kant's work has become the touchstone for most modern philosophical studies of autonomy, even with those who disagree with him.

Gerald Dworkin, distinguished professor of Philosophy Emeritus at the University of California, Davis, explains that autonomy gives someone the capacity to define their nature, gives their lives meaning and coherence, and allows them to take responsibility for themselves.[165] He characterizes autonomy as "a second-order capacity of persons to reflect critically upon their first-order preferences, desires, wishes, and so forth and the capacity to accept or attempt to change these in light of higher-order preferences and values."[166]

---

164. Ryff, "Psychological Well-Being Revisited," 10–28.
165. Dworkin, *The Theory and Practice of Autonomy*, 20.
166. Dworkin, *The Theory and Practice of Autonomy*, 20.

The terms *second-order capacity*, *first-order preferences*, and *higher-order preferences* require some explanation. Second-order capacity is a person's ability to make critical choices based on their judgment and act upon them. First-order preference is the behavior or desires targeted by the second-order capacity. Finally, higher-order preference is the value that we decide is valid. An example may help.

Let's say that one day I decide to follow my cardiologist's recommendations and change my diet for the good of my health. For example, maybe I decide that I will no longer eat beef. Along with this, let's say that I choose to drop alcohol, specifically beer, from my diet.

The fact that I can decide that my diet is poor and needs to be changed is a second-order capacity. What I want to eat and choose to eat would be the first-order preference. Finally, a higher-order preference would be accepting that the proper care of myself and maintaining my health is a value worth pursuing.

Whether I choose to change my diet or not, I'm still exercising my autonomy. Even if it's a wrong choice, the ability to choose is still an exercise in autonomy. The second-order capacity, first-order preference, and higher-order preference are still present.

It's important to note that Dworkin's autonomy model doesn't include substantive independence as a component.[167] Substantive independence is a concept advocated by some in which for an individual to be considered autonomous, the person's desires must be wholly independent of others. In other words, if substantive independence was a requirement of autonomy, then the act of deferring to the judgment of another would not be autonomous. According to substantive independence, I would have to not defer to my doctor's judgment concerning my diet to act autonomously.

There are several problems with substantive independence. One problem is a purely practical one. As our knowledge grows, it's becoming more difficult for one individual to decide independently. In today's world, one must, at times, defer to a professional for direction.

Another problem with substantive independence is that it's not value neutral. It declares one form of choice as "autonomous" and the other as "non-

---

167. Dworkin, *The Theory and Practice of Autonomy*, 27.

autonomous." According to substantive independence, only those choices against the grain of authorities are autonomous. The problem with this is that it deems certain choices as second class.

Any accurate model of autonomy cannot include substantive independence. It doesn't matter whether I choose to defer to my doctor's authority. Refusing to defer to my doctor's authority may cause my autonomy to conflict with other values. Wisdom tells me that I lack the knowledge, experience, and training my doctor has. Courage may be necessary to exert one's autonomy when faced with pressure to conform to others' wishes or in the face of one's fears. These are just a few of the virtues needed to be incorporated by the higher-order preference. Of all the virtues, the most important is the virtue of wisdom, for it is necessary to know which other virtues to apply based on the circumstances.

For Kant, an autonomous person isn't without laws. An autonomous person has laws, but those are not set by outside forces. Instead, they are laws the autonomous person sets for themself. The key is that these laws are determined not by external forces but by the individual themself.[168]

While autonomy allows one to defer to an authority for guidance, it does not allow one to defer responsibility for choosing to do so. Nor can one defer responsibility based on the directions of the other. I can use my autonomy to defer to my doctor in my choice of diet, for example, or not, but I'm still responsible for the decision either way. I'm also still responsible for what I eat, even if it's based solely on the doctor's orders.

The judgment of history laid the argument over deferring responsibility to rest years ago. The claim that one could defer responsibility became known as the "Nuremberg defense" because Nazi officials used it during the trials at the end of World War II. The international court ruled that the officers were still liable for their actions and were found guilty. The Nuremberg defense has been considered a fallacy ever since. One cannot defer responsibility for one's actions.

Earlier, we saw that a Dark Pagan understanding of a healthy Self would strive for authenticity. This existential striving for authenticity isn't separate from autonomy. John Christman, director of the Penn State Humanities Institute and professor of philosophy, political science, and women's studies, wrote

---

168. Dworkin, *The Theory and Practice of Autonomy*, 5.

that an autonomous individual would be their "own's person." According to Christman, an autonomous person's desires and considerations aren't externally imposed but authentic.[169]

Autonomy and Personal Sovereignty

Autonomy is closely related to personal sovereignty. To understand what personal sovereignty is, we must first review what it is not. While this isn't a book about politics, we need to rule out certain political distortions of personal sovereignty. Several far-right political groups, found in many nations, have hijacked the word *sovereignty* for their purposes. The personal sovereignty of Dark Paganism isn't, in any fashion, associated with extremist right-wing political movements.

Let us begin by stepping back and looking at a historical example of sovereignty. Our historical case takes us back to the mythic history of Ireland.

John Beckett has written extensively about personal sovereignty in his blog and as a contributor to the book *Pagan Consent Culture: Building Communities of Empathy and Autonomy*. Beckett's work has greatly influenced my understanding of personal sovereignty, and I will often refer to him in this section.

According to Beckett, there is an ancient Irish tradition that the land and the goddess of sovereignty, the Morrígan, granted sovereignty to the king. He referenced a myth concerning a stone in Ireland that would call out his name if touched by the true king. However, this didn't grant ownership of the land to the king. Claims of the divine right of kings were a Christian-era rationalization to excuse a claim of power and were not Pagan in origin. To the ancient Irish, sovereignty meant that the king had the right to rule and rule justly. Failure to rule with virtue and justice would result in the goddess Morrígan removing the king's sovereignty.[170]

We can build upon this Irish tradition, which is also found in different forms in various cultures, to develop a model of personal sovereignty. Personal sovereignty is about power over your own life. Beckett wrote that the individual has sovereignty just as the land does. The person has the right to rule themselves and to do so rightly.[171]

---

169. Christman, "Autonomy in Moral and Political Philosophy."
170. Beckett, "Culture of Consent, Culture of Sovereignty," 23.
171. Beckett, "Culture of Consent, Culture of Sovereignty," 23.

The source of each individual's sovereignty originates in the nature of the Self. As covered earlier, the Self is a divine being or god. It's a manifestation of pure consciousness, which is the divine bedrock of reality. As an individual unit of this pure divine consciousness, the Self, therefore, has an innate right to self-determination. It's from this right to self-determination that we receive our sovereignty.

Not everyone respects the personal sovereignty of individuals. Some groups strive to remove it. These groups can be some of the greatest threats to our exercise of personal sovereignty.

Many religions actively work against personal sovereignty. Elohim commands Abraham to offer his son, Isaac, as a sacrifice and stops him just before the act. Therefore, Abraham, who abandoned his sovereignty, is treated as a role model for faithfulness. The Christian canonical texts include a passage where Jesus of Nazareth said that a person had to become like a child to enter heaven. Of course, a child is considered incapable of exercising their sovereignty, which is held in regency by their parents. As a result, a faithful adult Christian should abandon personal sovereignty to God. And while the word *Islam* translates as "peace," it also translates as "surrender," meaning to surrender to Allah.[172]

There is a vested interest by the news media in removing our sovereignty. Their main tool is fear. They play on the fears of both sides of the political aisle to hook us and, in turn, help boost their profit margins.

We see similar efforts by the mad men of Madison Avenue. Advertisers attempt to manipulate us into buying goods. They work to create desires and needs that we wouldn't have on our own.

Both media and advertisers use similar methods to remove our sovereignty. Each attempts to tap into our desires to manipulate us. If they're able to combine our desires with the hopes and fears of the Shadow, then their influence increases exponentially.

Social media is a significant player in the attack on personal sovereignty. On all of the different platforms, we're bombarded by messages, positive and negative, meant to influence us. All too often, these messages become toxic and dangerous to the person's well-being.

---

172. Smith, *The World's Religions*, 222.

Last but not least, there are powerful forces in society that wish to remove a person's body sovereignty. Their target is primarily the sovereignty of women. Beckett wrote that we each own our bodies and no one else's.[173]

Dark Paganism pushes back against all agents that try to remove our sovereignty. Dark Paganism includes personal sovereignty equal to the gods. As the Greek philosopher Plotinus wrote, "Let the gods come to me, and not I to them."[174] Dark Pagans do not accept marketing and media attempts to take our sovereignty, and we certainly don't accept the attempts by some to regulate our bodies.

Ultimately, personal sovereignty is about living your life according to your terms as you see fit. It's a divine right that we each possess. Personal sovereignty is a birthright.

Autonomy, Personal Sovereignty, and Community

The appearance of COVID-19 and the 2020 pandemic has brought the issue of autonomy and personal sovereignty into the spotlight. Where do the rights of the individual end and the social control, such as governmental, begin? Are there limits to autonomy and personal sovereignty, or are they absolute and inviolable?

Previously, I mentioned that Albert Camus stated that autonomy and personal sovereignty aren't absolute. Making either absolute would result in the freedom of the weak being taken away by the strong. As a result, authorities can, and should, limit someone's autonomy and sovereignty when their behavior endangers other members of society. Demands can be made on us by societal institutions, such as governmental authorities, to protect the lives of others.

Reviewing the Concepts

Dark Pagans set our standards, are independent, and act for ourselves. An autonomous person has laws. The laws are not set by outside forces. They are laws one set for themself. Autonomy is closely related to personal sovereignty. Many social forces try to remove our personal sovereignty. Personal sovereignty is about power over your own life.

---

173. Beckett, "Culture of Consent, Culture of Sovereignty," 23.
174. Moore, "Neo-Platonism."

Autonomy and personal sovereignty aren't absolute. Making either absolute would result in the freedom of the weak being taken away by the strong. Societal institutions, such as governmental authorities, can make demands on us to protect others.

Questions to Consider

* What forces do you encounter that strive to remove your autonomy in your life?

* Autonomy and personal sovereignty became hot-button topics during the recent pandemic. What demands can society make on us? When does personal freedom end and the needs of others begin?

* What role does society play in our lives?

VII
PRINCIPLE 4: MAGICK

Fourth principle: Each person has the potential
for power to exert influence over reality itself.

Magick is a spiritual practice in that we change not only the world but also ourselves. The practitioner learns that the changes to the world resulting from an intensive magickal practice pale when compared to the changes that occur to themselves. This aspect of self-change is why magick is one of the nine Dark Pagan principles.

Magick changes a practitioner because of its intimate nature. As we shall see, magick involves the interaction of the Divine Self with a conscious universe. This interaction creates a feedback loop for the practitioner. Just as intensive physical activity will change a person's body over time, so will an intensive magickal practice.

Magick is a practice common among many Pagans, including Dark Pagans. John J. Coughlin dedicates a chapter to magick in *Out of the Shadows: An Exploration of Dark Paganism and Magick*. Raven Digitalis has written several books that include magick, such as *Goth Craft: The Magickal Side of Dark Culture*. The same is true about Konstantinos, who wrote about it in *Nocturnal Witchcraft: Magick After Dark*, *Gothic Grimoire*, and *Nocturnicon: Calling Dark Forces and Powers*.

Before diving into what magick is, the odd spelling of *magick* needs to be addressed. The use of the letter *k*, though bad grammar in contemporary English, is based on the word's archaic spelling. One example is Daniel Defoe's tome, *A System of Magick*, which used proper spelling when published in 1727.

Aleister Crowley began the practice of using this archaic spelling to differentiate the spiritual practice from stage magic.[175] Crowley's homophone and usage continue to be popular today among Pagans.

Homophones are common in modern English. Examples of homophones are *knight* and *night*. We need to remember that English is a fluid and living language. Sometimes the *right* way to *write* a word is complicated.

Understanding Magick

What do Pagans mean by *magick*? There have been numerous definitions presented over the years. Of all the different definitions, Anodea Judith provides the best and most concise one. She defines *magick* as "probability enhancement."[176] Judith's definition works because it builds on the essential nature of reality.

At its base, all of reality functions on probability. Some events are very likely, while others are less. Annie was right when she told the other orphans that sunrise was a sure bet. Nothing would stop the earth from turning. While not as likely as a sunrise, the odds are still pretty good someone in the United States will find a quarter on the sidewalk. After all, there are many quarters in public circulation. However, the chances of finding a roll of one-hundred-dollar bills just lying on the sidewalk are very low because currency of that size isn't common among most people.

The reason for the centrality of probability in the Cosmos is the role of Chaos. Chaos's role here isn't a reference to quantum mechanics or chaos theory. Some authors jump on the quantum mechanics bandwagon, which occultist Gordon White refers to as "quantum abuse."[177] Instead, as used here, Chaos is an esoteric principle that plays a profound, existential role in the Cosmos.

The primal role of Chaos exists in many Pagan myths. For example, in the Babylonian creation myth, after Marduk defeats the offspring of Tiamat, who embodied Chaos, he carves up her body, as if cleaning a fish, and uses one half for the sky and the other for the earth. He then uses her tears to make the rivers. Marduk then mixes the blood of her defeated demon children with mud to

---

175. Higginbotham and Higginbotham, *Pagan Spirituality*, 80.
176. Zell-Ravenheart, *Grimoire for the Apprentice Wizard*, 19.
177. White, *The Chaos Protocols*, 48.

create humans. In this creation myth, while order exists in the Cosmos, Chaos provides the building blocks.

Magick is a spiritual practice intended to influence the probability of an event. It might be to bump up the likelihood of a preferred event or lower the possibility of one that's unwanted. The Greek mathematician Archimedes wrote, "Give me a lever long enough and a fulcrum on which to place it, and I shall move the world."[178] We might say that magick is the practitioner's metaphorical lever and fulcrum. We're applying our will through ritual and correspondences (the lever and fulcrum) to influence an occurrence's probabilities that fit our desire.

Many writers will point out that the odds of magick being successful are partially dependent upon the probability of the goal occurring in the first place. Returning to the previous example of the odds of finding a quarter compared to a roll of one-hundred-dollar bills, the less the probability is of something naturally occurring, the more difficult it is to have a successful spell.

Why We Can Do Magick

Earlier we saw that, according to Bertrand Russell, humans are motivated by different desires. Of the various motivational desires, the greatest is the love of power. This love of power originates from our species' inherent nature to apply our labor force upon the physical world to modify it to our liking. Karl Marx called this productive activity humanity's "active species-life."[179]

Many of us living in the modern industrial world have lost touch with this aspect of our lives. This disconnect is especially true for individuals, like me, who spend their lives in large urban areas. We live day-to-day, exerting very little labor to obtain our wants and needs. This lack of exertion hides the fact that everything we have is the product of humans' collective applied labor upon the natural world.

This ability to modify reality goes beyond the application of physical and mental labor power. This active species-life is so central to who we are that we're capable of manipulating reality itself through the exertions of our divine will. Humans can become creators of reality.

---

178. Achor, *The Happiness Advantage*, 64.
179. McDermott and Lave, "Estranged Labor Learning," 110.

Magick, therefore, is a form of power that we exert upon reality. Understanding magick as a form of power isn't unique to Dark Paganism. The world wisdom tradition of Taoism has several paths or schools. Of these different schools, the oldest school is magickal Taoism. According to Taoist practitioner Eva Wong, magickal Taoism is called the "way of power." We would include divinational Taoism, which, according to Wong, is the "way of seeing" since knowledge is power.[180]

The origins of our power to influence reality begin with the role of consciousness. According to classic thought going back to the Greeks, consciousness is present throughout the Cosmos. As mentioned in chapter 4, the world is infused with spirit. Soul is present in all things, which many Pagans refer to as the fifth element. Author Jason Miller prefers the alchemical term *azoth*.[181] As conscious beings, we can interact with this Cosmic consciousness or azoth. This interaction is where magick begins.

Because of consciousness's role, the Cosmos exists in two different aspects or modes: material and spiritual. The material aspect is the playground of the scientific method, which operates on verifiable and systematic observation. The spiritual exists beneath the phenomenon and acts as its source.

We must not fall into the trap of thinking that the spiritual exists apart from the material. Everything exists simultaneously as one being with two aspects, both material and spiritual. There is not a separate soul that somehow interacts with the body. The material and spiritual are but different coexisting aspects of the Self. To understand this, we can look to science for an analogy.

Everyday experience tells us that something is always one thing at one time. A dog is a dog and not simultaneously a dog and a cat. However, that's not necessarily the case at the quantum level. A quantum entity, such as a photon, exists simultaneously as both a particle and a wave until observed. Upon observation, the photon collapses into either a particle or a wave. This dual existence until an observation is known as quantum superposition, and there have been many theories concerning it since its detection in 1927.

---

180. Wong, *Taoism*, 5.
181. Miller, *The Sorcerer's Secrets*, 61.

Quantum superposition is a helpful analogy for the dual nature of reality. Like the photon in quantum superposition, all things have a dual aspect of being simultaneously physical and spiritual. I term this ontological superposition.

One way of understanding ontological superposition is through lenticular art. Lenticular artwork consists of interlocking images that change based on the viewer's angle. An example is the novelty art sold during Halloween that appears to be a Victorian-era photograph of a person from one angle and morphs into an image of a hideous ghoul as you shift your perspective. My favorite contemporary lenticular artwork is by the artist Randy Noborikawa. Its appearance is of a skull with prayer hands from one angle, but it morphs into a goddess holding a flower at another angle.

The material and spiritual aspects of the Self and the Cosmos are like the different perspectives of a lenticular art painting. All sides exist at the same time and in the same place. By changing perspective, the image changes. Changes in consciousness create changes in the Self's function from the physical to the spiritual and vice versa.

Another reason we can practice magick is that each person is a miniature replica of the greater Cosmos. This belief was found in classic Greek thought and continued through the Middle Ages and by Renaissance alchemists. In her classic *Isis Unveiled*, H. P. Blavatsky, whose influence continues in contemporary Paganism, wrote that a person is "a microcosm inside the great universe."[182]

The Hermetic principle, which reads "As Above, So Below," is yet another reason for magick. Known as the law of correspondence, the Hermetic principle is often associated with the *Kybalion*, which was published anonymously in 1908. However, the principle dates much further back. The Hermetic principle is in the *Emerald Tablet*, which is attributed to Hermes Trismegistus. The *Emerald Tablet* begins, "That which is Below corresponds to that which is Above, and that which is Above corresponds to that which is Below, to accomplish the Miracle of the One Thing."[183]

In their book *Paganism: An Introduction to Earth-Centered Religions*, Joyce and River Higginbotham wrote that magick works "because everyone is immersed in the flow of an enfolding and the unfolding universe."[184] Humans

---

182. Hall, *The Secret Teachings of All Ages*, 223.
183. Zell-Ravenheart, *Grimoire for the Apprentice Wizard*, 281.
184. Higginbotham and Higginbotham, *Pagan Spirituality*, 81.

might seem separated and isolated, but the Cosmos is united and interconnected in the otherworld beneath it all.

The Higginbothams provide an excellent analogy using an iceberg to illustrate the interconnectedness of the Cosmos. Above the ocean surface in the North Atlantic, one will observe numerous spires of icebergs. Yet, if one looks below the ocean's surface, one will see that many of the spires aren't separate icebergs at all but are upward extensions for whole icebergs.

The material world is like spires protruding above the water from a massive, single iceberg. The appearance of each phenomenon as being separate is an illusion. The different phenomena interconnect below the surface in the spiritual world, just like the iceberg below the ocean surface.

Whatever term one prefers (interconnectedness, Hermetic principle, law of correspondences, etc.), the Cosmos is like a web. If you tug on one thread, it pulls another. To quote John Muir, "When we try to pick out anything by itself, we find it hitched to everything else in the Universe."[185]

This interconnectedness is similar to the metaphysics of the Neoplatonists. Plotinus viewed the Cosmos as a hierarchy of three substances, or *metastasis*: one, intelligence, and soul. Everything in the world, according to Plotinus, is a part of the lowest *metastasis*: the soul. In this model, nothing is truly separate from another. John Cooper, Henry Putnam University professor of philosophy at Princeton University, describes this model as presenting a "unity in plurality."[186]

Magick begins with an alteration of consciousness that changes the Self's inner world. Because of the Cosmos's dual aspect, changing the consciousness of the inner world of the material Self creates changes to the spiritual Self. Changes to the spiritual Self then ripple into the Cosmos because each person is a miniature of the Cosmos and interconnected. Interconnectedness allows the practitioner to interact with spiritual entities, such as those of natural substances, such as herbs, as well as gods. Ultimately, using Hermetic language, changes to the above (material) change the below (spiritual), which in turn influences the above (material).

---

185. Gifford, *Reconnecting with John Muir*, 25.
186. Cooper, *Pursuits of Wisdom*, 323.

While magick involves a change in consciousness, it doesn't have to be intentional on the practitioner's part. We see this in Carl Jung's concept of synchronicity, which often happens at the subconscious level. Ritual, or psychodrama, can enhance magick's effectiveness, but it doesn't need to occur. Some poltergeist activity results from unintentional magick caused by individuals.

A clarification is necessary. At the risk of contradicting myself, magick does appear to have a near-mechanical aspect. Because of this aspect, some magick users have identified what seems to be laws of magick. While magick involves alterations in consciousness, the magick user must consider this mechanical aspect and incorporate the proper correspondences and processes into their rituals.

Two Types of Magick

The Western system of magick comes in two flavors. There is thaumaturgy, and there is theurgy. These two share many features, and their boundaries get a little fuzzy. Sometimes, it's nearly impossible to tell the two apart. However, in theory, each has features that distinguish it from the other.

The word *thaumaturgy* is Greek in origin. The original Greek was *thaumaturgia*, which means "wonder-working." According to Oberon Zell-Ravenheart, "This is the use of magick to effect changes in the reality of the outer world— what we call practical magick."[187] Thaumaturgy is sometimes known as folk magick, low magick, kitchen magick, hedge magick, or sorcery. When discussing magick, thaumaturgy is the type referred to by most people, including both practitioners and critics.

In thaumaturgy, the focus for change comes from the practitioner. The practitioner usually applies their divine will, intent, or power through rituals called psychodramas or spells. Most spells include various correspondences to increase the probability of successful results. These correspondences include, but aren't limited to, performing the ritual on a specific day of the week; making an offering to the appropriate deity or planet; including a particular type of stone or plant; and wearing a talisman or the proper clothing color and burning the appropriate incense or color of candle.

---

187. Zell-Ravenheart, *Grimoire for the Apprentice Wizard*, 153.

Over the ages, archaeologists have found numerous thaumaturgical spells. For example, magickal spells have been found that were written down from the second century BCE through the sixth century CE. These are known as the *Greek Magical Papyri*. Many of the manuscripts were discovered in Egypt by Jean d'Anastasi in the nineteenth century. The Anastasi collection, along with papyri found by other collectors and archaeologists, has since been slowly translated, often with great difficulty, by various scholars. These precious spiritual documents were published within the last thirty years and are now available to the public for study and use.[188]

The word *theurgy* also comes from Greek and means "god-working."[189] Theurgy focuses on transcendence and changes through the help of a deity. The power behind theurgy comes from deities and not the practitioner. According to Iamblichus, only the gods have such authority and power.[190]

Like many philosophers of his time, Iamblichus opposed thaumaturgy. However, he was a strong advocate of theurgy, which, he held, made it possible to become cocreators with the gods. He viewed theurgy as being a form of "co-operative demiurgy." Iamblichus believed that the theurgist could imitate "the nature of the universe and the creative energy of the gods."[191]

According to Cooper, Iamblichus's treatment of theurgy as being different and superior to thaumaturgy is flawed. Cooper refers to Iamblichus's theurgy as "religious magic." Though Cooper doesn't endorse a belief in magick, he contends that since theurgy, like thaumaturgy, involves ritual rather than philosophical contemplation and the power of reason, it belongs to the realm of magick.[192]

For Dark Pagans, the differences between theurgy and thaumaturgy become even fuzzier. This blurring is because, as mentioned previously, of our nature as gods. If we insist on maintaining this two-part classification of magick, theurgy would be best understood as magick focused on deities outside the practitioner.

---

188. Betz, *The Greek Magical Papyri in Translation*, xiii–xiiv.
189. Zell-Ravenheart, *Grimoire for the Apprentice Wizard*, 153.
190. Shaw, *Theurgy and the Soul*, 93.
191. Shaw, *Theurgy and the Soul*, 24.
192. Cooper, *Pursuits of Wisdom*, 385.

What's in a Name?

While labels can be restrictive and are frowned upon by many, the practice of labeling seems to be part of human nature. People like to label things. Pagans are no different. There are a variety of labels that we give ourselves. The popularity of one title comes and goes like the seasons. What follows are a few of the common titles specific to magick users.

Witch

One of the most popular labels among Pagans is *witch*. The word *witch* is from the Old English word *wiććan*. *Wićća* was male, while *wićće* was female. The pronunciation of the letter *ć* is "ch." The meaning was "one who practiced magic and used sorcery."[193] Though commonly used to mean a female practitioner, many male Pagans now use the label.

Famous witches of literature and media include the weird sisters of *Macbeth*, often portrayed as three witches. There are also the Good and Bad Witches of the *Wizard of Oz*. In recent times we've seen witches in the Harry Potter novels and movies. On the small screen, we've had the witches of the series *Charmed* and the witches in the Netflix series *Chilling Adventures of Sabrina*, which is based on the graphic novel. Recently witches became the primary protagonists of the Freeform series *Motherland: Fort Salem* and *WandaVision* on Disney+.

Wizard

Wizard is like *witch* in that it has ancient origins. The word *wizard* is from the Anglo-Saxon word *wysard*, which means "wise one."[194] This word tends to be applied to men and is often representative of a magick user. However, today it's not uncommon to see the term applied to anyone who shows an uncanny ability, such as an internet wizard.

The title of a wizard is used by Oberon Zell-Ravenheart, a magick user, author, and highly influential figure in Paganism. The most famous wizard of literature is Merlin, most associated with the Arthurian myths. In modern pop culture, we hear Elton John sing of a "pinball wizard" in the rock opera *Tommy*, and many male characters in the Harry Potter series have the title.

---

193. Bonewits, *Bonewits's Essential Guide to Witchcraft and Wicca*, 137.
194. Zell-Ravenheart, *Grimoire for the Apprentice Wizard*, 1.

Warlock

Although this term is less common today, it's still used by some Pagans. *Warlock* is derived from the Old English word *wǣrloga*, meaning "one who breaks faith."[195]

In contemporary pop culture, the word *warlock* has returned. Its most recent incarnation is in the Netflix series *Chilling Adventures of Sabrina,* which uses it for male Satanic witches.

Magician

There should be no confusion about the meaning of the label *magician*. It's one who works with magick. However, the problem is that without context the assumption would be of an illusionist or stage magician rather than one who works with magick as a spiritual practice.

The term *magician* is used for the magick workers in the novel *The Magicians* by Lev Grossman. According to Wong, in magickal Taoism, the title *magician* applies to those who work with nature for magickal power.[196]

Magus

A magus is a master of magick. Historically, this title has had a misogynistic bias in that it was applied exclusively to men. One of the most famous in the last hundred years was magus Aleister Crowley.

Sorcerer

This is the label that I prefer for myself. The word *sorcerer* derives from the medieval Latin word *sortiarius*, which means "one who influences fate or fortune."[197] It's common for people to equate *sorcerer* with *wizard*. Historically, the title *sorcerer* is gender-specific in that it's been applied exclusively to men. The female equivalent is *sorceress*.

Some oppose the term *sorcerer*. One is Zell-Ravenheart, who associates it with destructive magick.[198] However, not everyone views it negatively. Miller

---

195. "Warlock," 2576.
196. Wong, *Taoism*, 99.
197. "Etymology of Sorcery."
198. Zell-Ravenheart, *Grimoire for the Apprentice Wizard*, 294.

uses the term because he believes it carries the message that magick is at the forefront of his practices.[199]

In magickal Taoism, the term *sorcerer* is for those that work with deities and spirits.[200] In classic literature, there is the eighteenth-century poem "The Sorcerer's Apprentice" by Johann Wolfgang von Goethe. In modern pop culture, we see it in Disney's animated classic *Fantasia,* where the apprentice from Goethe's poem is Mickey Mouse. The title also appears in the Doctor Strange comic book series as the character is declared the "sorcerer supreme."

Black Magick versus White Magick

Presented for your consideration, two doctors who lived in two different centuries. Each man was a success in his field, and each was an important inventor whose creation would affect the world for generations to come.

Professor Frank Pantridge was a leading cardiologist of the twentieth century. After returning from World War II, he settled into medical practice in his homeland of Northern Ireland. In the 1960s, he realized that CPR, which he had helped pioneer, wasn't enough. Another intervention was necessary. Pantridge invented the automatic external defibrillator from this realization, saving untold numbers of lives each year.[201]

George Edward Fell was an American doctor with a degree not only in medicine but also in engineering. In 1887 he used these two degrees to invent a mechanical device that provided an early form of artificial ventilation, saving many individuals suffering from opioid overdoses. However, Fell isn't remembered for his artificial ventilation device. He's most famous for his invention of the electric chair, which took its first life in 1890.[202]

Besides being created by doctors, these two inventions have in common that electricity powers each device. Electricity is neither good nor bad. As the cases of Pantridge and Fell show, what matters is how we decide to use it. With electricity, we can save a life or take a life.

Magick is like electricity in that it's also amoral by nature. It's neither good nor evil. The intention of magick is what makes it one or the other. This amoral

---

199. Miller, *The Elements of Spellcrafting*, 189.
200. Wong, *Taoism*, 99.
201. "Frank Pantridge."
202. "Discovering Buffalo, One Street at a Time."

nature of magick is like the eye of the storm. It's a void with all the potential but no purpose.

Historically, "black magick" is any magick used for evil purposes. This association continues today. For example, wizard Zell-Ravenheart wrote that magick, while morally neutral, if done with selfish intentions, is termed "black."[203]

The major problem is that the modern association of black with evil has explicit racist overtones. As mentioned previously, the color black as a pejorative has had historical racist roots with its connection to the slave trade. It was a small step to apply the racist association of the color black with evil to other areas, such as magick.

The racist association of black magick with evil doesn't mean that color has no place in magick. Color plays an essential role in magick. For example, in his classic book *Real Magic: An Introductory Treatise on the Basic Principles of Yellow Magic*, Isaac Bonewits, who opposed the idea that black magick was synonymous with evil, provided an extensive color-coding system of magickal practice.[204] In addition, many magickal systems designate different colors to be used in different spells.

If you want to call your style of magick "black," then go ahead. I can relate, for I, too, call my form of magick "black." For me, black magick is effective magick. As the founder of the Feri tradition wrote, "Poetry is White Magic. Black Magic is anything that works."[205] In addition, I prefer to use dark aesthetics associated with black magick in my magickal tools and rituals for the simple reason that they appeal to me.

As mentioned earlier, the color black, like darkness, has numerous connotations. Many of these apply to magick. The color black represents the infinite possibilities found in magick and the occult. Black is the historical color of power and sovereignty, which are benefits of a magickal practice. For me, magick is black, for it taps into the black fire that burns within. Finally, the color black reminds one that they are corporeal and that our time in this life is limited, for we will all someday leave this world.

203. Zell-Ravenheart, *Grimoire for the Apprentice Wizard*, 294.
204. Bonewits, *Real Magic*, 202.
205. Miller, *The Elements of Spellcrafting*, 65.

Whatever manner in which you wish to use color in your magickal practice is your choice. However, some practices need to stop. One of those is the racist practice of designating *white* and *black* to represent good and evil magick. Such a practice belongs in the ash heap of history.

The Efficacy of Magick

You might be wondering if magick really works. Or are successes nothing but confirmation bias? Some positive scientific studies on astrology show that birth charts can predict the risk of schizotypal personality.[206] And in 2011, the *Journal of Personality and Social Psychology* published a study that supported psi's existence.[207] However, I have to admit that these studies are the exceptions. Reliable scientific studies with statistically significant positive results are hard to come by.

I'm skeptical about there ever being scientific proof of magick. Scientific studies of both theurgy and thaumaturgy pose particular challenges. According to Richard Sloan, PhD, a behavioral medicine professor at the Columbia University Irving Medical Center, the scientific research of spiritual practices, such as prayer, does "violence" to the subject matter by reducing it to base elements. The result is "bad science and bad religion."[208]

All I have is my experience and the anecdotal experiences of people I trust regarding whether magick works. I, along with others, have seen the success of both types of magick. So in answer to the question of whether magick works, I would have to answer "yes."

My positive experience with magick makes its efficacy a personal truth for me. However, it doesn't make it an objective truth. Science does not—and cannot—accept personal experience as proof. You must decide whether my personal truth is sufficient for you, based on reason, to accept magick's efficacy. Even then, if accepted, it doesn't make it an objective truth.

Magick sometimes fails. This hard reality has been a challenge for some who claim that magick always yields positive results. The need to explain why magick fails is greater for thaumaturgy than theurgy. Theurgists can blame gods or spirits who may choose not to grant requests. However, thaumaturgy poses different problems when spells fail.

206. Hayden, "Science Confirms Astrology!"
207. Bem, "Feeling the Future," 407–25.
208. Carey, "Long-Awaited Medical Study Questions the Power of Prayer."

A spell can fail if the odds of success are poor since magick is a form of probability control. For example, magick performed to stop the sun from setting is guaranteed to fail. Not even a god can stop Earth from spinning, regardless of how literally the fundamentalists read the Hebrew myths. The odds are astronomically (pun intended) in favor of the sun setting and then rising the next day right on schedule. Probability effects are also why magickal practitioners aren't all lottery winners. The chances of winning the grand prize are so bad that the arcane power needed to nudge the odds in the magick users' favor is extraordinarily difficult to achieve.

Another reason a spell fails is user error. Did you apply your divine will, or did you phone it in? Did you use the wrong correspondences? Did you perform the ritual incorrectly? Spellwork is like cooking. Fail to properly follow the recipe and the result may be something inedible. As naturalist John Burroughs wrote, "A man can fail many times, but he isn't a failure until he begins to blame someone else."[209] In chapter 5, which focused on the principle of self-acceptance, I pointed out that blaming others is, as Jean-Paul Sartre wrote, acting in bad faith. If your thaumaturgy failed, don't look elsewhere for a cause. Instead, you should look in the mirror.

Reviewing the Concepts

Magick is the potential to exert influence over reality itself. It's a spiritual practice in that we change the world and ourselves. Of all the different definitions available, the best and most concise is that magick is "probability enhancement."

Magick works because each person is a miniature version of a larger, interconnected, and conscious Cosmos. We interact with the Cosmos by altering our consciousness, which influences the material world because of the Hermetic principle.

While magick is amoral, the terms *white magick* and *black magick* have been used to describe it as good or evil. These labels of *white* as good and *black* as evil carry racist overtones and should not be used.

---

209. Williams et al., *The Advantage of Leadership*, 99.

Questions to Consider

* How do you define magick?

* Do we all have magickal abilities, or is this a talent of a few people?

* Do you believe that magick originates outside the practitioner, from within, or from a combination?

* Do you believe magick is inherently good, evil, or amoral?

* Is it accurate to say that associating magick performed with evil intent with the color black has racist implications? If not, why not?

VIII
PRINCIPLE 5: CORPOSPIRITUALITY

Fifth principle: The Dark Pagan embraces the physical body's goodness
and knows that the material world is as sacred as the spiritual.

I n his book *Pagan Theology: Paganism as a World Religion*, Michael York, director of the Bath Archive for Contemporary Religious Affairs at Bath Spa University College, explains that the Pagan concept of divinity differs from monotheism in many ways. One significant difference is that while monotheism
conceives the Divine as being wholly other or transcendent, the Pagan concept
of the Divine is that it's immanent. The implications of an immanent divinity go
beyond the nature of deity. The result is that corporeal existence itself is divine.
York terms the belief of divine corporeal existence *corpospirituality*.[210]

Philosopher Brendan Myers wrote that he hadn't seen the term *corpospirituality* outside of York's work. He noted that he didn't understand why York used
the word *corpospirituality* when he could have used *pantheism*.[211] It's true that,
at first glance, pantheism and corpospirituality bear some resemblance to each
other. However, though similar, they're not the same.

Pantheism sees the god and goddess in the world. It ranges from Baruch
Spinoza's god to Gaia worship. In contrast, corpospirituality focuses on the
sacredness of the embodiment and divinity of the body. It emphasizes the blessings of sensuality and an encouragement to enjoy physical existence.

---

210. York, *Pagan Theology*, 13.
211. Myers, *The Earth, the Gods, and the Soul*, 11.

Corpospirituality also shares elements with animism, which, as we've seen, is a common characteristic of Paganism. Raven Kaldera defines animism as "The belief that not only all living things, but all natural things, and some man-made things, have an indwelling spirit/soul of their own."[212] This is a belief with ancient roots. Plato wrote in his dialogue *Timaeus* that "this world is indeed a living being endowed with a soul and intelligence." Because of animism, various natural landmarks may be considered sacred by Pagans. However, not only are dramatic landmarks deemed sacred, but all phenomena, such as trees, rocks, and streams, are considered sacred and living.

According to John Beckett, animism is an excellent alternative to materialism. By understanding that everything has a spirit or consciousness, we begin to see the world differently. Animism inspires us to relate to nonhuman persons, whether they're the family dog or a tree, using Martin Buber's "I-Thou" relationship rather than "I-It." Plus, it reminds us that everyone, human or otherwise, has dignity and deserves to be respected.[213]

It's important to note that while animism shares much with corpospirituality, they're not the same. Animism acknowledges the presence of the spiritual within the material. Corpospirituality recognizes the sacredness of matter not just because it's infused with spirit, as stated by animism, but because matter itself is sacred. The existence of spirit within matter is not the deciding factor in corpospirituality.

Another way to understand the corporeal in relation to the spiritual is through the human body as a metaphor. The outermost layer of the skin, the stratum corneum, is formed by dead cells that migrate up to the body's surface. Although the stratum corneum cells are dead, they're made of the same organic material as the living cells beneath the surface.

The corporeal realm is like the stratum corneum, while the inner layers are like the spirit. The outer and inner layers are made of the same stuff, but the former is dead, while the latter is living. Plus, the former is short-lived in that outer skin cells slough off relatively quickly compared to the inner. We might compare this to the corporeal realm, for, as in a quote often attributed to the

---

212. Kaldera, *Dealing with Deities*, 12.
213. Beckett, *Paganism in Depth*, 22.

Buddha but that might have been said by Marcus Manilius, "We begin to die from the moment we are born, for birth is the cause of death."[214]

Dark Paganism isn't alone in recognizing the material as sacred. Until the first century CE, Greek philosophy viewed the Self as embodied. Life in this world, not the next, was the focus of Greek philosophers before the Neoplatonists. According to John Cooper, pre-first-century Greek philosophers believed that "Our happiness is found, at least in part, within a well-lived animal life."[215]

It's tempting to say that the material is an expression of the sacred, yet that wouldn't be accurate. For example, a self-portrait is an artist's expression but isn't the same as the artist, regardless of how lifelike it might seem. To say that the material is an expression of the sacred would imply that the sacred is something else. Instead, the material realm is sacred in and of itself.

The principle of corpospirituality impacts Dark Paganism's view of science. Historically, science is a secular means to crack open the universe and learn its secrets. This intent is reflected in a quote, wrongly attributed to Francis Bacon, that science places nature on the rack to break her and force her to reveal her secrets.[216] This view that we are to conquer nature reflects a mindset that the corporeal realm is profane and lacks value. It holds that science is a powerful weapon used by many in a war between humanity and nature.

Dark Paganism, as presented here, views science very differently. Because of the principle of corpospirituality, rather than viewing science as a weapon, Dark Paganism considers science to be a sacred act. In the same way that one dedicates their attention to understanding someone they love dearly, science allows us to better understand the corporeal realm. Science isn't a torture device to break nature but a tool to understand her better.

The belief that science (i.e., systematically studying the world) is a spiritual act is rooted in several classic Pagan myths. The most widely known is the myth of Prometheus. According to the Greek tragedy *Prometheus Bound*, the Titan stole fire from the gods because he felt sympathy for humans. More importantly, for this issue, he also taught humanity writing, mathematics, and more,

---

214. Ramage, *Great Thoughts from Classic Authors*, 527.
215. Cooper, *Pursuits of Wisdom*, 306.
216. Pesic, "Proteus Rebound Reconsidering the 'Torture of Nature,'" 304–17.

which are essential to science. Because Prometheus had to trick Zeus to achieve this, Zeus punished both Prometheus and humankind.

Prometheus wasn't the only Greek deity responsible for the gift of science. The divine golden boy was Apollo. Apollo's different domains included mathematics, reason, rhetoric, and logic. These domains form the basis of the scientific method.

Another classic Pagan myth in which the gods give humanity the gift of science is the Sumerian myth of Inanna and the sacred mes. In this myth, Inanna visits the god Enki, and after a round of heavy drinking, he gives her the sacred mes, which was the body of all knowledge. She then had to fight her way back to Uruk, the center of her worship in Sumer. The Sumerian sacred mes included a wide variety of positive and negative aspects of society, several of which, such as wisdom, would form the basis of the scientific method.

Corpospirituality answers some mysteries about reincarnation. Why are we drawn to embodiment again and again? Are we trapped in a vicious cycle of karma? Or, as thought by Iamblichus, are we held down by daemons who, though meaning well, keep us stuck to the corporeal realm like someone whose shoes are stuck in the mud so that each time we die, we bounce back and reincarnate again? Rinse and repeat.

One answer the Greeks had was that embodiment was to bring the glory of the Divine into the world.[217] Instead, maybe we're drawn to embodiment because it's in our nature. There may exist an attraction to repeatedly incarnate in the same way a sea turtle is drawn back to a specific beach to lay its eggs.

Author Ptolemy Tompkins proposes an alternate answer. For Tompkins, embodiment occurs because it provides an opportunity for spiritual evolution. Each embodiment that we have has the goal of growing and progressing. The ultimate goal of this is for the Self to achieve godhood.[218] Therefore, embodiment would be an avenue for ascension to higher levels of being.

Would Tompkins's concept of embodiment as means to ascension conflict with corpospirituality's claim that embodiment is sacred? Divinity does not equal perfection. According to many myths, even the gods evolve and improve

217. Shaw, *Theurgy and the Soul*, 94.
218. Tompkins, *The Modern Book of the Dead*, 144.

over time. And change with the possibility of improvement is an essential feature of corporal life.

Corpospirituality has implications beyond science and reincarnation. Since
physical embodiment is sacred, sensual pleasures are blessings to be enjoyed
and not sins to be avoided. There is no sin in enjoying pleasures of the flesh, be
they food, drink, consensual sex, or other physical pleasures. Rather than hid-
ing away, corpospirituality calls us to be fully involved in the world. Embodied
life is to be lived to its fullness.

The World of Horrors

We must be careful not to romanticize embodiment. While many envision
the afterlife as a place of eternal happiness, this isn't true of life in the material world. For a complete understanding of corpospirituality, we must come to
grips with a hard, self-evident truth. Corporeal existence, while it has an inherent divinity, includes suffering.

Life begins with pain at childbirth for both the mother and child. The child
then experiences anxiety as it begins the rest of its life as an isolated being, separate from its mother. We experience sadness, pain, lost love, the death of loved
ones, and illness through the years. Many suffer from hunger and poverty. We
experience anxiety and fear. If we're lucky, we live long enough to grow old;
however, we also suffer ailments because we age. Invariably our existential fears
come true, and we die, sometimes alone, often preceded by fear and pain.

For many readers, this will look familiar. It forms the basis of the first Noble
Truth of Buddhism. According to Buddhism, suffering is inherent in the very
nature of physical existence.[219] The Dali Lama wrote that "we must die and
prior to death must all suffer inadequacies."[220]

In the Left-Hand Path ritual The Ceremony of Nine Angles, the physical
realm is labeled the "World of Horrors."[221] Indeed, there are horrors in this
world. One learns this by simply watching the evening news. Far too many
suffer from abuse, illness, hunger, and poverty. Add to this the existentialist
anxiety of realizing that one is responsible for oneself. The World of Horrors
captures everything of the first Noble Truth.

---

219. Smith, *The World's Religions*, 101–2.
220. H. H. the Dalai Lama, Tsong-ka-pa, and Hopkins, *Deity Yoga*, 3.
221. Chappell, *Infernal Geometry and the Left-Hand Path*, 88–89.

What is the cause of suffering in this World of Horrors? According to Buddhism, the source of suffering is our desires. To be more specific, the desire for private fulfillment, or tanha. As the cause of suffering, tanha is the second of the Four Noble Truths of Buddhism. Buddhism holds that tanha separates us and causes us to be more concerned about ourselves than others.[222]

In Dark Paganism, tanha isn't the source of suffering but a powerful liberation tool. As mentioned earlier in chapter 4, desire, which includes tanha, is what drives us toward greatness. We grant it's possible to twist tanha into something destructive to both the Self and others. It happens all of the time. History is replete with tales of people who destroy themselves and those around them in their drive for private fulfillment.

However, we should not confuse the abuse of something with the thing itself. The consumption of nutritious food is necessary for a healthy body. However, as mentioned, overeating, even nutritious food, is harmful. Healthy tanha, like a healthy diet, is essential to a healthy Self. As part of the Self's cultivation, Dark Pagans strive not to eliminate the desire for private fulfillment but to cultivate it.

While Dark Paganism differs from Buddhism on the desire for private fulfillment, Buddhist practices provide helpful tools to help the Dark Pagan maintain a healthy tanha. Buddhism's Eightfold Path, along with various Buddhist techniques, can be helpful. Along with identifying the different tanha, those same Buddhist tools can help a person increase healthy desires over unhealthy ones. In addition, these practices can act as a salve for the pain experienced during our corporeal existence.

If the desire for private fulfillment isn't the source of suffering, what is? What is the answer to the nature of the World of Horrors? In Dark Pagan thought, as presented here, it's the inevitable result of the creative interaction between Order and Chaos.

At the point where Order and Chaos meet arises creativity, growth, and self-organization. The dialectic tension between Order and Chaos is the driving force behind natural selection and evolution. Life is dependent upon the interplay of Order with Chaos. However, this creative interplay has painful

---

222. Smith, *The World's Religions*, 192–93.

consequences. Entropy, pain, and death also arise from this liminal zone.[223] The spot where Order and Chaos meet is the origin of the World of Horrors and the source of suffering itself.

The fact of suffering doesn't contradict the grandeur of physical existence because the World of Horrors is more than suffering. Indeed, there is pain, but there is also joy, even if it's fleeting. Max Ehrmann was right. Despite all of the pain of this world, it's still beautiful. To focus on only one aspect is to miss all of what embodiment entails. This narrow focus of the world was the mistake of the German philosopher Arthur Schopenhauer, who advocated an austere life as a solution to suffering. Another German philosopher, Friedrich Nietzsche, had a different solution. According to Nietzsche, we should embrace life to the extent that we would welcome repeating embodiment even with the pain.[224]

Within this World of Horrors, there exists the potential for greatness. Tompkins's speculation that the reason for embodiment is that it provides an avenue for ascension may be correct. One possible reason we choose to incarnate is that the struggles and pain that we experience while embodied may provide an avenue for growth.

One should not confuse this potential for greatness to be a theodicy explanation for suffering during embodiment. Those who look to theodicy to explain suffering have it wrong, for suffering during embodiment wasn't built into the world because of some divine purpose. The World of Horrors simply exists as it is. Creativity results in suffering. Suffering results in creativity. These two go hand in hand.

If we choose, we can turn our meaningless suffering in this World of Horrors into something meaningful. The poet Robert Herrick once wrote, "Man's fate is according to his pains."[225] Or, as we say today, "No pain, no gain." Just as the smelting of ore results in pure gold, we can choose to use the World of Horrors as the furnace by which we become the golden flesh of gods.

---

223. Waldrop, *Complexity*, 11.
224. Pollack, *Seventy-Eight Degrees of Wisdom*, 218.
225. Pollard, *The Hesperides & Noble Numbers*, 66, 320.

Reviewing the Concepts

The Dark Pagan embraces the physical body's goodness and knows that the material world is as sacred as the spiritual. The material world is itself divine. This belief in divine material existence is called corpospirituality.

Since physical embodiment is sacred, sensual pleasures are blessings to be enjoyed. Physical pleasures are not sins to be avoided. We're to enjoy life to its fullest.

Each embodiment that we have has the goal of growing and progressing. The ultimate goal is for the Self to achieve a higher level of godhood. Divinity does not equal perfection. According to many myths, even the gods evolve and improve over time. And change with the possibility of improvement is an essential feature of corporal life.

Suffering is the inevitable result of the creative interaction between Order and Chaos. At the point where Order and Chaos meet arises creativity, growth, and self-organization. We can turn our meaningless suffering in this World of Horrors into something meaningful if we choose.

Questions to Consider

* Do you agree that the physical world is divine? Or is divinity reserved for the gods?

* What is the reason for embodiment? Is embodiment a blessing or a curse?

* Why do we suffer? Is there a way to stop suffering, or do we just have to cope?

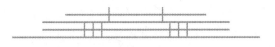

IX
PRINCIPLE 6: ENVIRONMENTAL MASTERY

Sixth principle: The Dark Pagan is a master of their world and not its servant.

The sixth principle of Dark Paganism is environmental mastery. Environmental mastery is closely related to autonomy. One might say that it's difficult to have one without the other. Environment, in this sense, isn't a reference to the climate. Instead, the environment is the individual's world that impacts them. Carol Ryff describes someone with environmental mastery as one who "has a sense of mastery and competence in managing the environment; controls complex array of external activities; makes effective use of surrounding opportunities; able to choose or create contexts suitable to personal needs and values."[226] Environmental mastery is mastery over your life.

I referenced Madison Avenue in chapter 6, the section on autonomy. Advertisers are continually striving to remove our mastery. Of course, this attempt isn't new. They honed their tools to manipulate us through the media during World War I as part of the US government's propaganda machine. After the war, those same propagandists left the government and became the mad men of the advertisement agencies. Since most advertisement firm headquarters were on New York City's Madison Avenue, the street became synonymous with advertising.[227]

Initially, Madison Avenue targeted the youth of the 1920s. Because no one had ever experienced such sophisticated marketing, the flappers and sheikhs of

---

226. Ryff, "Psychological Well-Being Revisited," 10–28.
227. Zeitz, Flapper, 197–200.

that time became easy victims of the advertisers' spells. Marketers thought they could use the latest psychology to manipulate young consumers into buying more goods. And they were very successful.[228]

An example of Madison Avenue's power is creating problems and needs that don't exist. One example is the epidemic of health issues that, before the 1920s, no one was very concerned about it. Halitosis, dandruff, dry or oily hair, acne, and others suddenly became problems. Each advertiser had the perfect cure—for a price, of course.[229]

If we can't control what and how much we consume, we fail to have mastery over our environment. By refusing to hear Madison Avenue's siren call of mindless consumerism, Dark Pagans can break their spell meant to remove our control.

The Virtue of Power

Earlier, in chapter 4, we learned that power is the strongest human desire. Environmental mastery is a form of empowerment. By mastering the environment around us, such as controlling our wealth, we exert tremendous power over ourselves and those who would control us. The corporeal Self isn't separate from the environment. The Self is embedded in the corporeal world. Therefore, mastering the environment is an exertion of power.

Unfortunately, power has a bad reputation. The most commonly referenced example of the dangers of power is the Stanford Prison experiment of 1971. In it, students had the power as prison guards over other students. The result was a horrible abuse of the students by the guards. While this experiment is now considered ethically unacceptable, it did seem to prove Lord Acton's famous words: "Power tends to corrupt, and absolute power corrupts absolutely."[230]

However, scholars have started to revisit the validity of the results drawn from the Stanford Prison experiment. In 2019 a paper published in the peer-reviewed journal *American Psychologist* concluded that the study was not just unethical, but the entire experiment was critically flawed. As a result, the

---

228. Zeitz, *Flapper*, 206–8.
229. Zeitz, *Flapper*, 205.
230. Bartlett, *Bartlett's Familiar Quotations*, 615.

conclusions about power and its abuse drawn from the experiment are no longer supported.[231]

The most common source of power is wealth. The greater one's wealth, the more power one has over one's world. Many assume that this must mean that the greater the wealth, the greater the chance of abuse of power. Some studies seem to support this assumption. The *Proceedings of the National Academy of Sciences* published an online study that found that upper-class individuals were more likely to exhibit unethical behavior than the poor and middle-class when subjected to various scenarios.[232]

However, one shouldn't be quick to conclude that the study proves that wealth automatically corrupts. It's just as possible that wealth and the resulting power simply allow those who are otherwise unethical to act upon how they wish. Unscrupulous individuals who lack power might simply lack the opportunity that wealth provides. We need a study to follow individuals before and after they acquire power.

In 2012 professor Katherine A. DeCelles, with the University of Toronto, published a study in the *Journal of Applied Psychology* designed to determine if ethical behavior changed after acquiring power. Her research found that the determining factor wasn't whether or not a person gained power. The determining factor was the "moral identity" of the individual before the acquisition. In the study, those who scored high for virtuous behaviors, such as compassion, on tests before acquiring power were more likely to use their new power virtuously than those who scored low before the acquisition.[233]

When we include DeCelles's study, we find that it's not as simple as "power corrupts." Rather than change a person's character, power allows the exhibition of it. If a person is already unethical, then power will make that characteristic of their personality apparent. If the person is virtuous, then gaining power allows them to act upon their virtue.

As mentioned in chapter 4, Bertrand Russell included the desire for power as one of humans' infinite desires. Gloria Steinem wrote that "Power can be taken, but not given. The process of the taking is empowerment in itself."[234]

---

231. Le Texier, "Debunking the Stanford Prison Experiment," 823–39.
232. Piff et al., "Higher Social Class Predicts Increased Unethical Behavior."
233. DeCelles, DeRue, and Ceranic, "Does Power Corrupt or Enable?" 681–89.
234. Beresford, *Participatory Ideology*, 120.

Power itself is not something to be avoided. The virtuous must acquire power. If the ethical don't, then the unethical certainly will.

Financial Mastery

Some abandon the world. People move to monasteries or buy a piece of land and try to live off the grid. While these are legitimate choices for some, they would not appeal to most, especially the majority of those living in the industrialized world. Then there are those in the industrialized world, many of them Pagans, who will tell you that they don't want to live like monks, but at the same time, they don't have an interest in money. They want to focus on the spiritual rather than the financial.

There are legitimate concerns about money. Placing a monetary value on something commodifies that thing, which turns it, to borrow terminology from theologian Martin Buber, from a sacred "thou" to a profane "it." The most famous critical saying is by the Apostle Paul, who wrote in 1 Timothy 6:10 that the love of money was the root of all evil.

With all of its faults, money, whether paper or electronic, is like magick in that it's amoral. Money can be used to feed a hungry child, or it can be used to buy a gun to murder someone. How money is used decides its ethical nature.

How one feels about money is irrelevant. Whether laissez-faire or social democracy, money is a requirement for life in our capitalist system. We can debate economics and whether our system is fair or should be changed. However, the reality is that money is still a necessity.

When it comes to money, many people, especially progressives, think they can eat their cake and keep it too. A person will often try to live a modern Western lifestyle while avoiding discussing or thinking about money altogether. The result is a tendency for some to go from one financial crisis to the next, casting emergency money spells just to make the rent.

Then some have an obsession with wealth. Wealth and money consume their thoughts and actions. Some strive to accumulate wealth to the point of destroying themselves and those they love.

Even if one doesn't obsess over wealth, our economic system will steal your financial mastery and destroy you if allowed. One shouldn't think of this as isolated to the United States. This characteristic exists around the globe. Our capitalist system values accruing monetary wealth over caring for human life and personal experience. The sorcerers of Madison Avenue and the priests of Wall Street strive to tap into Russell's desire for accumulation.

All of these examples involve surrendering one's financial mastery to others. Each grants power over our lives to someone or something else. If one tries to ignore the importance of money, one will regularly find it yanking them back like a choker leash on a dog. However, if you begin to obsess over money, you'll find both Madison Avenue and avarice leading you around like a bull with a ring through its nose. And if one dedicates one's loyalty to a corporation in exchange for the promise of money in the form of pay and benefits, one will soon find that employers will use them up and throw them away like a power plant uses coal and dumps the ash. The Japanese call this abuse *karōshi,* which translates literally as "overwork death."

Thankfully, these aren't our only options. There is another path that we can choose. The Greek Stoic philosopher Seneca wrote, "For the wise man regards wealth as a slave, the fool as a master."[235]

We don't have to abandon the modern world, nor do we have to be enslaved by it. It was P. T. Barnum who wrote, "Money is in some respects like fire; it is a very excellent servant but a terrible master."[236] We can learn to make wealth our servant by bringing it under our control. A Dark Pagan who knows how to master money has found one more way to empower themself.

I will admit that this isn't always easy. On a personal note, I once accumulated massive debt through my shortsightedness and by being enchanted by Madison Avenue's siren song. However, I've found that while it can be painful, it is possible to master your finances. While this book is about philosophy rather than financial advice, there are two philosophical aspects of finance to consider.

Defining Being Wealthy

What does it mean to be wealthy? In his book *Financial Sorcery: Magical Strategies to Create Real and Lasting Wealth,* Jason Miller writes that if you have indoor plumbing, clean water, electricity, access to health care, and food on the table, then you're already wealthy compared to most of the world's population.

---

235. Seneca, *Dialogues and Essays,* 108.
236. Barnum, *The Life of P. T. Barnum,* 176.

So being wealthy is a relative term. I agree with Miller's definition of being wealthy as "When your assets and sources of passive income are high enough to provide sufficient income to support your lifestyle without your having to work for a paycheck."[237]

Setting the Bar Correctly

What wealthy lifestyle should we strive to achieve? Many Americans believe that this means an extravagant lifestyle. As I was growing up, the television encouraged me to have "champagne wishes and caviar dreams." We were all advised by the Duchess of Windsor that "You can never be too rich or too thin."[238] Credit cards, which used to be hard to come by, became easy to acquire.[239] Now media tells us that shopping on Black Friday is essential to our nation's economy.[240] In fact, after 9/11, Americans were told shopping was our patriotic duty.[241] Recently, with echoes of the movie *Soylent Green*, one American politician went so far as to say to the public that senior citizens would be willing to die from COVID-19 if it meant a return to a strong economy.[242]

Americans' dream lifestyle is not only unrealistic but unhealthy. While wealth has numerous influences, negative and positive, on behavior, one of the most striking adverse effects is on the environment. According to Joel Kovel, a former professor of social studies at Bard College, our obsession with wealth and the dominance of capital results in "poverty, eternal strife, insecurity, eco-destruction and, finally, nihilism."[243]

The idea that unrealistic wealth can be dangerous isn't new. This fact was well established by classic philosophers. Their solution was to bring what we perceive to be our needs in line with the reality of what we need. The Greek philosopher Epicurus wrote, "If you wish Pythocles wealthy, don't give him more money; rather, reduce his desires."[244] While Epicurus advocated an austere lifestyle that most consider extreme, his basic principle is sound. Being

237. Miller, *Financial Sorcery*, 20–21.
238. Knowles, "Duchess of Windsor."
239. "A History of America's Credit Cards."
240. Davidson, "The Trouble with Black Friday."
241. Stewart, "How 9/11 Convinced Americans to Buy, Buy, Buy."
242. "Older People Would Rather Die than Let Covid-19 Harm US Economy."
243. Kovel, *The Enemy of Nature*, 82.
244. O'Keefe, "Epicurus."

satisfied with a realistic lifestyle that avoids the extremes of either extravagance or poverty makes achieving Miller's definition of wealth more likely.

Safety and Environmental Mastery

Environmental mastery is about more than financial matters. All the money in the world is meaningless if you live your life in fear. Therefore, safety is a necessary element of environmental mastery.

Some see danger around every corner. However, most of these concerns are myths. One myth is that there's an epidemic of child kidnappings by strangers. In reality, most child abductions are by relatives.[245] Therefore, any discussion of safety must not degrade into fear. As Russell wrote, "Fear is the main source of superstition, and one of the main sources of cruelty. To conquer fear is the beginning of wisdom."[246]

Then there's the other extreme. Some see the world as all rainbows and sunshine. There are those who live their lives feeling safe and secure in their tiny bubbles. This worldview is found more often in the Western world than in the Eastern.[247]

While we shouldn't live in fear, the reality is that there are risks in this world. Every year in the United States, more than thirty-seven thousand people die in road accidents.[248] On average, 635,260 die in the United States each year from heart disease. Another 598,038 die from cancer. And although the homicide rate in the United States is lower than it has been in decades, it's still a real problem. The national homicide rate in the United States is 4.9 per one hundred thousand inhabitants.[249] The pandemic of 2020 was a stern reminder of the dangers of this world.

The otherworld has its dangers as well. In his book *Protection & Reversal Magick: A Witch's Defense Manual*, Miller points out that not everything in the otherworld is friendly. He writes that once you practice magick, you become known to the otherworld. He quotes Paul Huson, who wrote, "The moment

---

245. Roman, "The Truth Behind 10 Popular Crime Myths."
246. Russell, *The Basic Writings of Bertrand Russell*, 96.
247. Joshi and Carter, "Unrealistic Optimism: East and West?"
248. "Road Safety Facts."
249. United Nations Office on Drugs and Crime, *Global Study on Homicide 2013*, 23.

you set foot upon the path of Witchcraft, a call rings out in the unseen world announcing your arrival."[250]

Like with finances earlier, this book cannot address all ways to stay safe. However, a few recommendations drawn from various Pagan practices can help.

Situational Awareness

We tend to walk through life as though we're somewhere else. We might be focused on our phones or staring off, deep in thought. All of this time, life is taking place around us. Sometimes the result of this distraction is injury by either accident or crime.

One way to reduce injury by distraction is through increased awareness, or more specifically, situational awareness. In an article written by Lisle A. Stalter, a government attorney who writes for the Illinois State Bar Association newsletter, understanding one's current environment and anticipating potential problems with effective actions is the key to safety.[251]

There are a variety of tools one can use to increase situational awareness. One tool is mindfulness meditation, which is based on the seventh element of the Buddhist Eightfold Path. Mindfulness meditation is so prevalent in the West today that it borders on being a fad. The numerous magazines and books available on the topic show that mindfulness is big business. Many claims by mindfulness proponents are questionable at least, and some go so far as to be quackery.

One of the few confirmed benefits of mindfulness meditation is its ability to put a person "fully in the moment." Generally, meditation quiets the voice in the head. The person experiences a sense of deep connection with the events and people around them at the time. Positive feelings, such as joy and contentment, often accompany these experiences. For safety, being in the moment also means being in a heightened state of awareness. I highly recommend *Beginning Mindfulness: Learning the Way of Awareness* by Andrew Weiss to learn more about mindfulness meditation.

---

250. Miller, *Protection & Reversal Magick*, 16.
251. Stalter, "Becoming More Aware."

Magickal Protection

As mentioned earlier in this chapter, not everything in the otherworld is friendly. The Hermetic maxim of "As Above, So Below" would necessitate this. Just as the material world has viruses and predators that can be hazardous, the otherworld has entities and forces that are hazardous. And as in the corporeal realm, where some humans are consciously dangerous, so are there conscious hostile entities in the otherworld.

There are many steps that magick users can take to protect themselves. Burning incense, such as Dragon's Blood, can be used for banishing and spiritual protection. Another common tool is to establish magickal wards around your house or apartment. You can also create magickal talismans that you and your loved ones can carry to provide protection when away from home. These are just a few magickal steps available.

There are several good books on magickal protection. I highly recommend Miller's book *Protection & Reversal Magick: A Witch's Defense Manual*. Another excellent book is *Practical Protection Magick: Guarding & Reclaiming Your Power* by Ellen Dugan.

Practical Wisdom

One of the essential tools in achieving environmental mastery is practical wisdom. Called *phronesis* by Aristotle, practical wisdom is sometimes translated as "prudence." Some describe it as "street smarts."[252] For the Self to flourish in this world, it must sail safely and avoid crashing onto the rocks. Practical wisdom is necessary to make this happen.

Practical wisdom can also increase one's *de*, which is the Chinese word for the power that results from virtue. Knowing how to maneuver in this increasingly complex and multicultural world opens doors, both financially and socially. The opportunities provided by practical wisdom make life easier and increase the chance of success in any endeavor.

Reviewing the Concepts

The Dark Pagan is a master of their world and not its servant. Environmental mastery is mastery over your life. Social forces are continually striving to

---

252. McKay and McKay, "Practical Wisdom: The Master Virtue."

remove our mastery. This assault on our mastery is especially true in our economic system.

With all of its faults, money, whether paper or electronic, is amoral. Money can be used to feed a hungry child, or it can be used to buy a gun to murder someone. How money is used decides its ethical nature. We can learn to make wealth our slave by bringing it under our control. A Dark Pagan who knows how to master money has found one more way to empower themselves.

Power by itself isn't bad. Nor does it always create abuse. Power makes it possible for people, good and bad, to act out their character. If the ethical people don't take power, the unethical will.

Safety is an essential part of environmental mastery. While one shouldn't live in fear, neither should one assume all is safe. There are various methods one can use to help increase one's safety.

Questions to Consider

* Do you feel like you're the master of your environment?

* Is it true that there are forces in your life trying to remove your mastery? If so, what are they, and how can you push back against these forces?

* Is power amoral? Or does power always corrupt?

* Do you feel safe in your day-to-day life? If so, are your defenses sufficient?

X
PRINCIPLE 7: PURPOSE IN LIFE

Seventh principle: Dark Pagans acknowledge that each
individual is responsible for creating their purpose in life.

For this measurement, according to Carol Ryff, someone with a life's purpose "has goals in life and a sense of directedness; feels there is meaning to present and past life; holds beliefs that give life purpose; has aims and objectives for living."[253] If knowing life's purpose or meaning is as vital to well-being as Ryff believes it to be, then how do we find it? What is the meaning of life?

There is no unified Dark Pagan view about the meaning of life. Neither John J. Coughlin nor Raven Digitalis write about it in their books. According to Konstantinos, our meaning or purpose in life is to return to the source of the Cosmos. We incarnate to experience as much as possible as a form of training for such an ascension. In addition, the paths our lives take are determined during our time in the afterlife.[254] Konstantinos's view is a classic idea held by many great minds over the ages.

Ikigai: A Japanese Method

Okinawa Island, one of the Japanese archipelago islands, is known for its citizens' longevity. The average age of men in Okinawa is eighty-four, and for women, it is ninety. It's not unheard of for an Okinawan to live to one hundred, making residents of Okinawa some of the longest-living humans. While some

---

253. Ryff, "Psychological Well-Being Revisited," 10–28.
254. Konstantinos, *Nocturnal Witchcraft*, 9–12.

credit the clean air, active lifestyle, and healthy diet to their long lives—and no doubt it all helps—some say their longevity is due to their philosophy of life called *ikigai*.

The age or health benefits aren't what makes ikigai special. *Ikigai*, which roughly translates as "life, to be worthwhile," is another way of saying "meaning of life" or "the reason for living." [255] Many Okinawans consider ikigai the reason they get up in the morning. It sets the tempo of their lives and gets them through their days.

According to ikigai, there are four elements to consider. They are what you love, what you are good at, what the world needs, and what you can be paid for. If you place these four elements in overlapping circles, where they intersect tells you your ikigai, or meaning for life.[256] Once you determine how these elements interact, you should, according to ikigai, allow them to guide how you live your life.

According to psychologist Katsuya Inoue, ikigai provides three possible directions for one's purpose: social, nonsocial, or antisocial.[257] The social direction focuses on the needs of society, while the nonsocial focuses on the Self. The antisocial is the focus of hateful or revengeful lifestyles.

The three possible directions of ikigai (social, nonsocial, or antisocial) are interesting from a Dark Pagan perspective. At the risk of cultural appropriation, the social and nonsocial directions resemble contemporary Paganism's lightside and darkside, respectively. The three directions of ikigai would place the antisocial direction outside either light or dark paths.

Ikigai is also very pragmatic, which should appeal to the Dark Pagan. It acknowledges that being paid should be an important part of choosing one's purpose in life. As mentioned in chapter 9, reality demands access to money. Therefore, one should consider the financial impact of one's choices on the purpose of one's life. Of course, this doesn't mean one must work in a field that pays well. But one should be prepared for the financial consequences of one's choices.

Another positive feature of ikigai is that it is human focused. Ikigai doesn't claim to draw from either the Cosmos or a god. Nor does it look to society as the guide, for that's only one of four considerations. The other three

255. García and Miralles, *Ikigai*, 11.
256. García and Miralles, *Ikigai*, 9.
257. Inoue, *Psychology of Aging*, 80–99.

considerations (what one is good at, what one loves, and what one is paid for doing) are Self-centric. Ikigai focuses on the needs and desires of the Self.

Western Concepts of Meaning

Here in the West, there are numerous attempts at finding meaning. There are so many different methods that whole volumes are written about the topic. For this book, I'm going to focus on only four.

Aristotle

We have historically looked to Aristotle for guidance on meaning. While Aristotle believed that the gods played an active role in the Cosmos, he didn't believe that the gods determined meaning of the Cosmos but were subject to its rules just the same as humans. He thought that the gods didn't grant eudaimonia. Instead, he believed that it was an integral part of the Cosmos itself. Aristotle believed that the universe was orderly and structured. Everything has its place, he believed. Therefore, once you deduced your rightful place in the universe, you would know how to flourish.[258]

Dark Paganism differs dramatically from Aristotle's beliefs. We've since learned that Aristotle was wrong about the Cosmos. While Order is present in the Cosmos, Chaos is an essential element. The beautiful complexity of the Cosmos arises from the interaction of Order with Chaos. There is no apparent meaning to the Cosmos, and therefore, we can't look to an orderly Cosmos as a source of meaning.

Plato

The Demiurge creates the Cosmos in Platonic cosmology and serves as an intermediary with the Source.[259] However, the Cosmos isn't laid out in an orderly fashion. Instead, it's a continual interplay between Chaos and Order. Instead of the Demiurge being a designer of the Cosmos, it's a mindless creative principle that creates without meaning. We can liken the Demiurge to Johnny Appleseed randomly sowing seeds of apples as he travels. While spreading

258. May, *A Decent Life*, 11.
259. Blackburn, *The Oxford Dictionary of Philosophy*, 98.

seeds was meaningful to him, where the seeds landed was random and without meaning.

Even if we go back to the hypercosmic gods of the Source, we find that the Source didn't intentionally create the Cosmos. Instead, the Source's contemplation of itself results in the Demiurge emanating outward. Creation is a meaningless by-product of a Self-centric Source.

Monotheism

Monotheism dominates much of modern Western thought on the meaning of life and is distinctly different from Aristotle's beliefs. The monotheist view is that the One God gives meaning. Westerners look to God for not only guidance on morality but purpose in living. Monotheism holds that God created the Cosmos and everything in it for a purpose. Therefore, according to monotheism, the meaning of life is something given by this Creator.

Dark Pagans can't discern meaning from monotheism, either. The One God is omnipotent, omniscient, and omnibenevolent in classic monotheistic thought. However, upon close examination, monotheism fails because the One God fails to meet these three criteria.

One severe failure of monotheism is in the problem of evil. How can evil exist if there is one omnipotent, omniscient, and omnibenevolent God? One of the most famous arguments is known as Epicurus's Trilemma:

> Is God willing to prevent evil but not able? Then he is not omnipotent.
> Is he able but not willing? Then he is malevolent.
> Is he both able and willing? Then whence cometh evil?
> Is he neither able nor willing? Then why call him God? [260]

While it's not certain if Epicurus wrote this, the argument is still sound. Polytheism lacks this problem. As we shall see in later chapters, polytheistic gods of contemporary Paganism, while some or all may be omnibenevolent, are not omnipotent or omniscient. Therefore, although not subject to Epicurus's Trilemma, even polytheistic gods fail to give meaning.

---

260. Miles, *Introduction to the Study of Religion*, 71.

Albert Camus

The existentialist philosopher Albert Camus went in a completely different direction than either Aristotle or the monotheists. Unlike Aristotle, Camus found no message of meaning in the Cosmos. By Camus's lifetime, the clockwork universe view was no longer valid, and Camus did not find meaning in god, who seemed absent from the cosmic stage. Camus found silence rather than a message of meaning, divine or cosmic.[261]

Camus found, paradoxically, that this silence carried a message. That message is that the Cosmos and all its inhabitants lack inherent meaning. There is no one god with a grand purpose for us. Nor will the "universe provide," as some like to say. Instead, we are tiny ants briefly crawling on a speck of dirt spinning around an average star in an average galaxy. All that we do turns to dust and is forgotten. Even Earth itself will someday die as our burned-out sun swells to boil away the oceans, leaving the planet lifeless.

However, humans have an instinctive opposition to this meaningless message. This pushback arises from our consciousness, which demands order and meaning in everything. As a result, we see patterns in the world, many of which are illusions. Examples are clouds in the shapes of animals or a person's face on the moon's surface and the mountains of Mars. Camus termed this conflict between our demand for order and the meaningless indifference of the Cosmos as the *absurd*. Hence, Camus's philosophy is termed *absurdism*.[262]

How should we respond to this absence of Cosmic meaning? If there is no inherent meaning to life, Ryff may be wrong. Maybe the healthy response would be to give up and accept that there is no hope.

According to Camus, there are three paths we can take in response to the absurd. Each person must decide for themselves which of these three paths they wish to follow. The three paths are suicide, faith, and acceptance.

In the first line of Camus's essay *The Myth of Sisyphus*, Camus wrote, "There is but one truly serious philosophical problem, and that is suicide."[263] Camus considered suicide in response to the absurd an invalid choice. It's an irrational escape that fails to confront the absurd honestly. Suicide, therefore, isn't a viable option.

---

261. May, *A Decent Life*, ix.
262. May, *A Decent Life*, viii–ix.
263. Camus, *The Myth of Sisyphus and Other Essays*, 3.

Faith is also an irrational choice. To flee from the absurd by having faith in a silent god who "works in mysterious ways" in the hopes that we'll have meaning is intellectual and philosophical suicide. Like physical suicide, faith in a god for meaning isn't a legitimate option.

The only valid path is, therefore, acceptance. Acceptance means embracing the fact that the Cosmos, and hence our lives, has no intrinsic meaning. It means that one faces this uncomfortable truth with honesty and courage. Once we accept the truth of the meaninglessness of life, we discover that we're each free. Each of us is free to create our meaning and live the life that's best for us.

Camus termed this freedom to create our meaning as a revolt. We refuse to allow the absurdity of life to draw us into nihilism and pessimism. Instead, we revolt against the meaninglessness of the Cosmos by creating our meaning. We should follow the advice of Dylan Thomas, who wrote, "Do not go gentle into that good night."[264]

Camus believed that revolting against the absurd provides guidance on living our lives. There are elements that Camus thought were part of the life of revolt. By incorporating these elements, one could create a meaningful life.

The first element within Camus's work is not to sacrifice your current happiness for the hopes of a happy future. We spend so much of our lives in mind-numbing jobs with the promise that someday we'll retire and can then enjoy life. And it's not just workers. Students tolerate long, boring classes with the goal of one day receiving a diploma that will, they're promised, lead to a successful career.

When possible, we should strive to find employment and degrees that inspire us, even if the result might be lesser pay or a less promising degree. Our current happiness is more important than a promised future. A happy future isn't guaranteed because the future itself isn't guaranteed. One day, we'll die, and for many, that day will be tomorrow.

However, the reality is that it's not always possible to work or study in an inspiring field. We have no choice but to work soul-draining jobs or take dry university courses all too often. Camus used Sisyphus as a metaphor for the revolt. As punishment by the Greek gods, Sisyphus was forced to roll a giant boulder up a hill every day to see it roll back down again, forcing him to start all over. Camus

---

264. Bartlett, *Bartlett's Familiar Quotations*, 887.

didn't imagine Sisyphus as one who suffered but instead one who revolted against the absurd by refusing to be sad about his punishment. Camus wrote, "The struggle itself toward the heights is enough to fill a man's heart. One must imagine Sisyphus happy."[265] We are to be like Sisyphus in that we, too, should make happiness an integral part of our revolt against the absurd, even as we toll through the drudgery of our day-to-day lives.

Another essential element for Camus's life of revolt is not to be ignorant. Like the classic philosophers, he believed that evil resulted from ignorance. He wrote that "The evil that is in the world almost always comes from ignorance, and good intentions may do as much harm as malevolence if they lack understanding."[266] We may intend well with our acts, but we can do more harm than good if we lack knowledge. Plus, not everyone that harms us does so with malicious intent. If we strive to understand where the other person is coming from, we'll often find their actions result from other issues.

According to Camus, another important element derived from our freedom is to be a rebel. Camus paraphrased Descartes when he wrote, "I rebel; therefore we exist."[267] Rebelling means to create our values and not live our lives based on the dictates of society. Some modern poets and artists, such as William Blake, often portray Satan as the ultimate rebel. Blake wrote of Satan as rebelling against divine injustice.

Finally, Camus believed the absurd means that love in its many forms is paramount. Camus wrote, "Nothing in life is worth turning your back on, if you love it."[268] If one is forced to choose between the love of someone or a commitment, one should take a chance and choose love. This choice for love also extends to work. Let's say that at some point, you have a chance to choose between a job in a field that you have a passion for or one that's mundane but has better pay; you should choose the one that you have a passion for, even if it pays less.

Dark Paganism and Meaning

Dark Paganism, as presented here, strongly agrees with Camus and his philosophy of the absurd. Even if we choose our paths during this incarnation in the

265. Camus, *The Myth of Sisyphus and Other Essays*, 110–11.
266. Sharpe, *Camus, Philosophe*, 365.
267. Camus, *The Rebel*, 104.
268. Akṣapāda, *Walking with Albert Camus*, 67.

afterlife, as proposed by Konstantinos, our lives still have no meaning. Any goal of connecting to the Source resembles a moth attracted to a flame rather than an actual purpose. The Cosmos and all within it are ultimately meaningless.

In chapter 4, I mentioned that while Dark Paganism, as presented, shares elements of existentialism, it isn't an existential philosophy. The same is true about Dark Paganism and absurdism. Absurdism sheds insight on meaning; however, Dark Paganism isn't the same as absurdism.

Camus would likely have opposed Dark Paganism just as he was against theistic existentialism. For example, Camus was a hard-core secularist. He only accepted what he could touch and considered anything else, such as the supernatural, a "construction."[269] Unlike Camus, Dark Paganism views the supernatural as a valid model of the Cosmos based on the historical experiences of mystics and occult practitioners. Admittedly, these experiences are subjective and not subject to scientific scrutiny, but our own experiences support many of these claims.

Camus would also oppose apotheosis, or self-deification, because he would consider it as providing infinite hope. However, he didn't oppose hope altogether. Camus believed that we should all have "finite hope," which is the limited hope of the here and now found in the freedom of revolt. He opposed "infinite hope" because it's similar to the false hope given by religion. According to Camus, such infinite hope returns us to the philosophical suicide of faith.[270]

This difference in the validity of the supernatural and belief in apotheosis doesn't mean that Dark Paganism completely disagrees with Camus. As mentioned, Dark Pagans share Camus's view that the Cosmos is meaningless. We understand that the creation myths are not literal, and therefore, the gods didn't create the Cosmos or bring order to it. Since the gods did not create us, they cannot grant our lives meaning. In addition, the gods are products of the same meaningless Cosmos we are.

Traditional esotericism indeed believed that the Cosmos is full of meaning and therefore grants meaning to life. However, Dark Paganism is a contemporary form of esotericism and, like the rest of contemporary Paganism, isn't the same as the classic. Dark Pagan esoteric thought doesn't find meaning in

---

269. Foley, *Albert Camus*, 7.
270. Foley, *Albert Camus*, 26–27.

correspondence as the traditional esotericism did. We do not confuse connections, or even messages, with meaning or purpose.

Like Camus, Dark Paganism believes that we're free to create our meaning and revolt against the absurd. We accept all of Camus's principles mentioned above. Dark Paganism also looks to additional sources for guidance. A prominent source of Pagan thought is Joseph Campbell.

In *The Power of Myth,* Bill Moyers asked Campbell about the meaning of life. Campbell replied that people aren't seeking life's meaning. Instead, according to Campbell, what we're seeking are experiences that would help us "feel the rapture of being alive." Therefore, rather than finding the meaning of life, we should strive to find what makes us experience the joy of being alive.[271]

A remarkable aspect of Campbell's reformulation is that it's consistent with the Dark Pagan principle of corpospirituality. It focuses on the joy of living as embodied beings. This rapture is more than just living. It's being fully engaged in living. This engagement is the source of our rapture and where we create our meaning.

How do we discover this rapture of living? Campbell advised that the key is to "follow your bliss." By this, he meant to do things about which you're passionate. I, for example, have many interests, but I feel a particular passion for three: the Jazz Age, the occult, and philosophy. Incorporating these interests into my life helps me follow my bliss.

Everyone has their passions. Not everyone's passion is grand, nor is one person's passion better than another's. We each must decide what is right for ourselves.

Also, there's no requirement to find only one purpose in life and stick with it. Don't let those who claim that each person has only one purpose limit you. Explore whatever your passion is at the time. If you find another passion, then follow that. If you never find one passion in your life, that's okay.

We have to accept that there are times when our suffering becomes so great that neither Camus's freedom nor Campbell's bliss is possible. There comes a time when the World of Horrors becomes apparent. However, even in these cases, we can—and should—create our meaning. Viktor Frankl, who survived

---

271. Campbell and Moyers, *The Power of Myth,* 4–5.

the Holocaust, living through four different concentration camps, found that establishing meaning for oneself is critical in surviving suffering.[272]

To some, creating a meaningful life may seem daunting. However, Dark Paganism, like existentialism, holds that there is hope. Jean-Paul Sartre described a "stern optimism" in that the "destiny of man is placed within himself."[273] Dark Paganism shares this stern optimism in that it holds that each of us can create meaningful lives for ourselves.

Because there is no inherent meaning to life, we must create our meaning. Only the individual, and no one else, can decide what's meaningful for their own life. Remember, no matter how many lives you might live, you'll never live this one again. So follow your bliss and embrace this life.

Reviewing the Concepts

Dark Pagans acknowledge that each individual is responsible for creating their purpose in life because there is no inherent meaning. The classic search for meaning in the Cosmos fails upon close examination. Therefore, the Dark Pagan must create their meaning in this meaningless Cosmos. Dark Paganism believes that we're free to create our meaning and, to use the words of Camus, revolt against the absurd.

Questions to Consider

* Is there an inherent meaning to life? If yes, what is that meaning, and how do you know it? If no, is it possible to create meaning, or is nihilism the only answer?

* If we create our meaning, how do we do so?

* What is its source if we don't create our meaning, and how do we know?

---

272. Frankl, *Man's Search for Meaning*, 163.
273. Marsak, *French Philosophers from Descartes to Sartre*, 492.

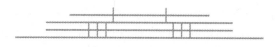

XI
PRINCIPLE 8: POSITIVE RELATIONS

Eighth principle: Dark Pagans understand that the Divine Self doesn't exist in isolation, and therefore, Dark Pagans strive to maintain healthy relationships with others.

According to Carol Ryff, someone with positive relations "has warm, satisfying, trusting relationships with others; is concerned about the welfare of others; capable of strong empathy, affection, and intimacy; understands the give and take of human relationships."[274]

It may seem odd that a worldview focused on the Self would strive for positive relations with others. But the reality is that the Self does not exist in isolation. We are all social animals. For each of us, our histories of relationships with others mold who we are. This molding doesn't end when we become adults. Relationships affect us from the cradle to the grave (and beyond). John Donne's famous poetic line "No man is an island" still rings true.

The fact that relationships are essential for the Self doesn't contradict the existentialist warning against following the herd. The opposite of following the herd isn't rugged isolationism. A healthy Self requires a relationship that is neither herd mentality nor isolationism.

Relationships are, therefore, obviously integral in the development of the Self. As a result, maintaining healthy relationships is essential for one's well-being. Because of this importance, Ryff included positive relations on her scale. It's also why it's one of the principles of Dark Paganism.

---

274. Ryff, "Psychological Well-Being Revisited," 10–28.

Since each person is a god, Earth is home to billions of gods who have to live together. If these minor gods don't try to live together, chaos and destruction ensue. With modern weapons, this destruction is great enough to wipe all life off the face of the earth. Stories of conflicts between gods appear in the myths of classic Paganism. Many living non-Abrahamic traditions, such as Shinto, are also replete with stories of gods in conflict with other gods.

John J. Coughlin wrote that ethics isn't necessarily a religious matter but is an aspect of humanity. Through ethics, we achieve an ability to coexist with each other peacefully.[275] Albert Camus wrote, "A man without ethics is a wild beast loosed upon this world."[276] Therefore, one cannot discuss relationships without also discussing ethics.

Ethical Systems

Over the ages, several different systems of ethics have developed. Deontology is one system, while another is consequentialism, to name just two. According to Christine Hoff Kraemer, the classic system of virtue ethics is the most popular among Pagans.[277]

The concept of virtue is ancient and very Pagan. The word *virtue* comes from the Latin word *vir*, which means "power."[278] While it has a clearly misogynist origin (it shares the same root word with *virility*), it has changed and lost its misogynistic emphasis over time. Many tend to think of virtue as a European concept. Yet, it's also in Eastern thought.

In China, animal bones and shells used for divination have been found dating back to the twelfth century BCE. Carved into these bones and shells was the Chinese word *de,* which means "virtue." According to Philip J. Ivanhoe, the Chinese word *de* means a form of power that a person had because they had acted favorably to another, whether the other was a person or spirit. He explains that acting "favorably" can include a sacrifice to a spirit or being kind to someone.[279]

---

275. Coughlin, *Out of the Shadows*, 99.
276. Freeman, *Seeds of Revolution*, 421.
277. Kraemer, *Seeking the Mystery*, xiii.
278. "Virtue," 2556.
279. Ivanhoe, *Confucian Moral Self Cultivation*, ix.

Another phonetically variant Chinese character of *de* is also related to virtue. However, in this case, it means that if someone has de, then they're able "to get" or "has some hold on" another person. Ivanhoe explains that while this character represents a form of power over others, it does not control or manipulate another, for then it would not be virtuous.[280]

Therefore, de was a source of social power to the ancient Chinese and a means by which to obtain divine beings' favor. For them, de was not a set of protocols but a force of nature like gravity. De was also very egalitarian. Not everyone has de, but everyone, from a commoner to the emperor, has the potential to possess it.

While most common people were thought to be capable of functioning in their daily lives with little or no de, the emperor was different. For the emperor to be successful, a strong de was believed necessary. To the ancient Chinese, an emperor with a strong de would receive a Mandate of Heaven, or *tianming*.[281] As long as the emperor was virtuous, he could gain the favor of the gods. However, ineffectiveness, natural disasters, or an overthrow were considered signs that the emperor lacked de and had lost his Mandate.

Andre Comte-Sponville, in his book *A Small Treatise on the Great Virtues: The Uses of Philosophy in Everyday Life,* writes that virtue is "a force that has or can have an effect."[282] He uses a knife to explain virtue. A knife's purpose is to cut. Therefore, if it's sharp, well-balanced, has a good grip, and is very good at cutting, that knife is said to have virtue. By comparison, a dull knife with a bad design that poorly cuts lacks virtue.

It's important to note a detail about the example of a knife's virtue that Comte-Sponville failed to mention. A knife's ability to cut well is not a virtue inherent to the knife itself. The object we call a knife could be dull yet serve as a highly efficient door prop. The knife's virtue, whatever that might be, is a value that we give to it and not one that's inherent to it.

Why is the fact that a knife lacks an intrinsic virtue important? As mentioned previously, it's important because we create our meaning and value. Therefore, our virtue is also something we create.

280. Ivanhoe, *Confucian Moral Self Cultivation*, ix–x.
281. Ivanhoe, *Confucian Moral Self Cultivation*, x.
282. Comte-Sponville, *A Small Treatise on the Great Virtues*, 2.

If we assign a knife the virtue of cutting well, what is a person's virtue? What is human excellence? According to Comte-Sponville, virtue is a capacity that a person has to be human.[283]

At this point, there is the risk of a tautological daisy chain. Therefore, we need to tighten Comte-Sponville's definition. According to Comte-Sponville, virtue is "an acquired disposition to do what is good."[284] This definition is very similar to the Chinese philosophers' belief. They referred to a virtuous person as having *ren*, which means "humaneness."[285] Virtue for a human, then, is a learned habit of actively doing good. It's not theoretical armchair speculation. It's practical.[286]

Classic philosophers, both Western and Eastern, have concluded that human virtue is the acquired habit of doing good. As we have seen, existential philosophers would agree that it's an acquired value rather than an inherent one. It might be due to facticity or transcendence, but it's acquired nonetheless.

The power of virtue is a positive influence on others, human and otherwise, leading to constructive change. It's important to note that de, or power from virtue, cannot intentionally harm someone. De can only arise from virtue, and virtue always requires a corresponding positive internal motivation. No matter how nice and effective, manipulative behavior isn't virtuous and wouldn't generate de.

Knowing that virtue is defined by human excellence and that virtue is the act of doing good is one thing; learning to apply virtue to real life is another. Chinese philosophers, especially Confucius, developed self-cultivation as a method by which one could become virtuous. For Chinese philosophers, this meant increasing one's sense of ren through a program consisting of eight steps.[287]

Of the different virtues possible, Comte-Sponville lists eighteen different virtues. While virtue ethics is popular among many Pagans, there is one virtue emphasized across Paganism. Though it's worded differently in various traditions, it's the same virtue. That virtue is justice.

---

283. Comte-Sponville, *A Small Treatise on the Great Virtues*, 3.
284. Comte-Sponville, *A Small Treatise on the Great Virtues*, 3.
285. Keenan, *Neo-Confucian Self-Cultivation*, xxiii.
286. Comte-Sponville, *A Small Treatise on the Great Virtues*, 3–4.
287. Keenan, *Neo-Confucian Self-Cultivation*, 40.

Justice is a complex topic, and there is no simple definition. The ancient Greek philosopher Epicurus defined justice as "neither to harm nor to be harmed."[288] This definition of justice by Epicurus is very similar to the Wiccan Rede: "If it harms none, do what you will."[289] While not all contemporary Pagan traditions include the rede, it is found in many and is referenced by many authors.

If we accept Albert Camus's premise that the world is without intrinsic meaning, how can we say that justice or any other virtue has merit? According to Camus, even though the world doesn't have meaning, humanity can because humans insist on having meaning. Therefore, we can decide what human virtue is and, according to Camus, "chose justice in order to remain faithful to the world."[290]

Justice is undoubtedly consistent with Dark Paganism. However, justice isn't a given, nor is it guaranteed to be here tomorrow. No matter how just a society you live in, there will always be injustices. Also, there will always be forces intent on removing justice in every culture. Therefore, a Dark Pagan must always be vigilant and work for justice for not only themself but for others.

Elements of a Healthy Relationship

According to the University of Washington, a healthy relationship is built on eight principles: mutual respect, trust, honesty, support, fairness/equality, separate identities, good communication, and a sense of playfulness/fondness.[291] Different types of relationships emphasize some principles over others. For example, a sense of playfulness or fondness wouldn't be appropriate for a working relationship, but all eight principles are healthy for a romantic relationship. Whatever type of relationship exists, it requires effort on the parts of everyone involved.

The University of Washington also lists the characteristics or actions of someone in a healthy relationship. There are two actions listed that are of particular interest to Dark Pagans. The first is to "Take care of yourself and have

---

288. O'Keefe, "Epicurus."
289. Coughlin, *Ethics and the Craft*, 8.
290. Foley, *Albert Camus*, 30.
291. University of Washington, "Healthy vs. Unhealthy Relationships."

good self-esteem independent of your relationship." The second is to "Maintain and respect each other's individuality."[292]

The emphasis on the Self in Self-centric philosophies such as Dark Paganism can challenge some individuals in maintaining healthy relationships. Sometimes, as a person progresses along the path of individualization, they can become stuck as they learn to accept the Self's centrality. The result can be selfishness rather than a mastering of the Self. These individuals fail to see the importance of healthy relationships. They become hardened to others and begin to make their interests the only ones that matter.[293]

It's essential for Dark Pagans not to fall into this trap. Part of the process of individualization includes developing healthy boundaries and maintaining healthy relationships with others. We need to remember that Dark Paganism is a Self-centric philosophy and not a selfish one.

Decency Ethics

As mentioned earlier, virtue ethics is the most common system found among Pagans. While it's the most popular among Pagans, it doesn't mean Dark Pagans are obligated to follow that system. Ethics are an individual choice. Dark Paganism doesn't mandate any one approach. Instead, it acknowledges that while an ethical life is part of healthy personal relations, the details are up to the individual. Each Dark Pagan must decide for themself which ethical system to apply to their life.

All of the various systems of ethics and all of their variations are inspirational. However, each school of ethics has problems when it comes to application. For example, in consequentialism, the ends justifying the means can allow one to act in morally questionable ways, even if the goal is positive.[294] And since the unconscious Shadow has such a strong influence, it raises the question of whether it's possible to be of "good character," which is at the heart of virtue ethics.

I find situational ethics very intriguing. In situational ethics, no one school of ethics dominates. Instead, one might imagine the various schools as tools in an ethical toolbox. As the idiom goes, "the right tool for the right job." Ethical

292. University of Washington, "Healthy vs. Unhealthy Relationships."
293. Coughlin, "An Exploration of Dark Paganism."
294. May, *A Decent Life*, 6–7.

behavior in one situation might require standing your ground for what you believe is right (deontology). Another situation might be to throw the rules out the window and focus on the consequences of your actions (consequentialism). Then again, the solution in another situation might be to strengthen your character and focus less on either some universal principle or consequence (virtue ethics).

No matter how good situational ethics appears, it lacks something. Situational ethics requires a standard to help decide what is the right tool to take from the ethical toolbox. Some, such as O. Sydney Barr, have recognized this problem. Barr advocated for situational ethics based on the Christian principle of "love thy neighbor."[295] While this is nice for Christians, for a Dark Pagan, who doesn't see Jesus as a role model, this doesn't help.

In his book *A Decent Life: Morality for the Rest of Us*, the philosopher Todd May reflects on the problems with trying to live by one of the three classical schools of ethics. He proposes a framework for ethical behavior, even in a world without a lawgiver to guide us. His framework is neither altruism nor moral nihilism. Instead, it proposes a pragmatic middle ground.

According to May, the goal should be to try to live a life that's "decent." It's not the life of sainthood or heroes, nor is it the life of selfishness or despotism, but one in which an everyday person can live and still be ethical. A decent life, according to May, acknowledges and acts upon the fact that all of us have lives that we're trying to live.[296] Decency ethics doesn't ignore the fact that I, too, have a life to live and that my needs are equally important, but it does not focus on just my own life while ignoring the lives of others. It seeks a golden mean between my needs and the needs of others.

May's decency ethics apply well to Dark Paganism's principle of healthy personal relationships. In Dark Pagan terminology, decency ethics begins by recognizing the divinity of the Self. I am a divine being with my own agenda and agency. It also acknowledges that you, too, are a divine being with your own agenda and agency. This mutual recognition is similar to the traditional Hindu greeting of "namaste." This phase has become widely known here in the West,

295. Barr, *The Christian New Morality*, vii.
296. May, *A Decent Life*, 37.

primarily due to the popularity of yoga. Meaning "the divine in me recognizes the divine in you," namaste acknowledges the divine nature of each of us.

Is May's decency ethics nothing more than "don't be a jerk" wrapped in the trappings of philosophical language? Being a jerk would certainly contradict decency ethics. However, limiting it to this fails to fully capture May's ethical philosophy. It's rather like saying that "do no harm," commonly associated with the Hippocratic oath, is the total of all medical ethics. Just as medical ethics is more complex, so is May's decency ethics.

Ethics and Humane Consumption

In his book, May expands decency ethics to nonhuman animals. He points out that he is a vegetarian.[297] His vegetarian diet arises out of his conviction not to treat any being cruelly, for they, too, have lives that they're trying to live. It's putting ourselves in their place. There are good Dark Pagan arguments for vegetarian and vegan practices.

May builds his conviction on the philosophical concept called moral individualism. According to moral individualism, we should consider each entity's situation and capacities, whether human or nonhuman, and act appropriately to each.[298] Moral individualism warns us against both speciesism, a form of bigotry similar to sexism or racism, and anthropomorphism, where we project onto nonhuman entities human attributes.

According to the common Pagan belief of animism, all of the world has a spiritual nature.[299] Human and nonhuman animal life, plant life, and inanimate matter have spirits. When we interact with anything, we are interacting with persons.

In addition to animism, another common Pagan belief is pantheism.[300] Pantheism goes beyond saying that spirits exist in the natural world. According to pantheism, the entire physical world is divine. This divinity is considered worthy of worship, and many Pagans regard it as a deity.

Therefore, vegetarianism and veganism allow us to honor divinity with all life. If all things are persons, then the ethics of decency would teach us to treat

---

297. May, *A Decent Life*, 109.
298. May, *A Decent Life*, 111–13.
299. Kraemer, *Seeking the Mystery*, xii.
300. Kraemer, *Seeking the Mystery*, xi–xii.

them the same as we treat other humans. Just as humans are just trying to get through this corporeal existence, so are all other entities in this world.

Vegetarianism and veganism are popular among Pagans. However, these two lifestyles aren't the only options available to Dark Pagans when it comes to the ethical treatment of nonhumans. There is an alternative to vegetarianism and veganism available to us.

We begin by acknowledging a hard truth. Living is dependent upon death. Even the strictest vegan must consume living things to survive. According to Joseph Campbell, all of life is dependent upon killing. He points out that even vegetarians and vegans must accept this hard fact. "You don't kid yourself by eating only vegetables, either, for they, too, are alive. So the essence of life is this eating of itself!"[301] We must acknowledge that all forms of killing and consumption, including that of vegetables, are acts committed against fellow persons.

Gregg Krech is an author and the executive director of the TōDō Institute in Monkton, Vermont. In his book *Naikan*, he wrote about being a vegetarian. However, Krech acknowledges that even vegetables are persons and that this is an ethical concern. Krech recognizes that his life depends on the deaths of the fruits and vegetables that he consumes. He then expresses gratitude to the fruits and vegetables for their sacrifices.[302]

Many vegetarians and vegans will argue that the consumption of plants is different from eating animals. They will point out that plants lack the complex nervous systems found in animals. Therefore, they argue that since they aren't conscious beings, they don't experience pain in the same way. Two responses are possible to this line of thought.

First, there is evidence that plants may indeed have some form of consciousness and knowledge of themselves and others. Undoubtedly, the past studies that seemed to show consciousness were poor, and the results were questionable. However, more recent studies that are better designed support that plants, such as trees, exhibit some form of consciousness.[303]

Second, even if further studies fail to support that plants are conscious beings, we know that the lack of external signs of consciousness doesn't mean there is no consciousness. Krech gives an example of a woman that awoke after

---

301. Campbell and Moyers, *The Power of Myth*, 50.
302. Krech, *Naikan*, 41.
303. Grant, "Do Trees Talk to Each Other?" 48–57.

a long coma. The medical staff didn't understand why she was impolite to one nurse after awakening while nice to the others. They later learned that during her coma, the patient was very much aware of her surroundings and that the one nurse would, at times, make rude comments about her when she came into her room. The lack of observable consciousness didn't mean that the woman wasn't conscious.[304] Even if we can't detect consciousness in plants, it doesn't mean it might not be present. While Krech is a vegetarian, his coma patient story provides a lesson that applies to meat consumption.

According to Campbell, hunting myths involve belief in a "covenant between the animal world and the human world." In some Indigenous cultures, there is a belief that an animal willingly gives its life for us and, in turn, through ritual, either transcends or returns through rebirth.[305] We see this in the customs of the Native Americans with the American buffalo and the Japanese *Mitagi* people with the Japanese black bear.[306]

How do we apply the ethics of decency to the hard truth that all corporeal life must consume others? I propose humane consumption as an answer. Humane consumption means that we may still ethically consume meat and dairy products if we so choose. However, as much as reasonable, we need to limit our consumption to animals raised and slaughtered in a way that causes the least suffering to the animal and the least ecological impact. This includes, but isn't limited to, buying produce from farms raising the animals with shelter, resting areas, sufficient space, and the ability to engage in natural behaviors; buying, whenever possible, from farms that practice humane slaughtering; and avoiding animal products in which the livestock was given hormones or unneeded antibiotics.

The principle of humane food consumption reminds me of a Japanese practice of meal etiquette. In Japan, it's considered proper etiquette to say *itadakimasu* with your hands put together in a prayer position and head bowed at the beginning of a meal. A literal translation of *itadakimasu* is "I humbly receive (this food)."[307] Most anime fans will notice that this translates as "Let's eat!" and the characters portray little reverence. However, the spirit of *itadakimasu* is one

304. Krech, *Naikan*, 56.
305. Campbell and Moyers, *The Power of Myth*, 90.
306. Campbell and Moyers, *The Power of Myth*, 91.
307. Krech, *Naikan*, 35–36.

of gratitude for the sacrifice of all that made the meal possible. Krech wrote that the act of saying *itadakimasu* before a meal recognized the provider's actions and the foodstuff's sacrifice. "We are taking, and others are giving."[308]

It's important to remember the role of the Self in all of this. In May's book, acknowledging the importance of one's own life is just as crucial as recognizing others' lives. The other isn't in a position higher or lower than oneself. In the Hindu greeting of namaste, one acknowledges that both the other and oneself are sacred. Finally, in animism, all things, oneself included, have a spiritual nature.

We now have a framework to apply to situational ethics outside Abrahamic teachings. Also, this ethical system applies to interacting with other humans and all things. Each encounter I have is an interaction with another person trying to get through their corporeal existence. This fact is true whether it's an interaction with another human, a nonhuman animal, a plant, a rock, or a lake. According to animism, everything is deserving of such consideration. Therefore, I'm to acknowledge the divine nature of all things. Also, I must respect each thing as an individual and neither discount its value, human or otherwise, nor project my own bias upon it. Every entity has a dignity of its own and is worthy of respect. Myself included.

Socio-Economic Relations

Most of us spend the majority of our waking hours either at work or commuting to and fro. A significant portion of our nonworking free time is spent navigating the marketplace. Even when we're not actively shopping, we're under assault by Madison Avenue as it tries to encourage us to purchase goods and services. These socio-economic relations are just as important as personal relations.

As mentioned, the ancient philosophers saw philosophy as a way of life. While they understood there to be different specialties of philosophy, such as metaphysics and ethics, the goal of each school of philosophy provided a complete package. Philosophy includes not only the individual but also society. The work of Plato is a good example. His book the *Republic* applied to not just the

---

308. Krech, *Naikan*, 36.

individual but society as a whole. Therefore, Dark Paganism needs to address personal relations on the socio-economic scale.

Let me start by saying that none of the works of the three prominent Dark Pagan authors (Coughlin, Digitalis, and Konstantinos) has expressed views on socio-economic matters. The Pagan community as a whole tends to be quiet on such issues. However, a few Left-Hand Path traditions have made some comments with socio-economic connotations.

Just as this book isn't about financial advice, this book isn't about economics or sociology. Therefore, in this book, I will not advocate in support of or argue against a specific socio-economic model. However, Dark Paganism as a worldview and as a philosophy has implications on socio-economic issues.

According to Camus, we are free; however, this freedom must be tempered with justice. Absolute freedom allows the strong to run over the weak while absolute justice crushes freedom. Both extremes are dangerous and must be avoided. Camus wrote extensively about this in his classic *The Rebel*.

Camus's balance of freedom with justice provides a guide from which we can build our Dark Pagan values. Dark Pagan values should strike a balance between individual freedoms and matters of justice. The following are a few fundamental Dark Pagan values applicable to socio-economics that impact freedom and justice.

One Dark Pagan socio-economic value is that the individual must be the focus of the system. The individual does not exist to serve the state, the people, the church, the market, or capital. Socio-economic structures exist to serve the individual, not the other way around.

This focus on the individual means that any socio-economic system must include both positive and negative rights. Negative rights are the individual's right from something, while positive rights are the individual's right to receive something. A typical example is the right to life. A negative right to life is the right against the taking of one's life by another, such as murder, which is not to be confused with the antiabortion use of the term. A positive right to life is the right to receive what's necessary to preserve one's life, such as food or health care.

A socio-economic system must include positive and negative rights because both are necessary to reach eudaimonia. Positive rights tend to be the most controversial.

In 1943, Abraham Maslow proposed that one fulfills a "hierarchy of needs to reach self-actualization." A typical illustration of his theory is in the shape of a pyramid. Maslow's hierarchy of needs begins with basic physical needs such as food and lodging, moves up to safety, social needs such as belonging and friendship, self-esteem, and finally, at the top, caps with self-actualization.[309]

Even if Maslow's hierarchy is a little simplistic, which some contemporary psychologists consider, there is truth. Maslow's hierarchy of needs is one reason why Dark Paganism's values support positive rights. For example, on a personal note, I consider the ability to acquire food, housing, a secure retirement, and medical care as fundamental positive rights. It's difficult to focus on self-esteem and, even less, self-actualization when struggling to find food and shelter. Since Dark Paganism includes cultivating the Self, positive rights would be a Dark Pagan socio-economic value for it aids in self-cultivation.

Negative rights are essential. They acknowledge the divinity of the Self and honor it. Such rights accept the fact that the Self is wise and can decide for itself what's best. Therefore, the maximum number of negative rights possible is a Dark Pagan value for any socio-economic system. The only acceptable standard for limiting a negative right is when that right harms others. As Thomas Jefferson wrote, "The legitimate powers of government extend to such acts only as are injurious to others. But it does me no injury for my neighbor to say there are twenty gods or no god. It neither picks my pocket nor breaks my leg."[310]

Another Dark Pagan socio-economic value is the support of the autonomy of the individual and personal sovereignty. Positive and negative rights are crucial for autonomy and personal sovereignty in the same way that they're essential for honor and supporting the individual. Also, any socio-economic system must recognize the individual's inherent power to control their own lives as long as it doesn't endanger others.

Personal sovereignty is under constant attack. Forces such as the media and Madison Avenue continually strive to control individuals' lives. These aren't the only social institutions trying to remove our sovereignty. Other institutions include the state, schools, churches, and, most recently, social media. Therefore,

---

309. Kaufman, *Transcend*, xii–xiv.
310. Jefferson, *Notes on the State of Virginia*, 165.

Dark Pagan socio-economic values would support a system that restrains forces that attempt to remove our sovereignty.

These Dark Pagan socio-economic values are the simple application of decency ethics in many ways. All of us are divine beings attempting to navigate through this corporeal existence. Allowing individuals to make their choices and live a life they believe is right acknowledges this fact.

Some wish to control the choices that individuals make. These attempts come from both ends of the political spectrum. People of all political persuasion want to decide what we can read, say, and eat, who we love, and whether or not we worship a deity and, if so, which one.

We saw how Madison Avenue and Wall Street attempt to control us. Social media creates a new form of control. However, rather than corporate control, social media platforms exert collective community control through such measures as bullying and social shaming.

What is the source of this drive to control others? It results from the dangerous convergence of the desire for power with the Shadow. Our failure to understand and incorporate these aspects of ourselves into our conscious lives allows them to manifest themselves in this toxic behavior.

Erroneous Dark Concepts

Several erroneous dark concepts permeate society today. These toxic concepts primarily involve misunderstanding the Self and its relationship with society. Three erroneous dark concepts deserve special attention. They are rugged individualism, objectivism, and social Darwinism.

Rugged Individualism

The idea of rugged individualism is a uniquely American concept. Primarily for the benefit of the non-American reader, the concept of rugged individualism needs some explanation. Rugged individualism, coined by Herbert Hoover in 1928, portrays the Self as completely self-reliant, self-made, and standing on its own. According to rugged individualism, people are to pull themselves up by their bootstraps without help from others, especially from the state.

During the early nineteenth century, the French diplomat and writer Alexis de Tocqueville identified two applicable concepts: egoism and individualism. According to Tocqueville, egoism is a "passionate and exaggerated love of the self that impels man to relate everything solely to himself and to prefer himself to everything else."[311] Tocqueville defined individualism as being "a reflective and tranquil sentiment that disposes each citizen to cut himself off from the mass of his fellow men and withdrawn into the circle of his family and friends, so that, having created a little society for his use, he gladly leaves the larger society to take care of itself."[312] He considered egoism the older and more primitive of the two concepts.

According to Tocqueville, early Americans tempered their individualism to recognize social needs. In his classic book *Democracy in America*, he wrote that nineteenth-century Americans strove to demonstrate the belief that enlightened self-interest guides their actions when they make sacrifices for others or the state. Tocqueville believed that this American doctrine couldn't last. Over time, he thought, individualism in America would break down. The result would be a degradation into egoism.[313]

Tocqueville's prediction was correct. The individualism that he saw in the young American republic did, over time, degrade into egoism. Hoover's term was nothing more than a repackaging of egoism with the veneer of a philosophy.

Rugged individualism's erroneous view of the Self has serious consequences. By portraying the Self as self-made, rugged individualism distorts its nature and breaks the natural bonds between people. People become isolated and shoulder their burdens alone. On a social scale, its disdain for any form of assistance, especially assistance from the state, results in social programs to help the poor and needy being either nonexistent or poorly funded. Decency ethics begin to unravel as each person looks after themselves.

Objectivism

On the surface, Ayn Rand and her philosophy of objectivism appears to be consistent with Dark Paganism. She was a passionate supporter of the individual. Rand described her philosophy as centered around "the concept of man as a

---

311. Ikuta, *Contesting Conformity*, 61.
312. Heath and Kaldis, *Wealth, Commerce, and Philosophy*, 285.
313. de Tocqueville, *Democracy in America*, 585.

heroic being, with his happiness as the moral purpose of his life, with productive achievement as his noblest activity, and reason as his only absolute."[314]

However, while Rand praised the Self, it's clear that she didn't understand its nature. Rand made psychological egoism and ethical egoism the bedrock of her philosophy. Psychological egoism is a thesis that holds that, whether or not we're conscious of it, our true motives are always our self-interest.[315] Ethical egoism builds on psychological egoism. It's the belief that people always act in their interest and that acting in their self-interest is the only ethical thing.[316]

Let's apply these two ideas to an example of a person running into a burning building to save someone. According to psychological egoism, the hero's motives weren't altruistic. Instead, they risked their lives for either praise or to avoid public ridicule if they had not acted. Ethical egoism would build on this and say that such an act is only ethical if it helped the hero somehow. If done out of a sense of duty or altruism, then ethical egoism would view it as an unethical act rather than heroic, for it went against one's self-interest to risk their lives in such a fashion.

Following this line of thought, Rand concluded that altruism and duty are evil. Any demand upon a person by others is wrong because it goes against their self-interest. Therefore, as Rand believed, any economic system that makes demands must also be unjust. According to Rand, the result was extreme support for laissez-faire economics that allowed for the maximum freedom for the individual.

In an essay titled "Psychological Egoism, and Ethical Egoism," Sandra LaFave, chair of the Philosophy Department at West Valley College in Saratoga, California, from 1986 to 2006, tackled these concepts.[317] I'm deeply indebted to her for this insight.

Psychological egoism takes one counterexample to prove it false. The previous example of someone risking their life to save another is one such counterexample. Any explanation that this selfless act is, in reality, selfishness pushes the level of credulity.

---

314. Badhwar and Long, "Ayn Rand."
315. Blackburn, *The Oxford Dictionary of Philosophy*, 115.
316. Rachels, "A Critique of Ethical Egoism," 80.
317. "Sandra LaFave Retired from West Valley College Philosophy Department."

Another problem is that self-interest is compatible with having an interest in the welfare of others. We see this in Adam Smith's invisible hand of the marketplace.[318] Leaving aside legal liability issues, a company knows that cheating its customers is bad for business and avoids such. Helping others helps oneself in the long run. Altruism is compatible with self-interest.

Psychological egoism also fails because human motives are more complex than granted by psychological egoism. It's simplistic to think that the benefit of the Self is the only motivation we have to act unselfishly. This is not to say that there are no individuals whose acts of altruism are performed for selfish reasons. As we've seen with the Shadow, some might not even be aware of their true motivations. Rand's error is to paint everyone with a broad stroke and treat all selfless acts as acts of selfishness. To assume only one motive for all human behavior flies in the face of reality.

Finally, the very premise of ethical egoism, that ethics must match human nature, is seriously flawed. Even if psychological egoism was valid, it does not make acting upon it ethical. For example, just because everyone has the capacity for murder doesn't make murder an ethical act. Human nature is only one among many criteria to consider when determining what is and is not ethical behavior.

Because Rand's objectivism is built on these two false principles, it becomes apparent that her philosophy is a house of straw. As a result, it's an erroneous dark concept.

Social Darwinism

Here in America, one can find social Darwinism promoted in many circles. And like the concepts mentioned above, social Darwinism fails upon close observation.

The term *social Darwinism* dates back to 1944, when the American historian Richard Hofstadter used it in his book *Social Darwinism in American Thought*. The *Oxford Dictionary of Philosophy* defines it as applying assumed facts of evolution ideas to ethical reasoning.[319]

The nineteenth-century English philosopher Herbert Spencer is popularly credited as the father of social Darwinism. Spencer's phrase "survival of the

---

318. LaFave, "Psychological Egoism and Ethical Egoism."
319. Blackburn, *The Oxford Dictionary of Philosophy*, 128.

fittest" was coined several years before Darwin used it as an alternative to his term *natural selection*. However, current historians are starting to reevaluate Spencer's traditional role as a social Darwinist, and his role in it is becoming less clear.[320]

According to social Darwinists, through competition, certain members of society rise to the top because of their fitness. Some social Darwinism advocates have used this dog-eat-dog belief as a rationale for laissez-faire economics and opposition to assistance for the poor and the oppressed. Social Darwinism was very popular during the United States' Gilded Age among the "masters of industry" and supporters who used social Darwinist ideas to justify their wealth and power. These views didn't end with the Gilded Age but continue today among some, although social Darwinism is generally held in disdain by scholars.[321]

The problem with social Darwinism begins with its misuse of natural selection. Contrary to the claim of social Darwinism, natural selection doesn't result in changes to the individual. It merely results in those who are best fit for their environment having more offspring. The prize of natural selection isn't a more fit individual. It's the transmission of genes from one generation to the next.

"Survival of the fittest" does not mean that individuals must compete with each other. While competition isn't ruled out, cooperation is just as possible, for it can also increase survival chances for the individual to procreate. Darwin understood this when he wrote that "communities which included the greatest number of the most sympathetic members would flourish best and rear the greatest number of offspring."[322] More and more studies support Darwin's understanding that cooperation evolved to be more potent than competition in humans.[323]

This cooperation doesn't mean that we lack self-interest. Nor does it mean we never act selfishly. However, it means that on a societal level, cooperation between self-interested parties, rather than competition, evolved to be the natural state for humans.

---

320. Weinstein, "Herbert Spencer."
321. Blackburn, *The Oxford Dictionary of Philosophy*, 128.
322. Darwin, *The Descent of Man, and Selection in Relation to Sex*, 79.
323. Axelrod, *The Evolution of Cooperation*, 8, 31.

Social Darwinism has been used to justify atrocities over the years. Evils such as eugenics, forced sterilizations, racism, and fascism have been rationalized by arguing that it was simply social Darwinism.

Rugged individualism, objectivism, and social Darwinism are all erroneous, for they all present a distorted view of the Self. Therefore, these three beliefs have no place in Dark Paganism.

Evil

Praises are heaped upon the ego and the Self throughout this book. I've written that the Self is a god. Trust the ego, I've said. All of this is still true. However, it's incomplete. There is one uncomfortable fact that has to be recognized. It's another truth from which we don't dare try to run away.

All of us harm others.

No animal on Earth can be as destructive and cruel as humans. People lie and cheat, even when honesty may result in a better outcome for all involved. We laugh at the pain of others. We murder our kind by the thousands annually.[324] Humans are one of the few animals known to hunt for sport. According to the United Nations, more than one million species are at risk of extinction due to human activity.[325] Our world is polluted and overheating from our greed. Like lemmings running off a cliff, our species is speeding toward collective suicide. At least the lemmings' suicide story is a myth. Our rush to extinction is genuine.

How do we reconcile these seeming contradictions between our divinity and cruelty? Can a god commit acts of evil and still be considered a god? Many of the ancients certainly thought so.

Zeus is the greatest of the Olympians. After freeing his siblings from Kronos's belly, he joined them to defeat the violent, primordial Titans. He then brought order to the universe resulting in the Cosmos. Life appeared under his command, and the world came to be as we know it.

However, Zeus is far from virtuous. His infidelity to his wife Hera is legendary. Many of his liaisons had nothing to do with romance. It's almost impossible to read some of his affairs as anything less than rapes. And Zeus was no

---

324. Roser and Ritchie, "Homicides."
325. Platt, "What Losing 1 Million Species Means for the Planet."

friend of humanity. The story of Pandora's creation was the Greek version of the Hebrew myth of the fall of man. Instead of a serpent tempting the first woman to eat a forbidden apple from a tree that Yahweh had planted, Zeus lured the first woman to open a box that he created to release all of its woes and suffering upon humanity. Let's not forget the pain and suffering Zeus inflicted on Prometheus for siding with humanity against him.

As we've seen with Zeus, a god can be just as cruel as a human. We will address the nature of the gods in further detail later. We need to understand that there is no conflict between our divinity and our potential for evil.

The fact that the gods can commit evil doesn't answer the more pressing question of the source of human depravity. The problem of human evil is an old question and is far beyond the scope of this book to cover adequately. However, there are some insights available to us.

The existence of human evil challenged the Greek philosophers of antiquity. The challenge arose because they viewed human nature as inherently good.[326] Therefore, evil posed a problem. If humans are good by nature, why do they commit evil acts?

The Greek philosophers' faith in reason provided them with an answer. In the *Republic*, Plato argued that people perform evil acts because they don't understand the consequences of their actions. The philosophers believed that all that was necessary for people to exhibit their good nature was to know the consequences of doing evil.[327] As mentioned, Camus later adopted this view of the source of evil.

However, this view is naive. Most people are aware of the consequences of their behavior. Contemporary philosophers refer to Plato's belief as "the Socratic fallacy."[328] The fact that most people know right and wrong, along with their consequences, isn't a new revelation. In a Buddhist parable, a poet asked his master what the main principle of Buddhism was. The master replied, "Do no evil, and perform what is good." The pupil replied, "Even a three-year-old knows that!" The master agreed, but he said that it didn't mean an eighty-year-old could do it.[329]

---

326. Hollis, *Why Good People Do Bad Things*, 2–3.
327. Hollis, *Why Good People Do Bad Things*, 2–3.
328. Hollis, *Why Good People Do Bad Things*, 3.
329. Hollis, *Why Good People Do Bad Things*, 24.

If we all know the consequences of virtue and vice, why do we so often not make the right choice? Why do we wrong others? One of the main reasons is what we discussed previously in length—the Shadow.

Carl Jung taught that although the Shadow is unconscious, it's never asleep. It's constantly placing pressure on the ego. The ego thinks it's in control, but in reality, it often builds rationalizations to support the influences of unconscious motivations and drives buried in the Shadow. Therefore, we are either blind to our behavior or rationalize its reasons.

It's important to remember that not all of our behaviors driven by the Shadow are evil. Of course, many saints sacrifice out of altruism. However, some seek out sainthood out of the desire for recognition and praise, no matter how humble they act.

When discussing the Shadow's role in our behavior, are we acting, to borrow a term from Jean-Paul Sartre, in "bad faith"? Is this nothing more than a psychoanalytical version of "the devil made me do it"? We will be acting in bad faith if we write our behavior off as being out of our control. However, there's nothing about the Shadow that negates our responsibility. Authenticity demands that we each take ownership of our conscious and unconscious actions. To quote Oedipus, "Apollo brought this fate upon me, but the hand that wounded me was mine own."[330]

What about the atrocities committed by nation-states? How can entire societies commit genocide and imperialism? What are the sources of systematic and institutional racism and misogyny? How can nation-states continue with oppressive socio-economic systems that deny negative and positive rights to entire classes of people?

While the Shadow explains much about the origins of personal acts of evil, it also provides some insight into institutional evil. According to James Hollis, just as individuals have their Shadows, so do entire societies. This collective Shadow is the product of the social interactions of the numerous personal Shadows. Hollis believes this collective Shadow is the driving force behind institutional evil.[331]

---

330. Hollis, *Why Good People Do Bad Things*, 28.
331. Hollis, *Why Good People Do Bad Things*, 128.

The existence of a collective Shadow shouldn't be a surprise. We see this with the documented studies of individuals who act differently in groups than on their own. This herd behavior is the product of natural self-organization inherent in complex systems. The complex systems are highly adaptive and exist on the edge where chaos and order meet.[332]

Caution is needed here. If we try to write off all evil as a product of the Shadow, we would be as naïve as the Greek philosophers who thought it was due to a lack of knowledge of the consequences. While the Shadow's influence provides valuable insight, it doesn't completely solve the mystery.

However, there should be no doubt that the Shadow Self is an essential piece of the puzzle of evil. The role of the Shadow is one reason why Dark Paganism places so much emphasis on Shadow work. First, to honor the Self, we must understand and accept all aspects of it, which psychologist Tara Brach calls "radical acceptance." Second, Dark Paganism claims that reason and rational analysis rest at its heart. If both are continually undermined and manipulated by the Shadow, we need to understand this source better. Otherwise, our dedication to reason rings hallow.

Reviewing the Concepts

Dark Pagans understand that the Divine Self doesn't exist in isolation, and they strive to maintain healthy relationships. Donne's famous poetic line of "No man is an island" still rings true. Relationships are, therefore, obviously integral in the development of the Self. As a result, maintaining healthy relationships is essential for one's well-being.

According to decency ethics, the goal of ethics should be to try to live a life that's "decent." It's not the life of sainthood or heroes, nor the life of selfishness or despotism, but one in which an everyday person can live and still be ethical. A decent life acknowledges and acts upon the fact that we all have lives that we're trying to live.

Healthy relations include more than just humans. Ethics also apply to how we treat other species. Vegetarianism and veganism are options for ethical treatment. Humane consumption is an acceptable alternative ethical response.

---

332. Waldrop, *Complexity*, 11.

Ethics also impact socio-economic relations. Decency ethics demand that we advocate for both positive and negative rights in society. Concepts such as rugged individualism, objectivism, and social Darwinism are erroneous and condemned.

Evil is a reality that we have to face. While it has many causes, one major cause is the influence of the Shadow upon us individually and collectively. Therefore, Shadow work is an integral part of Dark Paganism.

Questions to Consider

* How do you define a healthy relationship? By your definition, are all of your current relationships healthy? Is there room for improvement?

* Does decency ethics appeal to you as an ethical system, or do you prefer another?

* How does the ethical treatment of animals apply to your personal ethical system?

* To what degree, if any, do ethics apply to socio-economics?

XII
PRINCIPLE 9: MAGNUM OPUS

Ninth principle: The Dark Pagan is constantly striving
toward achieving higher and higher levels of being.

Carol Ryff includes personal growth as one of the indicators of well-being.
According to Ryff, personal growth is when one "has a feeling of continued development; sees self as growing and expanding; is open to new experiences; has a sense of realizing his or her potential; sees improvement in self and behavior over time; is changing in ways that reflect more self-knowledge and effectiveness."[333]

Personal growth plays a significant role in Dark Paganism. Most of the nine principles are centered around not only honoring but cultivating the Self. However, this raises the question: If we're already divine beings, why is there a need for personal growth? Don't the principles of self-knowledge and self-acceptance mean that personal growth isn't required?

We need to remember that we're minor gods. Iamblichus held that we're the lowest of divine beings. We exist at the bottom of the divine ladder.

Growth isn't unknown among the gods. The clearest example of divine growth is found with the goddess Inanna. Inanna's rise begins with her as a helpless maiden in the myth "Inanna and Huluppu Tree," where she's dependent upon the god-king Gilgamesh. She's then portrayed as a Promethean figure when she shrewdly acquires the sacred mes from Enki and fights to deliver them to humankind. Afterward, she has a series of conflicts, some she wins,

---

333. Ryff, "Psychological Well-Being Revisited," 10–28.

and some she loses. Each time her power and confidence grow. Finally, she descends into the netherworld, is murdered, hangs dead for three days, and is resurrected. After the resurrection, Inanna ascends to become queen of heaven and earth.

As the least of the gods, we too must fight to ascend. Like Inanna, we each must chart our paths to ascension. We'll have successes along our journey at times, while sometimes, we'll fail. Regardless of the difficulties faced, the ultimate goal of achieving a higher state of godhood will be worth the challenge.

The Great Work

In Dark Paganism, personal growth involves more than the corporeal Self. As in most esoteric thought, the development of the Self is also a spiritual process. This tremendous spiritual process is called the Great Work, or magnum opus.

Éliphas Lévi wrote the classic definition of the magnum opus. According to Lévi, the Great Work is the "creation of man by himself." It involves conquering his "faculties and his future" along with the "perfect emancipation of his will."[334] Upon achieving the Great Work, the magician would gain control of the primal alchemical elements and obtain the power to "upset and alter the face of the world."[335]

The Order of the Golden Dawn described the Great Work's goal in a similar way. It held that the Great Work's goal is "to obtain control of the nature and power of one's own being." Oberon Zell-Ravenheart wrote that such control was just the beginning. According to Zell-Ravenheart, the Great Work ultimately involves fostering consciousness's evolution to the next level, which he defines as apotheosis, or becoming divine.[336]

This-Worldly and Otherworldly

Greek philosophy before the first century was focused primarily on this-worldly life.[337] The previous eight philosophical principles emphasize embodiment in the same fashion. This emphasis is true even when speaking of the divinity of the Self. The principle of magnum opus and its goal of apotheosis change this

---

334. Lévi, *Transcendental Magic*, 113.
335. Lévi, *Transcendental Magic*, 12.
336. Zell-Ravenheart, *Grimoire for the Apprentice Wizard*, 59.
337. Cooper, *Pursuits of Wisdom*, 311.

focus from this-worldly life to possible otherworldly life. This ninth principle of Dark Paganism mirrors a change that occurred to philosophy in the ancient world. This change in philosophy in the ancient world would strongly influence the course of history.

According to scholars, in the first century CE, the Hellenistic world entered a "spiritual crisis" that would last for centuries. The Greco-Roman people had become dissatisfied with their institutions' answers. According to John Cooper, the Hellenistic world found a "shallowness" in the different schools' messages.[338] They wanted more than a focus on this-worldly life. People began seeking means of personal salvation from the anxiety of embodiment.[339] Some turned to religions from foreign lands, such as Christianity and Mithraism. However, not all Hellenists abandoned their philosophy for an alien faith during this crisis. Instead, one of the most historically significant schools developed, answering this spiritual crisis.

The Neoplatonist philosopher Iamblichus believed philosophy alone to be insufficient in providing personal salvation. He thought, in addition to philosophy, that ritual was also necessary. Through ritual, according to Iamblichus, one can perfect the soul and achieve immortality among the gods, which is apotheosis.[340]

For Dark Paganism, the magnum opus includes improving the this-worldly Self as well as the transformation of the otherworldly Self. Apotheosis, or the otherworldly Self's ascension, would be impossible without changing the Self's current physical or dayside manifestation. And improving the this-worldly Self while ignoring the otherworldly distorts one's perspective, leading to materialism and logical positivism.

Understanding Apotheosis

Of what does apotheosis consist? It's hard to explain without sounding poetic. One might say that apotheosis is the process of taking the spark of the Divine existing within the Self, the little god, and igniting it into the flame of fully realized godhood.

---

338. Cooper, *Pursuits of Wisdom*, 308.
339. Cooper, *Pursuits of Wisdom*, 21.
340. Shaw, *Theurgy and the Soul*, 57–58.

Historically, lightworkers have treated apotheosis as a future event. It was something that occurred after our death. Cicero wrote, "that to study philosophy is nothing but to prepare one's self to die."[341] In *Phaedo*, Plato wrote that, according to Socrates, a true philosopher should spend as much time as possible "in training for being dead."[342]

As we have seen, though, the existence of the corporeal Self is already divine. Therefore, we improve the entire Self by using magick to improve our existence in this corporeal state. Thus, improving our corporeal existence is an integral part of the process of apotheosis.

Personal Alchemy

We return to the Great Work of the alchemists referenced by Lévi. Most are aware of alchemists' seeming obsession with transforming base metal into gold. However, these attempts turned out to be in vain. The alchemists never succeeded. However, they did help lay the groundwork for the science of chemistry in much the same way astrology led to astronomy.

Gold has always been valuable. Not only is it rare, but it's amazingly pliable, along with being beautiful. Gold is associated with the sun because of its yellow color and reflective shine. This solar association has equated it with divinity, and it became known as the "flesh of the gods." Silver has always been right behind gold in value. The moon has been associated with silver, and therefore, silver has also been associated with divinity.[343]

While the search to transform lead into gold has been abandoned, the idea that a means exists to convert what is base into something of value continues. By applying magick to everyday needs, we are creating gold out of lead in a metaphorical sense. When we apply it to the Self, it becomes personal alchemy.

Unlike European alchemy, the explicit goal of Taoist alchemy is immortality, or to become *xian*. The ancient Chinese had two alchemy systems. They were *waidan*, or external alchemy, and *neidan*, or internal alchemy. In waidan, they strove to find an elixir of eternal youth to keep the body alive forever. In neidan, the Chinese alchemists focused on meditation and spiritual exercises to transform the soul by harvesting one's life force, or chi.

---

341. Fatić and Amir, *Practicing Philosophy*, 130.
342. Cooper, *Pursuits of Wisdom*, 115.
343. Gilchrist, *Alchemy*, 12–13.

According to Eva Wong, the internal-alchemical path of Taoism is the "Way of Transformation."[344] There are three steps in the Chinese internal-alchemical process. The first is to build a foundation by strengthening the body, in which there are several different methods. *T'ai-ch'i-kung* is one of the methods most widely known in the West. The second step involves refining various types of energy. I find it interesting that the terms used for this refining process include *fires*, *furnaces*, and *cauldrons*, which are similar to those used in Western alchemy. According to Taoist thought, the final step is returning the refined energy to the void and merging with the Tao.[345]

Amber Wolfe, psychotherapist and Celtic Pagan, defines personal alchemy as activation of individual choice. The individual chooses to transform oneself by consciously applying the power of the Self's internal aspect with nature's external forces. The individual can then achieve self-transformation.[346] Personal alchemy then turns the base material (human or little god) into gold (fully realized godhood).

Personal alchemy is the means. Apotheosis is the goal.

Apotheosis in Various Wisdom Traditions

Is apotheosis possible? Indeed, improving corporeal life is possible, but can one achieve ascendance to a higher state of being? Can one become a fully realized god? Pagan thought through the ages has said that it is possible. Wisdom traditions worldwide have also included the belief that it was possible to achieve a form of transcendence and divine status.

Greco-Roman

Ancient Greek mythology and religion included more than just the Olympians and the Titans. There were also dryads, nymphs, satyrs, and more. Along with these were the heroes, who were humans who had achieved excellence. Many were great warriors, but not all. Demodocus, for example, became a hero for his poetry and singing. The Greeks believed that the heroes achieved ascension

---

344. Wong, *Taoism*, 5.
345. Wong, *Taoism*, 178–83.
346. Wolfe, *Personal Alchemy*, xii.

to the Land of Bliss and were worthy of worship as demigods through their greatness.[347]

According to Iamblichus, one didn't need to be a hero to achieve apotheosis. He and the other Neoplatonists sought transformation through the practice of theurgy. They thought theurgy was necessary, for they believed a person couldn't accomplish this under their own will. According to Gregory Shaw, professor of religious studies at Stonehill College, "The goal of theurgy was to awaken the soul to the presence of the One that it bore unknowingly. And, utilizing the very components that bound the soul to its generative life, theurgy released the soul from their grip."[348]

The Hellenistic Pagans had *theios aner*, or "divine man." The term has a decidedly misogynistic wording, which shouldn't surprise anyone because the ancient Greeks were highly paternalistic. The idea of a divine man was that occasionally a person would be born who, though very human, had achieved a level of spiritual development that was divine. The classic list of divine men was Orpheus, Pythagoras, Empedocles, and Apollonius of Tyre.

Egyptians

The ancient Egyptians developed one of the most impressive systems for apotheosis. The Egyptian "Book of the Dead" has spells by which to become gods. The deceased would undergo a variety of challenges to ascend from the netherworld. If successful, the person would achieve "transformation into an *akh*, namely a transfigured, blessed dead, assimilated into the gods."[349]

Norse

There is an obscure class of divine being in Norse belief called the *disir*. The disir were benevolent female deities, much like the *bodhisattva*, who may have originated from ancestors.[350] A bodhisattva is one who has grown spiritually and could go to nirvana but stays to aid others.[351] If so, this change would be a form of apotheosis. The Norse also had *alfar*, or *alfs*, from which we get the

---

347. Mavromataki, *Greek Mythology and Religion*, 148.
348. Shaw, *Theurgy and the Soul*, 124.
349. Lucarelli, "Gods, Spirits, Demons of the Book of the Dead," 127.
350. Dougherty, *Norse Myths*, 119–20.
351. Shantideva, *The Way of the Bodhisattva*, 3–4.

English word *elf*. Elves could be dark or light. While the light elves were always bright and benevolent, the dark elves were more mischievous. Interestingly, the dark elves were to have been mortal and became elves after death, which would be a form of apotheosis.[352]

Shinto

Shinto focuses on life in this world rather than the next. However, it does allow for a person to become a kami. Many translate the word *kami* into *god*; however, its meaning is more nuanced and complex. According to author Aidan D. Rankin, the process of a human becoming a kami requires extensive spiritual cultivation.[353] A Japanese term for a person who has achieved being a kami is *genzai-shin*.[354] There is also an ikigami, or "living kami," who is someone revered as a divinity during their lifetime or afterward.[355] For example, the *mizugami* built great irrigation systems and were later declared "water gods." There are active shrines in Japan dedicated to the ikigami.[356]

Taoism

The search for apotheosis is also in Taoism. Taoism has spiritual beings called xian. While xian can include various entities, the word can mean a person who achieves immortality through Taoism.[357]

Buddhism

According to the Mahayana branch of Buddhism, Gautama wasn't the last Buddha. Any person can achieve a state called Buddhahood, which is a state of awakening. A person can cease *dukkha*, or suffering due to attachment, by achieving Buddhahood. Nichiren is a Japanese branch of Buddhism that holds that each person has the innate potential to achieve Buddhahood.

---

352. "The Ancestors in the Asatru/Heathen Religion."
353. Rankin, *Shinto*, 122.
354. Rankin, *Shinto*, 46.
355. Greer, *A World Full of Gods*, 96.
356. Greer, *A World Full of Gods*, 97.
357. "Xian."

In Buddhism, one may be reborn as many different beings. A *deva* is one of the many different entities. Though not immortal, they are longer lived than humans, have greater powers, and live better lives.[358]

The Pursuit of Excellence

The Great Work can be a lonely path. Dark Paganism isn't about trying to save the world. Any such attempt would be doomed to failure. Apotheosis belongs to the few and not to the masses.

The claim that apotheosis isn't universally available may seem elitist to some. And those individuals would be right. However, elitism isn't necessarily a bad thing. While the term has fallen out of favor in our egalitarian society, the truth is that there will always be those who will jump higher, run faster, and swim farther than all the rest. Yes, one might call this elitism, but it's not a negative. It's just the hard reality.

There are reasons that we refer to Olympic athletes as "elite" for their achievements of excellence in athletics. The same applies to those who earnestly strive for apotheosis. They are the Olympians of magicians.

A major reason for describing those who strive for apotheosis as "elites" is that achieving apotheosis requires personal sacrifice and dedication. And there's no guarantee of success. Those who have ascended to higher states of being don't radio back how-to guides for self-deification. There is no ready-made formula, regardless of what some will tell you. Therefore, it requires continuous study and effort by the serious magician.

It's important to remember that we should not allow our striving for excellence to lead us into hubris. In the poem *Desiderata*, Max Ehrmann wrote, "If you compare yourself with others, you may become vain or bitter, for always there will be greater and lesser persons than yourself."[359] We need to remember that there will always be those better than us. Human value isn't determined by ability but by the fact of being human. In this sense, while we're not all equal in aptitude, we are all equal in value.

---

358. Dhammananda, *What Buddhists Believe*, 305.
359. Ehrmann, *Desiderata*, 11–12.

Any Dark Pagan serious about reaching apotheosis needs to remember that only one person is competing. The Dark Pagan competes against no one but themself.

Reviewing the Concepts

The Dark Pagan is constantly striving toward achieving higher and higher levels of being. As the least of the gods, we, too, must fight to ascend. In Dark Paganism, personal growth involves more the corporeal Self. As in most esoteric thought, the development of the Self is also a spiritual process. This tremendous spiritual process is called the Great Work, or magnum opus.

For Dark Paganism, the magnum opus includes improving the this-worldly Self as well as transforming the otherworldly Self. Apotheosis, the otherworldly Self's ascension to a higher level of godhood, would be impossible without changing the Self's current physical or dayside manifestation. And improving the this-worldly Self while ignoring the otherworldly distorts one's perspective, leading to materialism and logical positivism.

Magick is the means to apotheosis. When applied to the Self, magick becomes a form of personal alchemy in which the base Self is transmuted into the gold of higher godhood. Personal alchemy through magick is the means. Apotheosis is the goal.

While the term *elitism* has fallen out of favor in our egalitarian society, the truth is that there will always be those who will jump higher, run faster, and swim farther than all the rest. But that's not a negative. It's just the hard reality.

Questions to Consider

* What does magnum opus or Great Work mean to you?

* If apotheosis is possible, what role does thaumaturgy play in it? Or is it purely a gift from the gods and therefore solely in the realm of theurgy?

* Is the word *elite* proper? Or is it inappropriate to use in any context within our democratic and egalitarian society?

PART III
DARK ENOUGH

"When it is dark enough, you can see the stars."[360]

—CHARLES A. BEARD

---

360. Sweeney, *Incredible Quotations*, 19.

XIII
DARK PAGANISM AND
THE LEFT-HAND PATH

John J. Coughlin has described the Dark Pagan approach to spirituality as being on the Left-Hand Path (LHP); however, he admits that not all Dark Pagans agree with him on this detail.[361] Raven Digitalis is a prominent Dark Pagan author who believes it isn't. He wrote that "most dark Pagans do not walk a Left-Hand Path."[362] Konstantinos makes no comment about the Left-Hand Path in any of his books.

Is Dark Paganism part of the LHP? If one only focused on illustrating the dual nature of spirituality, Dark Paganism is on the graph's left side. However, that would be a simplistic reason to declare it part of the LHP. As we've seen, Dark Paganism is more than its location on a hypothetical graph. Dark Paganism is a positive, life-affirming dark spirituality that focuses on honoring and cultivating the Self. By applying the nine principles of Dark Paganism, we strive to understand our divine nature better and cultivate it to achieve a higher level of being. What's needed is an understanding of the LHP.

Origins of the Left-Hand Path

The terms *Left-Hand Path* and *Right-Hand Path (RHP)* were introduced to Western esotericism by the Theosophists. Theosophy is a religion established by H. P. Blavatsky in 1875 and has dramatically influenced New Age and

---

361. Coughlin, *Out of the Shadows*, 131.
362. Digitalis, *Goth Craft*, 83.

contemporary Pagan thought. It blends Hellenist and Egyptian Paganism, Hinduism, Buddhism, Christianity, Western ceremonial magick, and more. According to Blavatsky, she was taught Theosophy by ancient spirits called "mahatmas."[363] Blavatsky and the Theosophists associated the LHP with a "black lodge" or evil magick users and the Tantra. In contrast, the RHP was associated with the "white lodge" or good magick users.[364]

Anthropologist Richard Sutcliffe explains that the LHP is from the Tantric term *vuma-marga*, which means "left-hand path." There are five practices in this Tantric system, known as *panchamakara*. Those five are *madya, mamsa, matsya, mudra,* and *maithuna.* These translate respectively as "wine," "flesh," "fish," "parched grain," and "intercourse." According to Sutcliffe, the Tantric LHP "involves the ritual transgression of certain taboos and incorporates ritual sexual intercourse."[365]

Over time the terms *Left-Hand Path* and *Right-Hand Path* in Western esotericism took on a life of their own. Various traditions arose, declaring themselves to be LHP. The LHP isn't static, and there are new traditions continually forming, some of which are Pagan. Plus, there's been tremendous advancement in the sophistication and development of LHP concepts and theories during the last forty years.

Comparing the Left-Hand Path and Dark Paganism

Coughlin wrote in a blog post that the LHP is a system that follows an internal approach to spirituality and contains a strong emphasis on the Self. According to Coughlin, the LHP places less emphasis on deity and ethics than the RHP. The LHP generally views such topics as being up to the individual to decide.[366]

Toby Chappell, author of *Infernal Geometry and the Left-Hand Path*, defines the LHP as "the assertion of absolute personal responsibility for enhancing and perpetuating the individual's self-aware, psyche-centric existence." The LHP, according to Chappell, does this by cultivating the person's will. The cultivation of the will, in turn, causes it to become a primary force in one's existence.[367]

---

363. Bonewits and Bonewits, *Real Energy*, 47.
364. Flowers, *Lords of the Left-Hand Path*, 237.
365. Harvey and Hardman, *Paganism Today*, 110.
366. Coughlin, "An Exploration of Dark Paganism."
367. Chappell, *Infernal Geometry and the Left-Hand Path*, 124.

Chappell describes the LHP as an "approach that emphasizes enhancing the sense of Self and Being, with its own techniques and aesthetics, and which is imperative to pursue responsibly and ethically."[368]

One of the sources often referenced by LHP adherents is *Lords of the Left-Hand Path: Forbidden Practices and Spiritual Heresies* by Stephen E. Flowers. Rather than providing a rigid definition, Flowers emphasized a set of criteria he considers necessary for someone or a tradition to be considered LHP. According to Flowers, to be considered LHP, two criteria must be met: self-deification and antinomianism. He defines self-deification as "the attainment of an enlightened (or awakened), independently existing intellect and its relative immortality."[369] Flowers defines antinomianism in the LHP as being that the "practitioners think of themselves as 'going against the grain' of their culturally conditioned and conventional norms of 'good' and 'evil.'" [370]

Joyce and River Higginbotham define the LHP as focused on "spiritual dissent" and looking to oneself for salvation rather than "deities or authority figures."[371] The element of spiritual dissent has its place. There are times to confront the majority's beliefs, especially if you're in the minority. The need to confront authority is essential here in the West, where Abrahamic religions and monotheism claim to be the norm while declaring all other religions alien or dangerous. Therefore, repeated expressions of dissent may be appropriate.

Once again, the application appears to be the critical difference. Rather than occasionally dissenting as needed, the LHP has a reputation of being in a state of perpetual spiritual dissent. Some members of the LHP seem to be constantly comparing themselves to mainstream spirituality. This state of perpetual spiritual dissent is in some of their choices of deities and tropes, which tend to be adversaries and rebels. Of course, this isn't unique to LHP. This can also be found among some non-LHP Pagans.

Perpetual spiritual dissent, whether explicitly stated or implied, is very limiting. It's like someone jilted by a past lover and just won't let go and move on. Rather than focusing on perpetual spiritual dissent, Dark Paganism, as presented here, focuses on developing a spiritual practice and lifestyle that stands

---

368. Chappell, *Infernal Geometry and the Left-Hand Path*, 4.
369. Flowers, *Lords of the Left-Hand Path*, 11.
370. Flowers, *Lords of the Left-Hand Path*, 11.
371. Higginbotham and Higginbotham, *Pagan Spirituality*, 121.

on its own accord regardless of the mainstream. Dark Paganism is certainly countercultural; however, this isn't the same as constant dissent spiritually.

Kennet Granholm has extensively studied the LHP and published numerous articles in peer-reviewed journals. He includes the LHP as part of Western esotericism and has given it five principal characteristics. They are emphasizing the individual over the collective, seeing human nature as both physical and psychic, focusing on corporeal life rather than the afterlife, self-deification, and maintaining antinomianism.[372] Granholm's five characteristics of the LHP and how—or if—they relate to Dark Paganism are important.

The LHP emphasis on the individual over the collective isn't unique to the LHP, especially here in the United States. However, Granholm states that the LHP raises individualism to an "explicit ideology."[373] There's a remarkable similarity between Dark Paganism and the LHP concerning the individual. The Dark Pagan principle of self-knowledge includes the individual's existential emphasis over Friedrich Nietzsche's "herd." Group thinking is known to lead to oppression and atrocities.

The confusion about individuality by some on the LHP appears to result from the mistaken belief that there are only two extreme choices. Some in the LHP paint it as though there is only a choice between rugged individualism or collectivism. Saying that these are the only selections is a false choice created by a false dichotomy. The truth is that individuality develops from a complex interplay between the individual and society. The Self's cooperative and social nature plays a critical role in creating a healthy, autonomous individual.

Granholm describes the LHP as viewing human nature as both physical and psychic. There's no degree of difference between the LHP and Dark Paganism on this matter. While some LHP traditions will focus on the spiritual more than others, it's safe to say that most consider the Self to be a mix of body and spirit.[374] This mind/body unity of the LHP is very much consistent with Dark Paganism.

The LHP traditions tend to focus on corporeal life rather than the afterlife. According to Granholm, many tend toward the view of eating and drinking for

---

372. Granholm, "Embracing Others than Satan," 87–89.
373. Granholm, "Embracing Others than Satan," 88.
374. Granholm, "Embracing Others than Satan," 88.

tomorrow we die.[375] Dark Paganism also focuses on the corporeal, as indicated by the principle of corpospirituality. While Dark Paganism allows for an afterlife, it does consider corporeal existence sacred and as something to be thoroughly enjoyed.

The importance of corpospirituality in Dark Paganism is a common ground we share with many LHP traditions.[376] The degree of focus, of course, varies from LHP tradition to tradition. However, it is a consistent feature found within them all.

Both Flowers and Granholm include self-deification as a critical element of the LHP. Some traditions view this as a metaphor for self-development and autonomy. Others take this literally and consider the person as either already being a god or having the potential to become one.[377] Miller points out that not all LHP traditions center on exalting the ego. Nor do all LHP traditions focus on our animal instincts. Some LHP traditions work on "refining and transforming our ego into something greater but still individuated from the rest of the universe."[378]

This approach to the ego agrees closely with the goals of Dark Paganism. Dark Paganism acknowledges the current divinity of the Self. The Self is a divine being with the possibility of apotheosis. Apotheosis is synonymous with self-deification. Not only can the individual improve their corporeal state, but, if they choose, they can strive for transcendence.

As a characteristic of the LHP, antinomianism is referenced by many different researchers besides Granholm. I would say that antinomianism may be the characteristic that is most widely associated with the LHP.

There's no doubt that antinomianism can, at times, be liberating and a step in personal growth and individuation. In a culture where a healthy view of the Self is under constant assault, even by some fellow Pagans, intentionally going against the grain can be positive. And it's important to remember that following an antinomianism philosophy doesn't automatically mean that one lacks a personal sense of ethics. Instead, it can merely mean that the person refuses to have their ethics dictated by society.

---

375. Granholm, "Embracing Others than Satan," 88.
376. Granholm, "Embracing Others than Satan," 88–89.
377. Granholm, "Embracing Others than Satan," 89.
378. Miller, "Strategic Sorcery and the Left Hand Path."

Once again, the difference appears to be in the application. The antinomianism found in many definitions of the LHP is why Digitalis states that most Dark Pagans aren't followers of the LHP. In his book *Goth Craft*, he describes the LHP as being "amoral" in that it fails to distinguish between what's moral and what's not.[379] If limited to ethical anarchism, antinomianism would be out of step with the Dark Paganism of Konstantinos, who describes Dark Pagans as having a good-dark or virtuous soul type.[380]

With this background, is Dark Paganism part of the LHP? If we focus solely on the characteristics of the LHP, we see that they're all found within Dark Paganism. All of Granholm's elements of the LHP are in Dark Paganism. Also, the constructive aspect of the Higginbothams' spiritual dissent is in the countercultural nature of Dark Paganism.

Differences appear in how some of the practitioners apply these characteristics. Some LHP members confuse individuality with rugged individualism. Others confuse antinomianism with ethical anarchy. And some appear to stay in a state of perpetual spiritual dissent rather than striving to build a positive, dark counterculture.

If we look at the two definitions provided by Coughlin and Chappell, we find no degree of separation between Dark Paganism and the LHP. Both Dark Paganism and the LHP are internal approaches to spirituality that emphasize the Self, just as Coughlin provided.

A similar agreement is with the definition provided by Chappell. Enhancing self-awareness is found in both the LHP and Dark Paganism. And both seek the positive transformation of the individual in responsible and ethical ways.

I agree with Coughlin on this matter. Dark Paganism is part of the LHP, for we're cut from the same cloth, even if we don't always agree on the application.

Reviewing the Concepts

Chappell describes the Left-Hand Path as an "approach that emphasizes enhancing the sense of Self and Being, with its own techniques and aesthetics, and which is imperative to pursue responsibly and ethically." Elements of the LHP include spiritual dissent, the emphasis of the individual over the collective,

---

379. Digitalis, *Goth Craft*, 83.
380. Konstantinos, *Nocturnal Witchcraft*, 15.

and human nature as both physical and psychic. It focuses on corporeal life rather than the afterlife, self-deification, and strong antinomianism.

When comparing the elements of LHP philosophy and Dark Paganism, any differences appear to be primarily about the application. As a result, Dark Paganism is part of the Left-Hand Path.

Questions to Consider

* Do you believe that Chappell's definition of the Left-Hand Path is accurate? If not, what is your definition?

* Do you believe that the Left-Hand Path is evil and the Right-Hand Path is good?

* Do you agree that Dark Paganism is part of the Left-Hand Path?

XIV
DARK PAGAN TRADITIONS

I must confess that I'm eclectic in practice and don't follow any specific tradition. It's not because I oppose traditions. I've simply never found one with which I could sufficiently agree. It may be because I'm independent. Although, it's just as likely that it's because I'm just too stubborn and egotistical to let someone else be in the lead.

Because of Dark Paganism's focus on the Self, it fits very well with eclecticism. As mentioned earlier, an eclectic Pagan draws from various sources to build their practice. For example, an eclectic Pagan may mix elements of Wicca with several other traditions. The eclectic Dark Pagan can create something highly personalized by mixing and matching. Often, eclectics are solitary practitioners, although some may join with other Pagans.

A Dark Pagan isn't limited to being eclectic or solitary. There are numerous traditions that one can join and still apply Dark Pagan spiritual philosophy to their lives. A tradition does not have to be identified as darkside or Left-Hand Path. Dark Paganism is perfectly compatible with Wicca, Asatru, Druidism, and other Right-Hand Path traditions.

There are many benefits to traditions. By following a tradition, one can benefit from generational knowledge. Many of the elders of these traditions share wisdom developed through years of experience. There's something to be said in not recreating the wheel.

Traditions also have their downsides. The first is the risk of herd mentality. Another is the risk of dogmatism. If the tradition imposes such demands, one risks losing individuality and autonomy.

Some traditions have in-person meetings. Since humans are social animals, these have multiple benefits. Studies have shown that belonging to a group increases overall well-being.[381] Not to mention the benefit of having an elder of a group share their wisdom with you in their presence. In addition, many group rituals can be inspiring and meaningful. Historically, Pagans have raised great power in group rituals.

However, participating in groups has its risks. Any group, including a Pagan one, can become toxic. The group can become autocratic or dogmatic and inhibit a person's growth. A group can also be much worse. There are far too many cases of gaslighting, exploitation, and mental and sexual abuse found within both large and small spiritual groups. The Pagan virtue of prudence can help identify healthy and unhealthy groups.

Sometimes prudence needs a little help. In his classic book *Real Magic: An Introductory Treatise on the Basic Principles of Yellow Magic,* Isaac Bonewits included a fifteen-point checklist that he termed the Cult Danger Evaluation Frame. He later expanded it to eighteen points and renamed it the Advanced Cult Danger Evaluation Frame, which government authorities, such as the FBI, have used to help identify cults.

He listed eighteen red flags in his evaluation that should be watched for in a group. Each red flag is rated on a scale from one to ten. A score of one indicates low risk and ten high. The greater presence of high numbers in the rating of the group indicates the more significant risks. The eighteen elements are internal control; external control; wisdom/knowledge claimed by leader(s); wisdom/knowledge credited to leader(s) by members; dogma; recruiting; front groups; wealth; sexual manipulation of members by leader(s); sexual favoritism; censorship; isolation; dropout control; violence; paranoia; grimness; surrender of will; and hypocrisy.[382]

Obviously, not all spiritual groups are toxic. We should take care not to stereotype groups, Pagan or otherwise. Many provide support to their members and cultivate a healthy environment that encourages personal autonomy and growth. Therefore, one shouldn't automatically avoid joining a Pagan group just because there are a few bad players.

---

381. Wakefield et al., "The Relationship Between Group Identification," 785–807.
382. Bonewits, "The Advanced Bonewtis' Cult Danger Evaluation Frame."

Defining a Dark Pagan Tradition

What standards should we use to label a tradition as being "Dark Pagan"? First, the tradition must be "Pagan." This requirement means that the tradition must be a contemporary form of esoteric spirituality built around a non-Abrahamic polytheism. Second, to be included, it must be "dark," which means that it must focus on honoring and cultivating the Self.

Does a tradition need to have a minimum number of followers to be included? If so, then how small is too small? While the idea of using numerical members as a guide is tempting, it poses some serious problems.

Paganism is a numerically small spiritual movement when compared to others. According to the 2008 survey in *The Pew Forum on Religion & Public Life*, only 0.4 percent of Americans describe themselves as Pagans. This translates to roughly 1.2 million people. While that might sound impressive, it's tiny compared to most other American religions. For example, 78 percent of all Americans self-identify as Christian.[383]

Dark Paganism is numerically far behind Paganism as a whole. Today, Dark Paganism is much like Wicca was in the early years. When Gerald Gardner went public with what would become Wicca, it was just one small coven with only a few members. While Wicca grew substantially in the next twenty years, it was still very small and didn't begin to grow significantly until the first decades of the twenty-first century. Dark Paganism is like Wicca was during its first few decades in that it's still a very young spiritual movement. While I'm aware of no studies on the number of people who currently consider themselves Dark Pagans, it's safe to say that we make up a very small percentage of Pagans.

Considering all of these facts, we must acknowledge that Dark Pagans are a minority within a minority. Because of this, we shouldn't consider the numbers in a tradition a factor.

Now that we've established some guidelines, we can explore various traditions. One will notice that many of these traditions self-identify as being part of the Left-Hand Path. I've chosen to include some LHP traditions in this list since, as I indicated, I share John J. Coughlin's opinion that Dark Paganism is an LHP philosophy.

---

383. "Parsing the Pew Numbers."

Nocturnal Witchcraft

The primary focus of Nocturnal Witchcraft is working with the dark forces found at night. According to Konstantinos, there are different esoteric energies at night than during the day. Nocturnal Witchcraft focuses on these nighttime energies, working with lunar powers and various dark spiritual entities.[384]

There are many resemblances between Nocturnal Witchcraft and Wicca in ritual and tropes. One might go so far as to say that Nocturnal Witchcraft is a close cousin of Wicca. For example, Nocturnal Witchcraft references the God and Goddess.[385] Nocturnal Witchcraft also follows the same Wheel of the Year as Wicca.[386] Nocturnal Witchcraft uses the same ritual tools, such as the athame and candles, as in Wicca.[387]

Yet, as the idiom goes, the devil is in the details. And it's in the details that we find significant differences between Wicca and Nocturnal Witchcraft. First, in Nocturnal Witchcraft, the altar cloth colors are limited to black, and so are the candles.[388] The reason for this emphasis on black is that the psychodrama (i.e., ritual) of Nocturnal Witchcraft aids the practitioner in tapping into the dark ether and other nocturnal forces.[389] Another difference is the centrality of the moon. Nocturnal Witchcraft, as the name implies, focuses on night energies. Therefore, in addition to the Wheel of the Year, Nocturnal Witchcraft closely follows the moon phases. Finally, another difference is the deities of Nocturnal Witchcraft. Nocturnal Witchcraft deities tend to be darker than the standard Wiccan deities. In *Nocturnal Witchcraft: Magick After Dark*, Konstantinos includes an entire chapter on Death as a deity. He also has a chapter on dark deities such as Hades, Nyx, and Anubis.

The best way to learn about the Nocturnal Witchcraft tradition is through Konstantinos's books: *Nocturnal Witchcraft: Magick After Dark*, *Nocturnicon: Calling Dark Forces and Powers*, and *Gothic Grimoire*.

---

384. Konstantinos, *Gothic Grimoire*, 5.
385. Konstantinos, *Nocturnal Witchcraft*, 30.
386. Konstantinos, *Nocturnal Witchcraft*, 24–28.
387. Konstantinos, *Nocturnal Witchcraft*, 31–36.
388. Konstantinos, *Nocturnal Witchcraft*, 33.
389. Konstantinos, *Nocturnal Witchcraft*, 32.

Temple of Set

The Temple of Set was established in the United States by Michael Aquino. Aquino had left the Church of Satan in June of 1975. A few days after leaving, he performed a ritual to invoke the "Prince of Darkness." The result of the ritual was an Unverified Personal Gnosis, or UPG, that he wrote down in a book titled *The Book of Coming Forth by Night*. A UPG is a personal belief that others cannot verify through scholarship. After publishing the book, roughly a hundred members left the Church of Satan and joined the Temple of Set. In October of that same year, the Temple of Set was incorporated as a religion in California.[390]

The Temple of Set uses the ancient Egyptian word *Xeper*, which translates as "to become; to be; to come into being." According to Aquino, *Xeper* has a magickal meaning of "transformation and evolution of the Will from a human to a divine state—by deliberate, conscious, individual force of mind."[391]

Setians believe that the ancient Egyptian god Set was the first "isolate intellect." According to Aquino's UPG, Set describes himself as "the ageless Intelligence of this Universe." Set's title is "Prince of Darkness" because a sea of darkness surrounds him.[392]

You can learn more about the Temple of Set in the book *Mysteries of the Temple of Set (Inner Teachings of the Left Hand Path)* by Don Webb, as well as on the Temple's official website: https://www.xeper.info/.

Draconian Path

There are a variety of paths and traditions in which the dragon is a primary focus. Asenath Mason, a prolific writer and founder of the Temple of Ascending Flame, has written about different Dark Pagan traditions. In her *Draconian Ritual Book*, she wrote of a tradition known as The Path of the Dragon or the Draconian Path.

Mason describes the Draconian Path as "a beautiful quest toward individual Godhood."[393] According to Mason, the dragon is "primal, raw energy." The

---

390. Flowers, *Lords of the Left-Hand Path*, 383–84.
391. Flowers, *Lords of the Left-Hand Path*, 384.
392. Flowers, *Lords of the Left-Hand Path*, 408–9.
393. Mason, *Draconian Ritual Book*, 32.

initiate uses the dragon to ascend to apotheosis through the Draconian Path.[394] The Draconian Path draws on various dark deities such as Lucifer, Leviathan, Lilith, Hecate, Belial, and more.[395] According to Mason, these deities originated in the "void." Self-deification is the ultimate goal of working with these dark deities.[396]

In her book *Grimoire of Tiamat*, Mason writes about another dragon-based Dark Pagan path called the Gnosis of Tiamat. The Gnosis of Tiamat builds upon the Babylonian creation myth of Marduk and Tiamat referenced in chapters 4 and 7. According to the Babylonian creation myth, the dragon is the world, and her blood flows through humanity. Within us there is a dragon consciousness. By tapping into this consciousness, we can achieve apotheosis. Apotheosis is the ultimate goal of the Gnosis of Tiamat.[397]

You can learn more about the Draconian Path in Mason's books *Grimoire of Tiamat* and *Draconian Ritual Book*.

The Sect of the Horned God

While not a tradition per se, the Sect of the Horned God is an influential and growing LHP organization. Founded in 2011 by Thomas LeRoy and Lisa Corrine, the Sect of the Horned God describes itself as an organization consisting of individuals who share a common goal of self-deification. Rather than simply declaring one's godhood, the Sect believes that time and effort through study and reflection are integral in achieving this goal.

On its website, the Sect of the Horned God describes itself as "an LHP Initiatory and Educational Foundation." There are five ascending orders within the Sect. Each order is named after a deity and has an esoteric element. The first order that a new member can join is Pan (earth). It's followed by Cernunnos (air), then Prometheus (fire), then Dionysus (water), and finally by Shiva (spirit).[398]

You can learn more about the Sect of the Horned God at its website: https://www.thesectofthehornedgod.com/.

---

394. Mason, *Draconian Ritual Book*, 14.
395. Mason, *Draconian Ritual Book*, 60–97.
396. Mason, *Draconian Ritual Book*, 58.
397. Mason, *Grimoire of Tiamat*, 12.
398. LeRoy, "The Sect of the Horned God."

Dragon Rouge

According to Kennet Granholm, Dragon Rouge is a Neopagan organization. Nature and the Divine Feminine are central to Dragon Rouge, which it shares with many Pagan traditions of the RHP. However, the organization also has many LHP elements, such as individualism, antinomianism, and self-deification, as a goal.[399] The organization defines its view of magick as being "dark" in that it involves "researching and awakening things that lie outside the structure we are situated in."[400] When we take these details together, it's clear that Dragon Rouge is Dark Pagan.

Thomas Karlsson founded Dragon Rouge. Karlsson reported having had mystical experiences since he was a young child. Around age twelve, he started experimenting with the occult, and by the time he was seventeen had surrounded himself with like-minded individuals. In the late 1980s, he studied the work of a group of LHP magicians known as Yezidi-Typhonian. Karlsson, while visiting Marrakesh, received a Dervish prophecy that "the old shall be destroyed and a temple shall be built for the Red Dragon."[401]

On December 31, 1990, based on the prophecy given to him, Karlsson started Dragon Rouge. At first, the organization was a local group in Sweden and held meetings in homes and privately in natural settings. Over time Dragon Rouge expanded to include international members. As of 2012, Dragon Rouge had nearly five hundred members.[402] About two-thirds of those members were not Swedish.[403]

You can learn more about Dragon Rouge at its website: http://dragonrouge.se.

Thelema

Thelema is the granddaddy of all Pagan traditions, including lightside and darkside. It's also one of the longest-lasting with loyal followers across the globe. The ceremonial magician and occultist Aleister Crowley founded Thelema during the early 1900s. Crowley was a complex and colorful person

---

399. Granholm, "Dragon Rouge,"132.
400. Granholm, "Dragon Rouge," 135.
401. Granholm, "Dragon Rouge," 132–34.
402. Granholm, "Dragon Rouge," 141.
403. Granholm, "Dragon Rouge," 134.

(probably an understatement). To understand Thelema, one must understand a little about Crowley.

Crowley was born Edward Alexander Crowley on October 12, 1875, in Royal Leamington Spa, England. While close to his father, he rejected his parents' fundamentalist Christianity and became interested in Western esotericism. After his education at Trinity College, Crowley became an avid mountain climber and poet. Crowley joined the esoteric Hermetic Order of the Golden Dawn in 1989 and later the Ordo Templi Orientis.

Crowley had a notorious reputation. He was proud that he was once called "the Beast" by his mother as a child. Crowley was known for his heavy drug use and his sexual proclivity. His lifestyle was a shock to many people, which was an effect that he loved causing. He reveled in the fact that the tabloids labeled him "Wickedest Man in the World." Bonewits described Crowley as "a genius whose brilliance was matched only by his neurosis."[404]

According to Crowley, a being called Aiwass contacted him while on his honeymoon in Egypt. This being then dictated to him a book that Crowley titled *Liber Al vel Legis* (*The Book of the Law*), which would become Thelema's principal book. This book contains the Thelema ethical principle "Do what thou wilt shall be the whole of the Law," which would become a source for the Wiccan Rede as well as the principles of what would become the Thelema tradition.

Thelema has the elements needed to be considered Dark Pagan. Thelema is polytheistic with multiple gods and goddesses, primarily Egyptian deities, although Thelemites differ concerning the nature of the gods.[405] Also, as in Dark Paganism, Thelema recognizes the divinity of humans. According to *The Book of the Law*, "there is no god but man."

To learn more about Thelema, you can read Crowley's *The Book of the Law*. You can also visit http://www.thelema.org/.

Vampyre Path

There are those today that see the vampire as more than just an entertaining fantasy character; they see it as a spiritual archetype. The vampire as a spiritual

---

404. Bonewits, *Real Magic*, 221.
405. Orpheus, *Abrahadabra*, 33–34.

archetype is one means to achieve the transformation of the Self. Magician and LHP author Michael W. Ford best describes the vampire's role in modern Paganism. He describes vampyre magick as focusing on "the inner drive to self-evolution and willed change."[406]

While I'm not a follower of the Vampyre Path, I will say that I find it intriguing. As an eclectic, I incorporate many of its concepts and tropes within my system. If I did choose to follow any Dark Pagan tradition, it would probably be the Vampyre Path.

You may have noticed the spelling of the word *vampyre*. Like the word *magick*, *vampyre* has an archaic spelling. The contemporary use of this archaic spelling is the same as Crowley adding the letter *k* to *magic*. Using the archaic spelling of *vampyre* helps differentiate the spiritual practice from the fictional character.[407]

Several Dark Pagan traditions use the vampyre archetype. I will focus on only two traditions that I believe best fit the definition of being Dark Pagan. While the different vampyre traditions have distinctive features, these share similar terminology, tropes, and concepts.

Order of the Vampyre

Within the Temple of Set, there is the Order of the Vampyre (OV). Because it's part of the Setian family, the OV shares terminology and concepts with the Temple of Set. Lilith Aquino and Robert Neilly cofounded the OV.

According to Webb, writer and high priest of the OV, Aquino provided seven essential techniques to the order. The seven techniques are the way of the animal companion, the way of reflection, the way of Circe, the way of the three valleys, the way of the bat, the way of the wolf, and the way of Suteck. Through these seven techniques, members of the OV work to incorporate the vampyre archetype within their lives.[408]

Through animal companionship, the vampyre learns the importance of instinct. In the way of reflection, one learns how to reflect the desires of others, have threats reflect fear and flee, or have others reflect virtues such as nurturing. The way of Circe is a technique to learn to control others. The way of

---

406. Sebastiaan, *Vampyre Magick*, ix.
407. Sebastiaan, *Black Veils*, 3.
408. Webb, *Energy Magick of the Vampyre*, 164.

the three valleys is inspired by the Chinese text *Anthology of the Cultivation of Realization*. The way of the bat teaches you to strike quickly and invisibly and to create your sense of navigating the world. The way the wolf focuses on faithfulness. The alpha walks behind to defend the pack, is loyal to family, and celebrates when happy. Finally, the way of Suteck teaches how to use one's natural desires as tools to achieve self-divination.[409]

A good source of information about the Order of the Vampyre is in Webb's book *Energy Magick of the Vampyre: Secret Techniques for Personal Power and Manifestation*. You can also learn more at the official OV website: https://www .xeper.org/ovampyre.

Ordo Strigoi Vii

The Ordo Strigoi Vii is a Dark Pagan tradition established by Father Sebastiaan that focuses on the Strigoi Vii, or living vampire. According to Corvis Nocturnum, the Ordo Strigoi Vii is a "dark spiritual pathway and Vampyric religion, designed for the Vampyre subculture."[410] Sebastiaan describes vampyre magick's goal as achieving immortality of the Self.[411]

The Strigoi Vii draws energy from various sources and sends it to spiritual entities it calls the *Strigoi Morte* through ritual. The Strigoi Morte then convert it to a form of energy called *Sorra*, which it sends back to the Strigoi Vii to strengthen the etheric body and allow for immortality.

The Strigoi Vii is about more than immortality. It also has an ethical code, which is called the Black Veil. The Black Veil originated in the early 1990s in the New York-based vampyre community. Written by Sebastiaan, the Black Veil covers seven rules of behavior. The seven rules address discretion, diversity, control, elders, behavior, donors, and community.[412]

Sebastiaan's books are the best source of information about Strigoi Vii. His books are *Vampyre Magick: The Grimoire of the Living Vampire*, *Vampire Sanguinomicon: The Lexicon of the Living Vampire*, and *Black Veils: Master Vampyre Edition 888*. You can also check out *Vampyre Magazine*, and the Ordo Strigoi Vii has a forum at https://www.strigoivii.org/.

---

409. Webb, *Energy Magick of the Vampyre*, 165–69.
410. Nocturnum, *Embracing the Darkness*, 98.
411. Sebastiaan, *Black Veils*, 6.
412. Nocturnum, *Embracing the Darkness*, 96–97.

Reviewing the Concepts

Because of Dark Paganism's focus on the Self, it fits very well with eclecticism, which takes from various sources to build a personal tradition. Eclecticism isn't the only option for a Dark Pagan. One can also follow a tradition or join a Pagan group, which has benefits and downsides. While Dark Paganism is compatible with many lightside traditions, several darkside traditions exist from which to choose. Those dark traditions include Nocturnal Witchcraft, the Temple of Set, the Pandemonium Mandala, the Draconian Path, the Sect of the Horned God, Dragon Rouge, Thelema, and the Vampyre Path.

Questions to Consider

* Which appeals to you the most: eclecticism or a tradition?

* If you prefer eclecticism, what sources do you draw upon for inspiration?

* If you prefer tradition, how do you decide which one is best for you?

XV
DARK GODS AND OTHER SPIRITS

Dark Pagans have a well-earned reputation for honoring dark gods. The Dark Pagan authors Raven Digitalis, John J. Coughlin, and Konstantinos reference dark deities in their books. Before we can understand what constitutes a dark god and why they attract Dark Pagans, we need to understand the nature of the gods. To do that, we need to begin with understanding spirits in general.

Understanding Spirits

According to occultist and author Judika Illes, "Spirits are powerful, independent entities who resist human efforts to define them."[413] In her book *The Encyclopedia of Spirits*, Illes provides a list of eleven characteristics of spirits. A few of the traits she describes are that they're non-corporeal, alive, can communicate with us, have their own needs and desires, and come in different types. Some interesting characteristics that Illes includes are that not all spirits are intelligent and that new ones are continually being born. Also, not all spirits are rulers, for some spirits serve.[414]

The idea that multiple spirits inhabit the Cosmos is not some fluffy New Age idea. There is an assortment of spiritual entities in Neoplatonist thought, especially that of Iamblichus and Plotinus. Most non-Abrahamic wisdom traditions, classic and contemporary, share a version of the ancient Greek belief that there are many different spirits. For the Greeks, these included the higher or

---

413. Illes, *Encyclopedia of Spirits*, 15.
414. Illes, *Encyclopedia of Spirits*, 15–19.

hypercosmic gods who were beyond contact with humans. They also had many encosmic gods of various ranks as well as angels, daemons, and heroes until reaching nature and embodied humans.

There are spirits associated with certain animals (such as crows, cows, and foxes) and life events (such as birth, death, and marriage) and with the four elements (water, fire, earth, and air), as well as landmarks (such as rivers, mountains, and forests). Of course, these are just a few, for there are many, many more types.

It's important to understand that while there are benevolent spirits, that's not true for all. The idea of dangerous spirits exists in Sumerian, Babylonian, Egyptian, and Greek Paganism. The belief that all spirits are kind and helpful is the product of our modern, leisure Western culture.

While ancient, dualism, in which the Cosmos is divided between good and evil, is a Right-Hand Path idea. Reality is much more complicated. Many spirits are not so much evil but primal or earthy. The sorcerer Jason Miller prefers to call these demons "sub-lunar beings."[415] These sub-lunar beings are often closer to the natural world than some other spirits. And nature, contrary to what we might think, isn't necessarily kind. As Lao Tzu pointed out, we shouldn't expect nature to follow human standards of ethics.[416]

It needs to be noted that just as there are conscious beings in the material realm who choose to act maliciously, some entities in the spiritual realm also consciously act with malice. Robert Bruce, famous for his work in astral projection, reports a terrifying encounter with a malevolent spiritual entity that nearly killed him in *The Practical Psychic Self-Defense Handbook: A Survival Guide*.[417] These are entities that one wants to avoid at all costs.

Understanding Gods

With this background, we can now turn our attention to the gods. All gods, dark and otherwise, exist as a particular form of a spirit. Their nature can be confusing. In his blog, Druid priest John Beckett compared humans discussing the gods' nature to a conclave of cats debating humans' nature. While cats, being our pets, do know something about their topic, the conversation would

---

415. Miller, *The Sorcerer's Secrets*, 140.
416. Tzu, *Tao Te Ching*, 8.
417. Bruce, *The Practical Psychic Self-Defense Handbook*, 204–8.

reveal more about them than us.[418] Since our knowledge of the gods is limited, maybe even more so than cats' knowledge about us, it should be no surprise that there is no one view of gods shared by all Pagans.

While Pagans, as defined here, are all polytheists, the polytheism takes many different forms. There are currently three popular views about the gods among Pagans. Those three views are archetypism, soft polytheism, and hard polytheism.

In archetypism, the different gods and goddesses are either psychological structures, similar to Carol Jung's archetypes, or different currents of arcane energy found in the Cosmos that are anthropomorphized.[419] Some archetypists consider the gods to be thought-forms created from worship and prayer by generations of believers. Over time these thought-forms may become egregores that exhibit some autonomy apart from their worshipers. One might imagine these gods along the line of Neil Gaiman's deities in the novel *American Gods*.

In soft pantheism, the different gods are different manifestations of a greater divinity. Also known as duotheism, soft polytheism views all male gods as manifestations of one unifying god, while the different goddesses would be different masks of one unifying goddess.[420]

Finally, there is the Pagan belief of hard polytheism, which is growing in popularity among Pagans. According to Christine Hoff Kraemer, hard polytheists view the gods as "objectively existing, independent personalities with whom human beings can have relationships." Though hard polytheists understand that the gods may be flawed, most still believe them worthy of honor and devotion.[421]

There is no one Dark Pagan view of the gods. While Coughlin expresses no personal position in his book *Out of the Shadows: An Exploration of Dark Paganism and Magick,* the other Dark Pagan authors differ about their nature. Digitalis appears to take a soft polytheist position in his book *Goth Craft: The Magickal Side of Dark Culture.* He writes that "the Craft divides the Great God and Great Goddess into multiple forms."[422] Konstantinos appears to take an

---

418. Beckett, "A Conclave of Cats."
419. Kaldera, *Dealing with Deities*, 13.
420. Kraemer, *Seeking the Mystery*, 26.
421. Kraemer, *Seeking the Mystery*, 33–34.
422. Digitalis, *Goth Craft*, 52–53.

archetypist stance. He notes that the gods and goddesses are direct links to the Source and are real in the minds of those who believe. He also goes on to write that groups of individuals can create gods.[423]

I'm a hard polytheist. My view of the gods is very much in line with Kraemer. I believe that multitudes of gods genuinely exist and have their agency and personality.

Believing that the gods are independent entities with personalities doesn't mean that they exist just as the classic Pagans presented. Such belief is as absurd as the fundamentalist Christians who claim their Bible to be historically accurate. The gods are much more complex.

A clarification is needed before exploring the nature of the gods. While this book explores their nature through the lens of hard polytheism, it doesn't mean there isn't truth to the other views. Duotheism, archetypism, and hard polytheism are complementary. The seeming incompatibility results from misconceptions, perspectives, and biases rather than reality.

Regardless of the positions of duotheists and hard polytheists, the gods have become archetypes because they have been present with us since our earliest prehominid days and possibly before. Therefore, they have become part of our deepest subconscious, collective and personal.

In duotheism, the different gods are masks of a singular god and a singular goddess. The term *masks* appears to have its roots in the work of Joseph Campbell. There is some truth to unity among the gods. Mystics often report experiencing reality as unified. This Cosmic unity isn't surprising since as we dive deeper into Cosmic nature, we find that reality is more unified. So, of course, the gods and reality begin to fuse at a deep level. At some point, all gods become a god, and all goddesses become a goddess. If we go further, we find that these two become one. For the Greeks, this unity was the Source. In Taoism, this unity is the Tao. According to Hinduism, it's Brahman.

None of this contradicts the hard polytheist view of the gods. It means that we shouldn't fall into the trap of using the word "only" when it comes to the gods. "The gods are only archetypes." "The different gods are only masks of the God and Goddess." "The gods are only independent personalities and cannot be something else."

---

423. Konstantinos, *Nocturnal Witchcraft*, 39.

The insistence that only one view is correct is wrong. Known as the "false dichotomy argument," it assumes an absolutist position. "It's my way or the highway." Hard polytheists are as guilty of this as the other two advocates.

Nature of the Gods: A Hard Polytheist View

According to Stephen Dillon, who is a hard polytheist, a god or goddess has three defining characteristics. The three are disembodied consciousness, power far more immense than evolved minds, and remarkable greatness.[424] While all spirits are disembodied consciousness and many spirits are more knowledgeable than we are, what distinguishes gods from the other spirits—and ourselves—is their remarkable greatness.

Dillon admits it's difficult to pin down remarkable greatness as a trait. The term reminds me of the famous definition of obscenity given by the US Supreme Court, which is that we know it when we see it.

Remarkable greatness is best understood as the sense one has in a god's presence. There's a sense of awe and wonder. Some feel both fear and attraction at the same time. This sense of greatness that one feels distinguishes gods from other spirits.

Most turn to myths to try to understand a specific god. However, one has to be cautious when using the myths for this purpose. Myths can be unrepresentative of the gods, which Socrates lost his life pointing out. The proper way to use the myths of gods is the same way we use contemporary myths. Although the story of George Washington and the cherry tree isn't historically accurate, it helps remind us that Washington had a well-earned reputation for honesty. Therefore, just as contemporary myths can teach us about a person's character, ancient myths can teach us about a specific god's character.

Most contemporary Pagans don't consider the gods to be perfect. Of course, this lack of perfection isn't limited to contemporary Paganism; it's also in other non-Abrahamic traditions. According to an ancient Tibetan proverb, "When people are desperate, they petition the gods. When the gods get desperate, they lie."[425]

---

424. Dillon, *The Case for Polytheism*, 4.
425. Miller, *The Elements of Spellcrafting*, 205.

There are characteristics that we share with the gods. Like the gods, we have agency and sovereignty. It's also true that the gods show love and hate much the same way as humans. These shared characteristics help make it possible for us to have relationships with the gods.

While we share some characteristics with the gods, we need to be careful not to fall into the trap of anthropomorphizing them. The gods are different from us and not just in the degree of power or lifespan. The Greek sixth-century-BCE philosopher and theologian Xenophanes warned against treating the gods as though they're the same as us.[426] Xenophanes's warning reminds me of F. Scott Fitzgerald's comment that those born rich are different than the rest of us.[427]

Another aspect of gods is that many seem to have something akin to a symbiotic relationship with the surface realm. We see gods associated with land, sea, and air. There are gods associated with nearly everything.

This close relationship between the surface realm and the gods may explain why they appear as psychological phenomena. The interaction between humans and the gods seems to be filtered primarily on the subconscious level. Because of this, we tend to project our personal biases upon them. We create the gods in our image, making it difficult to discern their true nature. On a positive note, we can use this effect to better understand and cultivate our Selves through Tantra and deity yoga practices.

We also need to remember that the socio-economics of each culture impact our understanding of the gods. Every culture applies its bias to its understanding of the gods. An example is the Sumerian goddess Inanna. Cultures throughout Mesopotamia worshiped her for thousands of years. To the Babylonians, she was Ishtar. To the Semitic people, she was Astarte. Different cultures also had different variations of her myths.

Finally, many classic Pagans organized their gods into pantheons. Each pantheon is usually hierarchical. The Greeks referred to their gods as the Olympians. The Egyptian pantheon was the Ennead, and the Canaanites called their pantheon of gods Elohim (yes, the same name used by the Hebrews in their creation story). This practice of organizing gods into pantheons continues today in contemporary Paganism.

---

426. "Xenophanes."
427. Fitzgerald, "The Rich Boy," 7.

Virtue and Gods

Are the gods virtuous? Socrates certainly thought so. So did the Neoplatonists. Beckett has expressed similar opinions.[428]

The main problem I have with this belief is that there's little support that each god is by nature virtuous, and there's a lot to support that many are not. While I mentioned that we have to be cautious about using myths to understand the gods, they are our primary source. The myths portray most gods as not being very virtuous. Indeed, the myths show some gods as more virtuous than others, and others lack any form of virtue as we know it.

Giving Beckett credit, he admits that the gods' portrayal in their myths does pose a challenge to his view. He agrees that it's challenging to reconcile myths with his belief in the gods' innate virtue. One answer he gives to resolve this conflict is a reminder that we shouldn't fall into the same trap as Christian fundamentalists. We need to make sure that we don't read the myths literally. This warning is good advice I firmly agree with.

However, I don't believe that one must read the myths literally to see the message that few gods are consistently virtuous. Whether we try to read the myths as metaphors or other nonliteral methods, we still get back to the same conclusion: virtue among the gods often seems lacking in many of the myths.

Raven Kaldera offers a way to reconcile the myths with a belief in virtuous gods. According to Kaldera, gods have a vertical characteristic. He uses the analogy of the stalactite that expands upward to the top of a cave. In this model, the gods have lower aspects that resemble their representation in myths. However, they also have a higher or a transcendent nature that resembles those that Socrates advocated and for which he died.[429] Kaldera's model, therefore, allows the gods to be virtuous while having less virtuous qualities as well.

Should We Worship the Gods?

If not all gods are virtuous, we must ask if they're truly worthy of worship. Not everyone believes that they are worthy. Some, especially some on the Left-Hand Path, hold that we should worship no god but ourselves. Is this the correct answer?

---

428. Beckett, "6 Thoughts on Gods Claiming People."
429. Kaldera, *Dealing with Deities*, 33.

As an animist, I believe that all beings, the gods included, are inherently worthy of respect. Respect isn't something earned but inherited by one's divine nature. This inherent entitlement to respect includes humans (living and dead), animals, plants, and the very ground we walk on. Spirits, which include gods, are just as worthy of respect. A being can lose the right to be respected by their actions, but they begin with it by default. Therefore, by its divine nature, a god is worthy of respect unless it proves otherwise.

However, worship or reverence is different from merely paying respect as we would give to each other. And it's more than what Carl Rogers termed "unconditional positive regard." Most definitions of worship include respect that's "extravagant."[430] Also, worship can include devotion. The question then is whether the gods are worthy of such reverence.

The power that gods wield is undoubtedly one reason to give them extravagant respect. If a person points a loaded gun in my direction, I will respect their power with the firearm. When it comes to power, the gods are to an average spirit what a hurricane is to a tornado. Other spirits are to us what a tornado is to a dust devil.

Honor is a variant of extravagant respect. I can respect someone's power without honoring them. Earlier, I mentioned someone pointing a gun at me. While I would be an idiot if I didn't exhibit respect for what that person could do, it doesn't mean that I would honor that individual.

Gods are worthy of honor for their place in the Cosmos. Most Pagan thought over the ages has held that the gods are necessary for the material and spiritual realms' proper functioning. They can also play an essential role in assisting us in our ascension. These all impact us, and therefore, it would serve us well to honor these beings.

As mentioned, worship can go beyond extravagant respect and honor. If worship only included honor, then it would be shallow and empty. It would resemble two mob bosses who honor each other despite their mutual hatred and continue to do so because of tradition and their fear of each other's power. Honor keeps the peace, but it's hollow and superficial.

Anyone who worships a personal deity will tell you that a deeper form of worship includes mutual respect and devotion. Some might go so far as to say

---

430. "Worship," 1445.

that it also includes mutual affection. Worship at this level becomes more than showing honor based on power or position. At this level, worship becomes an intimate relationship between the god and the human.

Mutual respect, devotion, and mutual affection are some of the characteristics found in healthy personal relationships. A healthy personal relationship is one where all parties recognize the autonomy and personal sovereignty of each person involved. There should also always be respect for personal space and boundaries. This need for healthy relationships is true whether one discusses humans' relationships between other humans or gods.

Some elements are never in any healthy relationship. A healthy relationship never includes any form of mental or physical abuse. Gaslighting should never be part of a relationship. No one in the relationship should ever fear the other. A person in a relationship should never feel forced to do something they don't want to do. And sexual assault is never, ever acceptable. All these limits apply not only to human relationships but also to relations between gods and humans.

Virtue isn't a required element for being a god. Yes, some gods exhibit virtue more than others. But there's no evidence or reason to believe that all gods are 100 percent virtuous. More important is whether these spirits, regardless of whether one considers them gods or not, are worthy of worship. At a minimum, gods should be extravagantly honored (i.e., worshiped) for no other reason than their power and status. If one is lucky, one will have an opportunity to have a relationship with a god or gods that involves mutual love and respect. Such a relationship is the most profound form of worship.

"Dark" Gods

We're finally in a position to understand dark gods. First, Coughlin points out that we shouldn't put too much weight into the terms *dark* and *light* when applied to deities. All deities are multifaceted.[431] For example, Apollo is the golden boy of the Greek pantheon of gods with many positive traits.[432] According to Kaldera, Apollo was a god of physicians. As a physician's god, he held the epitaph *Apollo Latros*. However, Kaldera explains that Apollo also had a dark

---

431. Coughlin, *Out of the Shadows*, 154.
432. Illes, *Encyclopedia of Spirits*, 195.

side, for he was the bringer of disease and epidemics. In this aspect, Apollo is *Apollo Parnopius.*[433]

Just as gods associated with light can have dark sides, dark deities can have light sides. For example, Kaldera writes that psychopomps, spirits that guide those who have just died to the afterlife, though stern to the living, act very differently to the deceased. To those who have died, they're loving, kind, and compassionate.[434]

If all deities have dark and light sides, what makes specific deities dark? According to Coughlin, the distinctive difference between light and dark deities is that deities considered dark are raw, intense, and unpredictable. There's a sense of mystery with dark deities. The combination of these aspects is often frightening to some. Therefore, some individuals are fearful of these dark, unpredictable deities.[435]

In many ways, this resembles the role of the Shadow of the human psyche. As mentioned, the Shadow is the creation of those aspects of our personality that we've shoved down and denied. It's common for the Shadow to be raw, unpredictable, and frightening—just like dark deities.

To understand what makes a deity dark, we need to compare different deities. Venus is commonly known as a love goddess and is generally considered a light deity. Some mistakenly think Inanna is a love goddess, but she's not. Inanna is a goddess of sex and war. She is not a light deity. She is a raw and passionate dark deity. Venus is a light goddess, while Inanna is dark. Interestingly, Venus and Inanna share the same stellar object: the planet Venus.

There are dark deities, but humans decide the classification. While the gods exist as independent entities with their agency, we still create the gods in our image. That includes projecting our hopes and fears upon them. And that makes some deities dark.

Reviewing the Concepts

To understand the nature of gods, we much first understand spirits. Spirits are non-corporeal, intelligent beings with their own needs and desires. There are spirits associated with locations, life events, and the four elements.

---

433. Kaldera, *Dealing with Deities*, 33.
434. Kaldera, *Dealing with Deities*, 113.
435. Coughlin, *Out of the Shadows*, 151–52.

In Paganism, there are three main views of the gods: archetypism, soft polytheism, and hard polytheism. There is no one Dark Pagan view about the nature of the gods. The viewpoint presented here is from a hard polytheism perspective.

The gods share three characteristics from a hard polytheist viewpoint: disembodied consciousness, immense power greater than evolved minds, and remarkable greatness. Remarkable greatness is best understood as the sense one has in a god's presence. There's a sense of awe and wonder. Some feel both fear and attraction at the same time. This sense of greatness that one feels distinguishes gods from other spirits.

The gods share many characteristics with us. Like us, they're not perfect or all-powerful. They have their agency and sovereignty as we do. It's also true that the gods show love and hate much the same way as humans. These shared characteristics help make it possible for us to have relationships with the gods.

While they share some characteristics with us, the gods are different from us and not just in the degree of power or lifespan. Another aspect of gods is that many seem to have something akin to a symbiotic relationship with the surface realm. Like all spirits, we see gods associated with land, sea, and air. There are gods associated with nearly everything.

At a minimum, gods should be extravagantly honored (i.e., worshiped) for no other reason than their power and status. If one is lucky, one will have an opportunity to have a relationship with a god or gods that involves mutual love and respect. Such a relationship is the most profound form of worship.

There are dark deities, but humans decide the classification. While the gods exist as independent entities with their agency, we still create the gods in our image. Dark gods are those deities considered raw, intense, and unpredictable.

Questions to Consider

* What is your definition of a spirit?

* What do you believe best describes the nature of the gods? Archetypism, soft polytheism, or hard polytheism?

* Are there dark gods? If so, what differentiates gods from light and dark?

XVI
SPIRITUALITY AND THE DARK ALLURE

D ark Pagan aesthetics and tropes tend to be dark. It's not surprising that the three founders of Dark Paganism have roots in the goth subculture. Raven Digitalis places the goth subculture at the heart of Dark Paganism, which he defines as a "deep-seated interest in the mysteries of magick and mysticism, combined with a dedication to the gothic subculture or another dark lifestyle."[436] In his book *Out of the Shadows: An Exploration of Dark Paganism and Magick*, John J. Coughlin considers dark aesthetics and dark lifestyles essential. Konstantinos has written several books emphasizing dark aesthetics, dark deities, and nighttime magick.

Sometimes it seems that we darksiders take our dark aesthetics a little far. Jason Miller is critical of the insistence by some on the Left-Hand Path that everything we do should be spooky. He refers to this over-the-top insistence as being "darke fluff."[437] Our dark aesthetics are not always in good taste. The fine art community considers much of it lowbrow.[438]

A good example of misplaced dark aesthetics is the deity Lucifer. Christians long ago took a word out of context from Isaiah 14:12 in the Hebrew Bible.[439] They then combined it with material from the Hebrew noncanonical texts and some passages from the Christian New Testament, also taken out of context.

---

436. Digitalis, *Goth Craft*, 2.
437. Miller, "Strategic Sorcery and the Left Hand Path."
438. Becket-Griffith, *Gothic Art Now*, 8.
439. Coogan and May, *The New Oxford Annotated Bible*.

The result was the myth that Lucifer was the name of a fallen angel who became evil incarnate.[440]

This misassociation by Christians has had a lasting impact on Lucifer's image through the years. It's next to impossible to mention the Roman god Lucifer without someone associating it with the Christian "fallen angel" as a dark and sinister embodiment of evil. Today entertainment, ranging from rock songs to television shows, continues this misassociation of Lucifer. Pop culture and some Pagan groups, primarily on the LHP, while no longer considering him evil, continue to associate Lucifer with the dark and ominous tropes given to him by Christians.

If Christians and others are wrong about Lucifer, then what is his true nature? Lucifer, whose name translates as "light-bringer," is a god of the Greco-Roman pantheon. He's associated with the planet Venus as seen at sunrise and known as the morning star. While the Romans called him Lucifer, he was Phosphorus to the Greeks. Lucifer was the son of Aurora, who was the goddess of the dawn, and was the father of Ceyx. According to the Roman poet Ovid, Lucifer's primary task is creating order in the heavens.[441]

Pagans are slowly starting to return to a classic understanding of Lucifer. Since the mid-1920s, several occult societies have arisen that advocate Lucifer as a bringer of wisdom and enlightenment, much like Prometheus. In his book *Nocturnicon: Calling Dark Forces and Powers*, Konstantinos describes a UPG that he had about Lucifer. While suffering from serious medical issues, Konstantinos encountered an angelic being emitting a pure blinding light. The being described himself as the "Light-Bringer." According to Konstantinos, Lucifer focuses on bringing knowledge and freedom to humanity.[442] Konstantinos's UPG isn't the only one of this type. I'm aware of other UPGs involving Lucifer that are very similar.

We now have a very different understanding of Lucifer. Christianity's dark, spooky, evil fallen angel Lucifer doesn't exist. We know his nature to be closer to the Roman god Lucifer, whose wisdom allowed him to set order to the heavens and who gave the stellar bodies the freedom of the sky. Many Pagans now understand Lucifer as a god of light whose goal is to share his wisdom and

---

440. Kastor, *The Satanic Pattern*, 57.
441. Ovid, *Metamorphoses*, 28.
442. Konstantinos, *Nocturnicon*, 123–29.

bring freedom to humanity. Any attempt to apply dark aesthetics to such a being as Lucifer is a mistake.

Dark Allure

While Dark Paganism started as part of the goth subculture, nothing about the Dark Pagan worldview presented in this book requires the practitioner to follow a dark aesthetic or dark lifestyle. If dark aesthetics and dark lifestyles don't appeal to a Dark Pagan, then that person is under no obligation to incorporate them into their practice. What matters most is that a person is authentic to themself. A person can have light and shiny aesthetics and still be a Dark Pagan. Following the herd isn't okay—even if that herd consists of Dark Pagans.

However, this chapter isn't about being light and shiny. It's about the fact that there exists a prominent role of dark aesthetics and dark lifestyles in most Dark Paganism. We, therefore, return to the question at the beginning: Why do dark aesthetics and lifestyles so dominate Dark Paganism? As it turns out, there are a variety of factors involved.

We need to begin by briefly addressing a simple fact. Without a doubt, there exist those for whom the dark aesthetic is nothing more than a superficial attraction. For some, it's nothing more than a matter of preference. The same as preferring chocolate over vanilla. Individuals preferring dark aesthetics can be found both in and out of Dark Paganism.

However, a difference in personal taste doesn't explain every person. For some Dark Pagans, like myself, it goes beyond a personal preference in fashion or art. There is a spiritual side to our dark aesthetics. Konstantinos labels the deep and spiritual draw of dark aesthetics felt by some Dark Pagans as a "dark allure."[443]

Dark Art

Artwork with a dark aesthetic is far from being a new phenomenon. Arnold Böcklin painted one famous example in the nineteenth century. Titled *Self-Portrait with Death Playing the Fiddle*, Böcklin painted himself leaning back onto a skeleton playing a fiddle behind Böcklin's left ear. Another example is Mary Queen of Scots, who is reputed to have worn a silver watch shaped like a skull. Engraved upon the timepiece was a quote from Horace written in Latin.

---

443. Konstantinos, *Nocturnal Witchcraft*, 15.

It meant, "Pale Death with impartial tread beats at the poor man's cottage door and at the palaces of kings."[444]

Böcklin's painting is part of a broader genre of art called *danse macabre,* in which death is a skeleton shown among the living. Sometimes the skeletons interact with the living by conversation or dance. While similar illustrations can date back to prehistoric times, the Western art style of the danse macabre is believed to date back to France during the fifteenth century.[445]

Historically, the skull in art, such as the watch of Mary Queen of Scots, was meant to remind individuals of the Latin expression *memento mori,* which translates as "remember, you will die." While the term *memento mori* is commonly associated with Christianity, the idea didn't originate with it. The belief in the importance of being aware of one's mortality dates back to ancient times. The Stoic philosopher Epictetus wrote that when one kisses a child or a friend, one should temper their happiness by remembering their mortality.

Skulls continue to be a part of contemporary dark aesthetics. They're on clothing, jewelry, artwork, and more. Portrayals of skulls range from cute to creepy and everything in between. According to the artist Ilya, the current trend began in London during the winter of 2004.[446] Of course, anytime something becomes widespread, it becomes commodified in our postmodern culture, which means that skulls will likely soon become passé as people grow tired of the flood of corporate-made skull art.

The dark art movement is another form of contemporary dark aesthetic. Dark art emphasizes the macabre and disturbing. It's closely related to protest art in that dark art either transmits a message or elicits a response. Surrealism dominates the dark art movement. Shades of black and gray are common colors.[447]

One of the most famous painters of the dark art movement was H. R. Giger, who became widely known for his design work on the horror/science-fiction movie *Alien.* One of my favorite contemporary dark artists is Billelis. According to Billelis's website, the artist is a "freelance 3D Illustrator & Art Director specializing in dark visuals and decorative art."[448] The seeds of the dark arts

---

444. Bartlett, *Bartlett's Familiar Quotations,* 107.
445. Wendell, *Necromance,* 5.
446. Ilya, *The Mammoth Book of Skulls,* 6.
447. "Dark Art Movement."
448. "About."

movement were planted by artists long before Giger. Artists such as Hieronymus Bosch, Henry Fuseli, and Salvador Dali are considered pioneers of the dark arts movement.

Goth Subculture

Dark aesthetics goes beyond illustrations and sculptures. As mentioned, Dark Paganism's roots are in the goth subculture, which has a well-earned reputation for preferring the dark aesthetic in nearly everything. This preference is especially true for goth fashion, which tends toward a Victorian theme, although there are different goth styles. While the color black isn't mandatory for goths, they do have a reputation for wearing black clothing. Of course, the modern goths weren't the first to prefer black or dark clothing. The late eighteenth-century European youth known as the Romantics preferred black. This taste for dark colors in fashion, which I admit to sharing, can present a challenge to those of us who live in warmer climates.

It's challenging to develop a universal definition of goth. One reason is that members of the goth subculture are, by nature, highly individualistic. According to author Corvis Nocturnum, goth is characterized by a compulsive drive toward "creativity and self-expression" along with a "deep fascination with all things frightening, odd, and mysterious."[449]

Dark Fiction

One of the typical dark tropes found in horror novels and movies is the vampire. While vampires, also known as revenants, are commonly associated with central Europe, they are found in many cultures. One example is the Babylonian *lamastu*.[450]

The portrayal of the vampire in modern fiction is often different than that of folklore. While John Polidori's nineteenth-century novel *The Vampyre* wasn't the first vampire story in Western fiction, it first portrayed the vampire as a sophisticated creature. Today most individuals don't think of Polidori's novel when they think of the vampire. Instead, most people think of Bram Stoker's novel *Dracula* and especially of the 1931 Universal Pictures adaptation starring

---

449. Nocturnum, *Embracing the Darkness*, 19.
450. Black and Green, *Gods, Demons, and Symbols of Ancient Mesopotamia*, 115–16.

Bela Lugosi. Over time the portrayal of the vampire has continued to evolve. The modern vampire is now often shown as a sympathetic and tragic figure. At times the vampire is even heroic.

The contemporary obsession with the virtuous vampire began in the 1960s with the daytime soap opera *Dark Shadows*. The series had only been on the air for a few months and was on the verge of being canceled when the producers introduced a new character: the vampire Barnabas Collins. *Dark Shadows* went from teetering on the edge of being canceled to a roaring success. Barnabas Collins, played by Jonathan Frid, was different from the stereotypical vampire. While he was still dangerous, Collins was complex, tragic, and sympathetic. He had a sense of ethics and was capable of love.[451] In one episode, Collins said, "If a man can become a monster, then a monster can become a man."[452]

Even though *Dark Shadows* ended in 1971, the series had a long-lasting effect on the vampire myth. The next major step in the vampire's rehabilitation was Anne Rice's landmark novel *Interview with the Vampire,* published in 1976. In the 1980s, the movie *The Lost Boys* portrayed the vampire as cool and stylish. Later, in the late '90s, the movie *Blade,* based on the comic book by the same name, continued portraying vampires as cool. Possibly the biggest hit for noble vampires was the *Twilight* novels and their film adaptations. Virtuous vampires are also found in numerous small-screen series, from *Buffy the Vampire Slayer* to *The Vampire Diaries* and more.

Dark Music

Dark aesthetics is also present in some styles of music. Genres such as gothic country, neoclassical darkwave, and dark cabaret are musical styles that emphasize macabre and darker themes. One example of dark musical aesthetics is the work of the Australian composer Peter Gundry. His compositions consist of dark symphonies with titles such as *Waltz of the Bone King, The Serpents Tongue, Dance of the Damned,* and *The Vampire Masquerade.* Another example is the band *Nox Arcana.* Its album *Necronomicon* has a dark ambient composition inspired by H. P. Lovecraft's work, and the band's *Carnival of Lost Souls* album is essentially a dark cabaret.

---

451. Melton, *Vampire Gallery*, 102–5.
452. Thorne, *Vampires*, 15.

Various Dark Non-Pagan Spiritualities

Dark Paganism isn't the only spirituality with a dark aesthetic. Various non-Pagan spiritual traditions incorporate dark aesthetics. While some have Abrahamic connections, all examples presented here have classic non-Abrahamic roots.

Día de los Muertos

Día de los Muertos is a festival popular in Mexico and among some in the United States. The iconic image of Día de los Muertos is the sugar skull, or *calavera*. It's often in makeup or masks worn by participants, in artwork, and in pastries. Many Día de los Muertos participants construct altars for the deceased. Some participants lay flowers, such as marigolds, on adults' graves and toys on children's.[453]

While Día de los Muertos is a Christian festival, its roots are deeply Pagan. Before the European invasion, the Aztecs celebrated a festival dedicated to the dead at the start of August. The Aztecs dedicated this festival to the goddess Mictecacihuatl. Because one of the European invaders' goals was to eliminate the Indigenous peoples' religion and culture, they replaced the Aztec festival with the Christian All Saints' Day. However, they weren't wholly successful at eliminating the Pagan roots. Elements of the original Aztec festival and worship of the Aztec goddess Coatlicue survived and blended with the Christian festival.[454]

Santa Muerte

The following of Santa Muerte is a quickly growing and highly controversial faith with strong dark aesthetics. Santa Muerte's iconography combines elements of the Grim Reaper with the Virgin Mary. Sometimes her hands are pressed together in prayer. Other times she's shown holding a scythe in one hand and scales in the other. There is usually a halo made up of light, roses, or both behind her.

---

453. Romo, "Why Marigolds, or Cempasúchil, Are the Iconic Flower of Día de los Muertos.";
    Strom, "Día de los Angelitos: Remembering Children on the Day of the Dead."
454. Prower, *La Santa Muerte*, 36–37.

Like Día de los Muertos, Santa Muerte has her roots in Mexico. The oldest written account of Santa Muerte comes from the eighteenth century when the Spanish clergy claimed to observe someone demanding miracles from a figure that appeared to be a skeleton. They claimed that the practitioners referred to the figure as "Santa Muerte."[455]

According to author Tomás Prower, the deity Santa Muerte results from a fusion of several Aztec deities with Spanish images of death. The same two Aztec goddesses, Mictecacihuatl and Coatlicue, who played a part in Día de los Muertos, were influential in her development. Another important element was the Spanish portrayal of death as a feminine entity named la Parca. These combined to become Santa Muerte.[456]

Santa Muerte's popularity stems from her two main characteristics. First, she's nonjudgmental because, as Horatio pointed out, death comes equally for us all. Because of this nonjudgmental nature, Santa Muerte doesn't judge your requests' ethics before granting them. Due to her neutrality, both police and criminals venerate her. This nonjudgmental nature has also made her popular among some LGBT+ individuals and sex workers. The second reason is that she's the deity of the desperate. Some will turn to her after their lightside deity fails to answer their prayers.[457]

Her spooky appearance is one reason she's controversial. The idea of venerating a deity that resembles the Grim Reaper frightens some. However, the main reason Santa Muerte is controversial is her popularity with criminals. The revelation that some of her worshipers are drug traffickers working on the US-Mexico border shocked many people.[458]

Santa Muerte is interesting from a Pagan standpoint. Indeed, most of the iconography for Santa Muerte is Christian, and there's a strong Catholic element to the language of the prayers and rituals. However, according to Prower, not all followers are monotheists. Some of her devotees are polytheists.[459] In addition, her roots are firmly Pagan.

---

455. Prower, *La Santa Muerte*, 37.
456. Prower, *La Santa Muerte*, 36.
457. Prower, *La Santa Muerte*, 14–16.
458. Prower, *La Santa Muerte*, 17.
459. Prower, *La Santa Muerte*, 10.

Santa Muerte has received recent attention on the small screen. The Showtime series *Penny Dreadful: City of Angels* included Santa Muerte as a reoccurring character. While her portrayal is not entirely accurate, she is portrayed positively.

Tantra

Of all of the different Buddhist traditions, Tantra is the one that Westerners find most intriguing and the one that they least understand. A quick search online of the word *Tantra* will result in multiple hits about "Tantra sex" or "How to increase your sexual performance through Tantra." Much of this results from Westerners' prurient interests rather than Tantra itself. While it's true that eroticism and sexuality are part of Tantra, sex makes up only a small aspect. Tantra is far more complex.

There's much about Tantra to which Pagans can relate. According to psychotherapist Rob Preece, for Tantra, the division between reality's material and spiritual aspects is fuzzy and hard to distinguish. As a result, the Tantra worldview includes animism with entities inhabiting trees, rocks, and rivers. Tantra practitioners pay tribute to different entities for successful crops and protection against spirits that bring disease.[460]

An intriguing aspect of Tantra for the issue of the dark allure is its wrathful deities. Tantra's wrathful deities are a collection of divine beings who exhibit frightening iconography. The wrathful deity Yamāntaka, for example, is described as blue, having a head of a bull, an erect phallus, and multiple arms and legs (the numbers vary), and wearing a garland of heads and animal skin. A massive cloud of flames surrounds him as he stands on numerous bodies.

According to Preece, Yamāntaka and the other wrathful deities embody the power to control the Shadow Self. They don't do so by repressing it. The wrathful deities control the Shadow Self by absorbing its forces into their nature. According to Preece, wrathful deities' frightening appearances allow them to work with the Shadow Self rather than bright and cheerful images.[461]

---

460. Preece, *The Psychology of Buddhist Tantra*, 1.
461. Preece, *The Psychology of Buddhist Tantra*, 182.

Origins of Dark Allure

So, with all of this background, what is the origin of the Dark Pagan dark allure? How is it that some of us see spirituality within the dark aesthetic? Unfortunately, there doesn't appear to be one answer. Instead, there seems to be a variety of variables that come in to play. Some are mundane, while others are esoteric.

As mentioned, classically the skull was a symbol used to remind us of the certainty of death and our mortality. Yet, there are those today who see it differently. In issue 5.2 of the magazine *Content*, the artist Stephanie Metz, known for her biomorphic abstract sculpture, stated the meaning of skulls isn't a symbol of death. Instead, each bone speaks about someone's life.[462]

We can view modern dark aesthetics in much the same way as Metz. Our dark allure isn't an obsession with death. Instead, by acknowledging our mortality, we're reminding ourselves to enjoy our mortal life for one day it will end.

Preece's understanding of the wrathful deities is helpful because it provides us with another piece of the puzzle of our dark allure. He draws upon Carl Jung's theory to explain that wrathful deities aid in gaining power over the Shadow Self, which ties nicely into another of Jung's theories. According to Mark D. Griffiths, Jung believed that horror films "tapped into primordial archetypes buried deep in our collective subconscious."[463]

The appeal of dark aesthetics, using Jungian thought, arises from the Shadow Self. When the Shadow Self manifests, it does so in symbols, myths, dreams, and desires, like all other aspects of the subconscious. Because the Shadow is the product of the aspects of one's personality that have been repressed and stigmatized, they tend to manifest themselves as dark tropes and an attraction to the macabre or dark subcultures.[464]

However, dark aesthetics and tropes are more than the manifestations of the Shadow. Dark aesthetics and tropes aid in gaining control over the Shadow Self. Like the wrathful deities, they assist in incorporating the subconscious's Shadow Self with the conscious.

---

462. Ilya, *The Mammoth Book of Skulls*, 5.
463. Griffiths, "Why Do We Like Watching Scary Films?"
464. Goldstein, *Why We Watch*, 188.

The meaning of illustrating death in art isn't limited to physical life and death. Death can also represent transformation. The Death card in the tarot is one example. While it can represent physical death, most writers interpret it as commonly signifying change. However, the Death card is more nuanced than often thought. According to Rachael Pollack, author of the classic *Seventy-Eight Degrees of Wisdom: A Tarot Journey to Self-Awareness*, the Death card isn't about change per se but represents the moment we give up something. One might say that aspect of yourself dies. After the removal of the blockage, then change will occur.[465]

Death

Occult author Michelle Belanger wrote that in Tibetan Buddhism it's believed that we die many times over during our lifetime. In this sense, death occurs whenever we let go of some aspect of ourselves. Therefore, symbols of death, such as the Death card, can represent this form of constructive loss or death.[466]

Finally, there might be a spiritual origin to our dark allure. Konstantinos believes that each person has a different soul type. Certain soul types include an innate attraction to a dark aesthetic or a dark allure, while others are repulsed by it. According to Konstantinos, each soul type is fundamental to who a person is. He believes that each person's soul type is set during the afterlife before rebirth.[467]

We can see that no one answer sufficiently explains the dark allure common in Dark Paganism. Different factors come into play. A combination of factors might also explain why dark aesthetics is so attractive. That the dark allure results from various factors shouldn't come as a surprise. Most things in life aren't simple.

Reviewing the Concepts

Dark Pagan aesthetics and tropes tend to be dark. Dark aesthetics is found in art, the goth subculture, fiction, music, and various dark non-Pagan spiritualities. There are various reasons, such as the influence of the Shadow and spiritual alignment, why Dark Pagans tend toward dark aesthetics.

---

465. Pollack, *Seventy-Eight Degrees of Wisdom*, 102.
466. Belanger, *Walking the Twilight Path*, 4.
467. Konstantinos, *Nocturnal Witchcraft*, 15.

While dark aesthetics and dark lifestyles are common among Dark Pagans, a Dark Pagan is under no obligation to incorporate them into their practice. What matters most is that a person is authentic to themselves. A person's aesthetics can be light and shiny, and they can still be a Dark Pagan. Following the herd isn't okay—even if that herd consists of Dark Pagans.

Questions to Consider

* Do you share the attraction to dark aesthetics common in Dark Paganism? If not, why not?

* Why do you think some people are attracted to a dark aesthetic? Is it a personal taste, for a philosophical reason, or because of something else?

* Can you think of some examples of dark aesthetics not listed here?

XVII
A DARK OCEAN

The ancient Greek philosophical schools were complete packages. Along with providing a way of life, each philosophy included a highly sophisticated model of the Cosmos. Therefore, this chapter explores how Dark Paganism's philosophy addresses the more arcane metaphysics and cosmology subjects.

With metaphysical concepts, we always speak in metaphorical language, using the words *higher*, *lower*, *above*, and *below*. That's not to say that there is no truth in metaphysics. It means that our experience as a corporeal being is limiting. As a result, the reality addressed by metaphysics is so alien that our language can't adequately describe it. Because of this, we inevitably speak in metaphors to try to understand the subject the best we can.

Since most wisdom traditions are externally focused, they couch most metaphysical concepts in external themed metaphors. However, since Dark Paganism is an internally focused spirituality, I believe it's time to use different metaphors. While the ideas used in Dark Paganism are similar to those found in classic Western esotericism, we should reimagine many of the tropes and elements to be consistent with the internal spirituality at the heart of Dark Paganism.

Before exploring dark metaphysics, a disclaimer is required. This section is the most speculative of all in this book. The majority of the musings in this chapter are mine alone and should not be considered essential components of Dark Paganism. One could have a very different model of metaphysics and still be a Dark Pagan.

That this chapter is speculative should not be a surprise. All metaphysics is speculative. The philosopher Immanuel Kant described metaphysics as "a dark ocean without shores or lighthouse, strewn with many a philosophic wreck."[468] Now let's dive into the dark ocean of metaphysics.

Esoteric Planes

Most Pagan cosmology describes the Cosmos's structure as consisting of a spectrum stretching from the Divine Source at one end and our denser material plane at the other.[469] Along this spectrum, various planes and subplanes exist between the material and the Divine Source. Those planes closer to the Divine Source are more sublime than those farther away.

This spectrum model of the Cosmos relates closely to that of the Greek philosopher Plotinus, who divided the intelligible world into three substances, also known as hypostasis. The three hypostases were the One, the Intelligence, and Soul, with the material realm being an extension of the Soul. According to Plotinus, the One overflows, or emanates, to the Intelligence and then overflows to create the Soul.[470] One might visualize this process as resembling a tiered waterfall similar to Western Australia's beautiful Mitchell Falls.

The Neoplatonists believed the material realm to be the end of the line for creation. The Neoplatonists thought that the material world was exhausted by the divine creative energy. The result is that the creation process ends with the material realm rather than creating additional planes.[471] One might say that our material plane is where the Demiurge runs out of gas.

This concept of a loss of energy at the material realm provides an exciting possibility. Maybe the tiered waterfall metaphor is wrong. Rather than the material universe being denser, perhaps it's less dense. Nature offers a different metaphor that can help us here.

Ice forms when water loses energy in the way of heat. Bodies of water in cold regions, such as North America's Lake Michigan, regularly develop a thick layer of ice on the surface during the winter. It's important to remember that ice, while it acts dense, isn't. Ice is lighter (i.e., less dense) than water, which is

468. Ouis, *Humorous Wit*, 541.
469. Miller, *The Sorcerer's Secrets*, 25.
470. Blackburn, *The Oxford Dictionary of Philosophy*, 290.
471. Wildberg, "Neoplatonism."

why it floats and why Lake Michigan develops a layer of ice on top of the body of liquid water.

The German philosopher Friedrich Wilhelm Joseph von Schelling wrote that "all existence is spirit. Just as ice is water, so matter is also spirit. Mineral, vegetable, animal, or human—all are a condensed form of spirit."[472] Rather than describing the material realm as "denser," we ought to describe it as more "solid" than the other planes. This way of looking at the material realm turns the Cosmos upside down to the external traditions. Instead of looking at the material realm as being at the bottom of reality, like the last waterfall tier, we should visualize our material realm as the Cosmos's highest layer.

The material realm floating at the top of the Cosmos is intriguing from a Dark Pagan perspective. Historically, the rest of the Cosmos, such as the otherworld, has been imagined as being higher. The next plane from us was higher, or astral, with each one that follows being higher and higher. Instead of looking above for the sacred, we should look below. The reversed view of the Cosmos reminds me of something the Pagan author Ursula K. Le Guin wrote:[473]

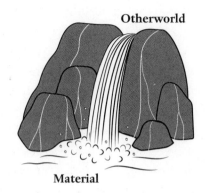

Otherworld

Material

Tiered Model

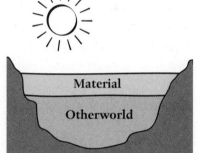

Material

Otherworld

Ice Model

> *Our roots are in the dark; the earth is our country. Why did we look up for blessing—instead of around, and down? What hope we have lies there. Not in the sky full of orbiting spy-eyes and weaponry, but in the earth, we have looked down upon. Not from above, but from below. Not in the light that blinds, but in the dark that nourishes, where human beings grow human souls.*

---

472. Steiner, *True Knowledge of the Christ*, 12.
473. Le Guin, "A Left-Handed Commencement Address."

A Few Words about *Infernal*

If the world is less dense and rests over the otherworld, then we might be jus-tified in calling the otherworld *infernal*. You may assume that my use of *infer-nal* is a not-too-subtle reference to hell in Christian theology. Indeed, if one searches on the internet for the meaning of the word *infernal*, the overwhelm-ing number of results would reference the Christian belief. However, this would be a misunderstanding of my usage. To better understand my use of the word *infernal*, we need to explore its linguistic source.

The English word *infernal* is from the Latin *infernus*, which means "below" or "lower regions." Yet, *infernus* means so much more. According to *A Copious and Critical Latin-English Lexicon*, published in 1849, its usage also includes the lower parts or lowlands; lightning from the earth; the abdomen, lower parts of the body; the river Styx; and someone or something devoted or sacred to the infernal gods.[474]

I would be disingenuous if I didn't admit that the word *infernal* did have some appeal to me because of its common association with hell. Yes, there's a touch of a double entendre in my usage. However, any devilish attempt at humor on my part (oops, I did it again) shouldn't negate the use of the word in this context. Based on its original meaning, *infernal* directs our focus down-ward rather than upward.

Infernal Subtle Bodies

Christine Hoff Kraemer writes that the concept that a person consists of mul-tiple souls, usually referred to as subtle bodies, is gaining popularity among Pagans.[475] This idea is not new in any sense. The ancient Egyptians believed that a person had three souls, the *ka*, the *ba*, and the *akh*.[476] In Theosophy, along with the physical body, there is the etheric body, astral body, mental body, and causal body.[477] According to Qabalaistic thought, there are four subtle bodies. Those are *yechidah* (absolute), *neschamah* (spirit), *ruach* (mental), and *nephesh* (astral/etheric/physical).[478] Some Shinto traditions accept a philosophy called

474. Riddle, Georges, and Arnold, *A Copious and Critical English-Latin Lexicon*, 466.
475. Kraemer, *Seeking the Mystery*, 91.
476. Miller, *Protection & Reversal Magick*, 188.
477. Bonewits and Bonewits, *Real Energy*, 47–51.
478. Barrabbas, *Magical Qabalah for Beginners*, 185–86.

ichirei shikon, which means "one spirit, four souls." The one spirit is the *naohi-nomitama*, while the four souls are *aramitama*, *nigimitama*, *sachimitama*, and *kushimitama*.[479]

Most traditions portray each subtle body as more subtle or refined than the other. A good example is Theosophy, which believes that the Cosmos and everything within it exist in a hierarchy of ever-ascending vibrations.[480] Therefore, according to Theosophy, the etheric body exists at a higher vibration level than the physical body. The astral body exists at a higher vibration level than the etheric body and so forth.

Just as the orientation of the esoteric planes was reimagined, it's possible to reimagine the subtle bodies. Earlier, we reimagined the material realm as more solid than the otherworld rather than denser. Therefore, rather than being less dense, we should reimagine the subtle bodies as less solid than the physical.

Another change is the directional metaphors used. An infernal model of subtle bodies should go internal rather than external. A good analogy would be Russian stacking dolls buried within each other. Each subtle body then would take us deeper and deeper into the Self.

At the risk of being repetitious, it's important to remember that the subtle bodies are not things apart from the physical. The Self's various bodies are not separate from each other like layers of an onion (or a cake, as a certain donkey would insist). These bodies, subtle and gross, are but different aspects of the Self. Each one coexists in an aspatial manner with the other.

Occultist Don Webb describes a magickal Self model that he refers to as the four levels of dynamism. Webb's four levels are surface, medial, core, and daemonic. For Webb, these four levels of dynamism, or essences, are necessary for understanding the magickal Self. According to Webb, understanding the magickal Self can create change.[481]

According to Webb's model, the surface is the "here and now." Some changes at this level have far-reaching consequences, while others don't. The medial is our hopes, dreams, and desires. Some are realistic, while others are fantasies. The core is our uniqueness or individuality. It contains the seeming contradictions of being

---

479. Yamakage, *The Essence of Shinto*, 130.
480. Bonewits and Bonewits, *Real Energy*, 48.
481. Webb, *Uncle Setnakt's Essential Guide to the Left Hand Path*, 9.

unchanging yet ever dynamic. Finally, the daemonic level is magickal. It both acts upon the Cosmos and is acted upon by the Cosmos.[482]

Webb's model of the magickal Self isn't a subtle body model. One could use his model and not believe in subtle bodies. However, Webb's magickal Self model is a helpful template for this purpose. We can take his model and modify it to apply to subtle bodies that look down rather than up. To be successful means keeping what works and changing what doesn't.

A subtle body model built on Webb's four levels would begin by keeping his terminology and order. Therefore, we would have the esoteric four bodies named surface, medial, core, and daemonic. Importantly, these would not exist at higher levels but at lower in descending order. It would begin with the surface and go down to the daemonic.

I find the fact that this model has the same number of bodies or souls as the Shinto concept of ichirei shikon intriguing. The ichirei shikon translation of "one spirit, four souls" applies here. Because all of the bodies are aspects of the Self, we can paraphrase the Shinto concept of ichirei shikon and say that this infernal model is "one self, four bodies."

We can now present our new model of subtle bodies. The Self has four esoteric bodies that coexist in descending order. The surface body is the corporeal, the medial body is the soul, and the core body is the sapient, which Theosophy calls the mental body. Finally, the daemonic body resembles the causal body of Theosophy in that it is closest to the source from which we came.

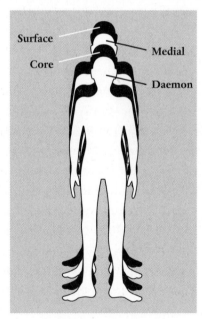

Infernal Subtle Bodies

Surface Body

Of the different aspects of Self, the surface aspect is the easiest to describe. It's the face that looks back at you from the mirror. It's the blood that rushes through

---

482. Webb, *Uncle Setnakt's Essential Guide to the Left Hand Path*, 9–11.

your veins as you exercise. It's your stomach growling when you're hungry and aching when you've overeaten. Your surface body is the pounding of your heart when a lover touches you, and it's your eyes that shed tears when your heart breaks.

We see the nature of the surface body in our evolution. Our path to humanity began when our ape ancestors had a genetic mutation allowing greater cooperation and less social fear. Over time we obtained the ability to walk upright through environmental pressure and fortuitous genetic mutation, which improved our locomotion and freed our hands to better use tools. Our body hair dramatically reduced, allowing our naked bodies to cool our growing brains and giving us the ability to travel greater distances. And these ever-increasing brains, in turn, allowed for more complex behaviors and structural changes to the face and throat to allow for complex speech.[483] Likely these steps were closely tied together, and one could not have happened without the other.

From a Dark Pagan perspective, this surface level is how the Self manifests its divinity in the surface realm. As flesh and blood beings, we experience the wonders of being human. The embodiment allows the Self to experience the wonders of being born, aging, and dying. Through physical existence, the Self loves and is loved. The Self can experience success and failure through the surface aspect. Through physical existence experiences, the Self can develop and evolve in ways that other forms of existence won't allow.

Spirit Body

Between the surface aspect and the next aspect is a liminal zone, which constitutes the beginning of the Self's spiritual aspect. In Spiritualism, this liminal zone is the body double.[484] Often this liminal zone is referred to as spirit to differentiate it from the soul. Esoterist Robert Bruce refers to this as the "human energy body."[485] For this purpose, this liminal zone is referred to as the spirit.

The contemporary Western esoteric model of the spirit is a mix of elements borrowed (or appropriated) from traditional Chinese medicine (TCM) and Hinduism, along with some Theosophical and New Age revisionism. According to Bruce, the spirit has seven primary energy centers known in Hinduism

---

483. Masterson, "From Grunting to Gabbing: Why Humans Can Talk."
484. Yamakage, *The Essence of Shinto*, 136.
485. Bruce, *Astral Dynamics*, 67.

as chakras, hundreds of secondary energy centers, three storage centers known in TCM as *dan tians*, and thousands of energy-exchange pores. A complex network of pathways that TCM calls meridians connects all of these.[486]

Each chakra has a color and role associated with it. Traditionally, the colors of the seven chakras are red for the base or root, orange for the sacral or groin, yellow for the solar plexus, green for the heart, blue for the throat, indigo for the third eye or brow, and white for the crown.[487] According to author Nancy Kilpatrick, some goth Pagans changed the colors to black (root), white or gold (groin), blue (solar plexus), crimson (heart), green (throat), silver (third eye), and purple (crown).[488] Vampyre magick modifies the role of each chakra: the root is for grounding of the Self, the groin is self-gratification, the solar plexus is self-empowerment, the heart is self-love, the throat is self-expression, the third eye is the vision of the subtle layers of reality, and the crown is the Seat of Immortal Self.[489]

If we apply the Hermetic principle, we can say with some degree of confidence that the spirit should have some form of structure, which we find in the surface. Also, I will say that I find the similarities between the TCM and Hindu models interesting. Both describe the life force or energy that flows along interconnected pathways built around hubs or centers within the spiritual body. This similarity, I think, gives us some degree of confidence in the traditional models.

However, we need to remember that the TCM model is different from the Hindu. The fact that these models contain significant differences shows that we need to exercise humility in describing the details of that structure. This humility doesn't mean that we must throw out all of our models of the spirit. We can believe in the models of TCM, Hindu, Theosophical, New Age, or any other that we prefer. What matters is that we avoid hubris in any model that we adopt.

Medial Body

The medial aspect is classically called the soul. It's the eternal expression of the Self. This eternal expression brings together all of the manifestations of the

---

486. Bruce, *Astral Dynamics*, 67.
487. Bonewits and Bonewits, *Real Energy*, 220.
488. Kilpatrick, *The Goth Bible*, 264–65.
489. Sebastiaan, *Vampyre Magick*, 134.

Self, resulting in wholeness. According to Iamblichus, the soul is immaterial and indestructible. It's Self moved and has autonomy and freedom. Iamblichus described the soul as a mediator between the material and the Cosmic Divine.[490]

Core Body

The core level is the mental or sapien body. Neoplatonist philosophers thought intelligence was the central human trait, placing it at the individual's core. According to John M. Cooper, the Neoplatonists believed that the soul was "simply identical with the capacity of intellect and power of rational insight."[491]

Sapience is more than just the ability to think logically. This word is the equivalent of *wisdom*. The *Cambridge Dictionary* defines *wisdom* as "the ability to make good judgments based on what you have learned from your experience or the knowledge and understanding that gives you this ability."[492] Without the sapiency of the core, the Self would be empty and random. Sapiency gives the Self structure. Through the core, the Self creates an identity out of the many mortal lifetimes.

Humans certainly aren't the only sapient beings in this corporeal world. We know that sapiency is in other animals such as elephants, apes, dolphins, and others. Recent studies show that it might also be in the octopus. Sapiency is not limited to these few, and we now know that there's a spectrum of different degrees and types that stretches across all life-forms on Earth.

As the name implies, the core is the heart of the Self. A good analogy is that the core is to the Self what the genetic code is to the physical body. The core redefines the Self as it evolves with its assimilation and reconciliation of its experiences during each embodied lifetime.

Daemonic Body

The daemonic level is the deepest part of the Self. It is the seed of Ipseity from which the Self grows. The word *daemon* is the Latin equivalent of the Greek *daimon*, which means "spirit." To the Hellenist Pagans, a daemon could be good

---

490. Shaw, *Theurgy and the Soul*, 47.
491. Cooper, *Pursuits of Wisdom*, 317.
492. Cambridge Dictionary, "Wisdom," accessed November 27, 2021, https://dictionary.cambridge.org/us/dictionary/english/wisdom.

or malevolent, and they had a variant word for each. Christians later classified all daemons as hostile and changed the spelling to *demons*.[493]

The nature of the daemonic level is dualistic. Duality should not be confused with dualism. Dualism is the belief that everything divides into ethical opposites. Good versus evil is an example. In contrast, duality is the belief or representation of something in twos. There are two sides to a coin, for example. Duality differs from dualism because it doesn't place an ethical value on either side.

The duality of the daemonic level is characterized by Order and Chaos. Humans prefer order. We plan our cities, drain swamps, and build orderly canals. Even if we can't see order, the priests of our civic religion of scientism tell us that everything happens according to underlying laws. Nothing is random, they tell us. Chaos has been banished.

However, this order isn't permanent. As soon as we think we have everything under control, our lives turn upside down. Our faith in order turns out to be hubris as chaos returns to our lives. Entropy is inevitable.

As disturbing as chaos is, wisdom tells us that it's necessary. Perpetual order leads to stagnation. Chaos is a necessary element for growth. Tapping into the Chaos of the daemonic level of the Self is essential for apotheosis. Friedrich Nietzsche wrote, "I say unto you: one must still have chaos in oneself to be able to give birth to a dancing star."[494] Asenath Mason refers to this primal creative chaos as "The Womb of the Dragon."[495]

In chapter 4, we learned that the heart of the Self is nothingness. We used the cyclone metaphor, for its eye resembles the nothingness residing at the center of the Self. The creative Chaos at the daemonic level of the Self is the same nothingness or void addressed previously. Just as the Cosmos perpetually arises from Chaos, so does the Self.

Narrative

There is one addition to the infernal model not found in Webb's model. There is a unifying feature throughout the four levels of the subtle bodies. This unifying feature is the narrative.

---

493. Illes, *Encyclopedia of Spirits*, 344.
494. Bell, *Philosophy at the Edge of Chaos*, 63.
495. Mason, *Draconian Ritual Book*, 26.

According to psychologist Dan P. McAdams, narratives build personal identities. We each create our identity in the form of a story in which we are the protagonist. This protagonist is never a villain. As John Barth wrote, "Everyone is necessarily the hero of his own life story."[496] Through the combination of memories and our hopes and dreams, we create our myths, which we, in turn, use to build our identities.[497]

The Self builds an identity by weaving a narrative that connects all aspects of the Self. As we have seen, the Self lacks an inherent meaning beyond its existence. Meaning is created by compiling and reconciling its experiences through its different lives. Each surface incarnation as a physical being provides another chapter in the personal myth of the Self. The result is more than a set of facts for the Self. Instead, the narrative creates a story with meaning and substance. Now the Self has meaning beyond just existence. The personal myth means that the Self has made its essence.

Locus of Control

In all of these bodies, where does consciousness reside? Is it in the medial, or is it an emergent property of the surface? Clinical neurologist Steven Novella summed up the two opposing positions on consciousness's nature during an online debate about consciousness. One side holds that something more than the brain is necessary for consciousness. In contrast, the other side maintains that the brain is more than sufficient.[498]

There is another possibility. Maybe the debate over the source of consciousness is the wrong one to be having. Perhaps the question for our purpose here shouldn't be where consciousness resides or how it originates. The animist position is that some form of consciousness exists within everything. Therefore, if consciousness is everywhere, maybe we should ask where the locus of control (LOC) of the Self is. Is the physical body driving itself, or is it operated as a drone by remote control by the spiritual Self?

According to Iamblichus, humans are tied to our physical bodies by daemons. In *De Mysteriis*, Iamblichus wrote that daemons lead our souls into the natural world. Even though, according to Iamblichus, ascension demanded that

---

496. Barth, *The Floating Opera and the End of the Road*, 337.
497. McAdams, *The Stories We Live By*, 11.
498. "Michael Egnor, Cartesian Dualism, David Chalmers, and the Hard (Non)Problem."

the individual break free from the "bonds of generation," he didn't consider the daemon evil. Nor did he share the Gnostic view that embodiment was an evil existence to escape. Instead, according to Iamblichus, the daemon would "bring into manifest activity the invisible good of the Gods."[499] In other words, daemons tie us to the material world, which blesses us and all of the surface realm.

Iamblichus differed in many ways from several other Neoplatonists, such as Plotinus. Plotinus believed that the soul didn't fully become manifest during embodiment. Whereas Iamblichus thought that such a state would divide the Cosmos and run the risk of falling into the trap of Gnosticism, which considered the material world evil. Iamblichus believed that at embodiment, the soul fully descended into the body. No external soul was controlling the body by remote.[500]

An embodiment in matter requires total immersion in the material aspect of existence. If the choice is between remote control, as the dualists advocate, or local control, as most scientists advocate, then the complete immersion (the soul's total descent) as an embodied being would appear to favor the LOC as being located in the physical body during embodiment and not the soul.

We see this full immersion in action when we consider the amnesia we experience in our embodiment. The fact is that while some individuals, primarily children, appear to have some memories of past lives, the vast majority of us don't. It's as though we all drank from the River Lethe before birth. Amnesia makes sense if we place the LOC within the surface. The current manifestation of individual consciousness (i.e., ego) didn't exist before birth. Instead, it developed over a lifetime. The ego's previous nonexistence supports that the LOC rests in the physical (what Novella referred to as the "brain") during its existence.

However, the story doesn't end with the LOC being an emergent property of the brain. Since consciousness exists throughout the Cosmos, the potential for LOC is in more than just the surface. It's also in the medial since that's also an aspect of the Self. However, while the surface level exists, the LOC of the medial is only a potential. We might think of the medial as sleeping while the surface level lives.

---

499. Shaw, *Theurgy and the Soul*, 44.
500. Shaw, *Theurgy and the Soul*, 13–14.

The fact that the medial sleeps while the surface lives doesn't mean it's not active. The physical body, for example, is very active while sleeping. While we are sleeping, there's an increased release of growth hormone, which is why our skin cells regenerate and our hair grows as we sleep. Healing occurs during sleep. The brain is also very active during sleep. For example, at Cardiff University in Wales, researchers found that the brain continues to process events that had occurred during the day and works on finding solutions to problems.[501]

Just as the physical body is active while one sleeps, so are the subtle bodies. During embodiment, the spirit is still active, which is why Chinese medicine works by more than just releasing natural painkillers. It also adjusts the flow of chi in the spirit. The same is true about other spiritual practices such as meditation, yoga, and tai chi. Also, while the medial sleeps, it's processing the Self's experiences during its physical life.

We could look to redundancy in air and space technology as a metaphor for how the surface body and medial body work together. A SpaceX rocket, for example, uses a three-redundant computer system. If one computer unit fails, then another immediately picks up the ball.[502] Or we could look at nature. Redundancy is like your two kidneys. If one fails or is removed, the other continues to function and keeps you alive. When the surface dies, then the Self continues through the medial.

The analogy of redundancy answers the scientific materialist who says that consciousness as an emergent property won't allow life after death. After the surface dies, the LOC function awakens in the medial. To use contemporary terminology, the LOC comes online in the medial after the surface goes offline. It's because of handing the ball from the surface to the medial that there is life after death. To borrow a phrase from radio broadcaster Paul Harvey, immortality because of the LOC transfer is the "rest of the story."

Infernal Cosmology

Because of the esoteric principle of microcosm/macrocosm, the infernal model is more than just about the Self. It also provides us with a new and exciting

---

501. Yong, "A New Theory Linking Sleep and Creativity."
502. "Dragon's 'Radiation-Tolerant' Design."

vision of the Cosmos. The infernal model gives a new meaning of "As Above, So Below."

Surface Level

The surface level of the Cosmos is the mundane material world that you encounter every day. It's the brisk morning air in autumn and the leaves' vibrant colors on the trees as they begin to fall to the ground. It's the sight of a squirrel burying nuts in preparation for winter.

At the surface level, we experience both pain and joy. As mentioned, this level is the World of Horrors in the Left-Hand Path's Ceremony of Nine Angles ritual. While the World of Horrors has terrors, it also provides opportunities for joy and growth.

One will sometimes hear that the Cosmos's surface level is an illusion. From a Dark Pagan perspective, the surface level is functionally real. Jump off the Empire State Building, and you'll die regardless of whether the surface level is an illusion. To quote philosopher William James, "A difference which makes no difference is no difference at all."[503] Hence, Dark Paganism treats the universe as real for practical reasons and leaves such topics to scientists and mystics.

Another important detail is that the surface level follows the laws of physics. By this, I mean that materialist cause and effect govern events at the surface level. While spirits and magick are real and can have real effects, not everything that happens to you occurs because of divine intervention, karma, or the Wiccan threefold law. One might say that rarely does something happen for those reasons. Not everything is an omen. Usually, an eagle flying overhead is just looking for its next meal rather than acting as a messenger from the gods. Freud was correct in saying that sometimes a cigar is just a cigar.

Medial Level

The medial level, also known as the otherworld or etheric, is the land of spirits. It's also the resting place where our medial aspect sleeps during our time as surface beings and our domain after the surface body dies. Finally, it's the LOC for the Self after our surface aspect dies.

---

503. William, *The Essential Writings*, xiii.

There have been numerous attempts by mystics and occultists over the eons to map the medial. As mentioned, the Theosophists describe the Cosmos as having five planes.[504] According to Bruce, tradition holds that there are seven planes, each containing numerous subplanes.[505]

Core Level

The Cosmic core level is similar to what Plato called the hyperuranion, meaning a "place beyond heaven," for he thought it was above the gods. For Plato, the hyperuranion was the intelligible realm that held the forms. Platonic forms are arcane entities from which all of the surface and medial are derived.[506] We may think of the core as being the realm of potentialities.

Daemonic Level

The daemonic level is the heart of the Cosmos and is the realm of absolute consciousness or divinity. Konstantinos refers to the Divine as the Source and the origin of all of the Cosmos.[507] There are two different views of the Source that we will explore. One is the Greek view, and the other is the Chinese Taoist view.

To the ancient Greeks, this Cosmic consciousness was the *nous*. This word is challenging to define. Over the years, many have translated it as "intellect." However, according to Christian Wildberg, *nous* is better translated as "consciousness."[508] Wildberg described the consciousness of the nous as "pure and absolute" as well as "pre-embodied."

In Plotinus's cosmology, consciousness, or nous, was the first principle. According to Plotinus, the nous was the foundation, or *arkhe*, of all existence. To borrow a phrase from theologian Paul Tillich, the nous is the "ground of all being." The nous had two aspects to its inner activity. One aspect was to contemplate itself. The other was "to meditate upon the thoughts that are eternally present to it, and which constitute its very being." For Plotinus, thought was the same as being. Plotinus wrote, "To think and to be are one and the same."[509]

---

504. Bonewits and Bonewits, *Real Energy*, 48.
505. Bruce, *Astral Dynamics*, 247.
506. Cooper, *Pursuits of Wisdom*, 313.
507. Konstantinos, *Nocturnal Witchcraft*, 37–39.
508. Wildberg, "Neoplatonism."
509. Moore, "Plotinus."

According to Neoplatonism, the nous "turns back" to contemplate its nature. The result is the ongoing process of creation.[510] What does the Source find as it gazes inward? Hesiod wrote in his *Theogony* that at the very base of reality is Chaos.[511]

Chaos isn't a level as much as it's a principle. It's the underlying principle of the Cosmos. It has no identity or division from the other levels of the Cosmos. To the ancient Greeks, there is nothing below Chaos. According to some Greek cosmogonies, it's from Chaos that the primordial divinities, such as Nyx (night) and Gaia (earth), appeared.[512]

In understanding the daemonic level, we're not limited to classic mythology or cosmogony. The building of mythology didn't end in antiquity. J. R. R. Tolkien coined the term *mythopoeia* for the literary process of creating contemporary mythology. While Tolkien's Middle Earth may be the widely known example of mythopoeia, another contemporary mythology better serves Dark Paganism in this case. As Dark Pagans, we look to the haunting contemporary mythology of H. P. Lovecraft.

Lovecraft is most famous for the short science-fiction horror stories he built around his philosophy, which he called "cosmicism." Cosmicism is not only the belief that there is no omnipotent god giving meaning to the universe. It, unlike humanism, emphasizes how insignificant humanity is in the Cosmos, which is at best indifferent to us and at worst hostile.[513] Lovecraft's universe is commonly referred to as the Cthulhu mythos, although he, tongue planted firmly in cheek, labeled it "Yog-sothothery."[514]

Lovecraft drew the name for his fictional universe from one of his primary supernatural entities: Yog-Sothoth. Yog-Sothoth was first introduced by Lovecraft in his story *The Dunwich Horror*. In the story, we read that "Past, present, future, all are one in Yog-Sothoth."[515] In the story *Through the Gates of the Silver Key,* he described Yog-Sothoth as "an All-in-One and One-in-All of limitless being and self." According to Scott Jones, such descriptions place Yog-Sothoth

510. Wildberg, "Neoplatonism."
511. Scully, *Hesiod's Theogony*, 91.
512. Fry, *Mythos*, 4.
513. Lovecraft, *Annotated H. P. Lovecraft*, 12.
514. Jones, *When the Stars Are Right*, 23.
515. Lovecraft, *Bloodcurdling Tales of Horror and the Macabre*, 111.

on the same mystical level as the Tao and Plato's ideal.[516] According to philosopher Huston Smith, the Tao in Taoism is the counterpart to Plotinus's One.[517] In other words, Yog-Sothoth is the nous.

However, Yog-Sothoth was not the most primal of entities in Lovecraft's mythos. In the Chthonic mythos, a different entity rests at the heart of the Cosmos, and he called it a "blind idiot god." Lovecraft named this blind idiot god Azathoth, and it is Chaos. In his short story *The Haunter of the Dark,* Lovecraft wrote that Azathoth was the "Lord of All Things" and that he was ever surrounded by a "flopping horde of mindless and amorphous dancers, and lulled by the thin monotonous piping of a demonic flute held in nameless paws."[518] If the Source is Tillich's "ground of all being," then Lovecraft's blind idiot god, Azathoth, is its dark, dank, cobweb-covered basement.

There are aspects to the Ceremony of the Nine Angles found in the daemonic level. The founder of the Temple of Set, Michael Aquino, developed the ceremony in the early 1970s. Over the years, he and other magickal practitioners refined it. Aquino took the Cthulhu Mythos and adapted them to a magickal ritual involving nine angles. Each angle has meaning. According to the ritual, the first angle is Chaos, and the deity is Azathoth, while the second angle is Order, and the deity is Yog-Sothoth.[519]

In these two characteristics of the Cosmic daemonic level, Order, and Chaos, we find the same duality as we saw in the daemonic level of the Self. In Yog-Sothoth, we find Order. And in Azathoth, we find Chaos.

Taoism gives a different picture of the daemonic level. In Taoism, the Tao has eternal wholeness. Yet, there is also a polarity known as the yin and yang. Within the whole Tao, there is the polarity of white/black, positive/negative, male/female, and so forth. We see this in the yin-yang symbol of Taoism, where one side is white and the other black with a dot in each half of the other, all within a unifying circle.[520] In Taoism, Order isn't built on Chaos. Each is a different side of the same coin.

---

516. Jones, *When the Stars Are Right*, 25.
517. Smith, *The World's Religions*, 198.
518. Lovecraft, *Bloodcurdling Tales of Horror and the Macabre*, 220.
519. Chappell, *Infernal Geometry and the Left-Hand Path*, 21.
520. Smith, *The World's Religions*, 214–15.

Whether you're looking at a Taoist, Greek, Lovecraftian, or some other model, at the balancing point between Order and Chaos, where they neither lock in place nor dissolve into turbulence, self-organization and creativity arise.[521] This edge of Chaos, a term by physicist M. Mitchell Waldrop, builds and destroys. It's the ultimate creative principle. The Greek philosophers called this creative principle the Demiurge.

Dark Current

The Demiurge is the Cosmic equivalent of the narrative for the Self. It weaves through the Cosmos, creating infinite diversity while also uniting it. The Cosmic narrative has been called different names over the eons. While some Greek philosophers thought the world-soul was the same as the Demiurge, this view wasn't universal. For some Dark Pagans, this Cosmic narrative is known as the dark current.

The term *dark current* is favored by Konstantinos.[522] One can visualize it traveling through the Cosmos like the mighty Amazon River. As it flows, the dark current perpetually gives birth to the Cosmos through its constant emanation of creative potentiality. The flow of the dark current ends here in the surface realm.

What does the dark current carry with it? Like the mythical Phlegethon, the dark current carries the black flame from the daemonic level. The black flame is consciousness according to many LHP traditions. Rather than "black flame," Konstantinos calls divine flowing consciousness the "dark ether," but I consider it the same. The dark ether may be the same as what the Taoists call "Chi" and the Shintoists call "ki." It may also be the same as what Hinduism calls "prana" and the alchemists call "azoth" or "quintessence." The dark ether might be the "dragon's flame" of the Draconian Path. It might be the same as Lévi's "astral light." Whatever it is called, it's the raw, random power of creation and transformation. The dark ether is what powers magick and apotheosis.

Some may decide to use the word *god* when discussing the Source from which the dark current flows. However, one shouldn't think they can have a personal relationship with this hypercosmic divine being. This "god" is not the

---

521. Waldrop, *Complexity*, 12.
522. Konstantinos, *Gothic Grimoire*, 5.

personal god of monotheism but more like god as philosopher Benedict de Spinoza envisioned. As Albert Einstein wrote in 1929, "I believe in Spinoza's God, who reveals Himself in the lawful harmony of the world, not in a God who concerns Himself with the fate and the doings of mankind."[523]

Reaching the Stars

If the dark ether of the dark current makes apotheosis possible, where does apotheosis belong in this dark metaphysics? As we've seen, the surface realm is the highest aspect, and the rest of the Cosmos is below. What metaphor or analogy shall we use when the Self achieves apotheosis or godhood?

Classic thought has long considered the stars capable of foretelling human affairs and playing a significant role in the growth and development of humans. According to Gregory Shaw, Iamblichus believed that the "stars were vehicles of the encosmic gods who themselves were vehicles of the hypercosmic gods."[524] Toby Chappell wrote that the stars belong to the "realm of transcendence."[525] He quotes Aleister Crowley, who said, "every man and every woman is a star."[526]

The starry sky represents multiplicity rather than unity. Chappell points out that most stars have their own planetary systems. He draws an analogy between the Self and stars. The night sky's grand diversity of stars is representative of the vast multitude of Selves.[527]

The fact that stars are gigantic balls of plasma held together by the dialectic tension of gravity and fusion doesn't mean they lack a transcendental aspect. As animists, Pagans understand the reality of the corporeal aspect of stars while knowing that each star has its divine nature. And something as grand as a star must have a spirit of such grandeur as to be a god.

It's not only stars that have grandeur. So do the planets. While the ancients didn't understand the planets' corporeal nature, they did understand that planets are noteworthy among the other objects in the sky. And studies confirm

523. Numbers, *Galileo Goes to Jail and Other Myths about Science and Religion*, 192.
524. Shaw, *Theurgy and the Soul*, 100.
525. Chappell, *Infernal Geometry and the Left-Hand Path*, 56.
526. Chappell, *Infernal Geometry and the Left-Hand Path*, 40.
527. Chappell, *Infernal Geometry and the Left-Hand Path*, 55–56.

that, at least for birth charts, the planets' positions at birth have some degree of accuracy in predicting someone's personality.[528]

The domain of planets and stars in the sky makes it part of the surface. To be more specific, the night sky. The moon and Venus, which appear during the day, are brightest and most glorious at night. Therefore, when we think of the stars, we think of the night.

The darkness of the night is a characteristic the surface shares with the infernal realms. Both are dark, and both can be frightening. One source of this fear is that the darkness cloaks all that dwells within. As Lovecraft wrote, "The oldest and strongest emotion of mankind is fear, and the oldest and strongest fear is fear of the unknown."[529]

However, the Dark Pagan doesn't fear the night. The Dark Pagan considers the night sacred. We see this in the Dark Pagan tradition Nocturnal Witchcraft. We're most in tune with the dark current and the flow of the dark ether during the night. The night and the tropes associated with it, both mythical and real, are revered by us. As Van Gogh wrote, "I often think that the night is more alive and more richly colored than the day."[530]

The night is, therefore, an extension of the infernal. The nighttime sky reflects the darkness of the infernal realms yet also houses the glory of the stars. Each star in the dark nighttime sky promises transcendence or apotheosis. The astral is the realm of gods, making the gods truly "encosmic" since space, planets, and stars make up the Cosmos. Therefore, an astral body is not the soul apart from the corporeal body. The astral body is the Self transformed into a fully realized god. It's similar to the *devi/deva* of Hinduism. It's like the Egyptian akh or the immortals of Taoism.

While the night is an extension of the infernal, it is, relatively speaking, higher than us. Hence, even in this revised cosmology, the traditional metaphors of "higher" and "ascension" are still appropriate when discussing the astral. For the Dark Pagan, the divine astral body, shining in the infernal darkness, is the Great Work's ultimate goal.

---

528. Bonewits and Bonewits, *Real Energy*, 131–32.
529. Lovecraft, *The Supernatural Horror in Literature*, 1.
530. Naifeh and Smith, *Van Gogh*, 164.

Reviewing the Concepts

The ancient Greek philosophical schools were complete packages. Along with providing a way of life, each philosophy included a highly sophisticated model of the Cosmos. For Dark Paganism to be complete, a new way to look at arcane metaphysics and cosmology subjects is helpful.

Most Pagan cosmology describes the Cosmos structure as consisting of a spectrum stretching from the Divine Source to our denser material plane. The Neoplatonists believed that the material realm is the end of this spectrum. The Neoplatonists thought that the material world was exhausted by the divine creative energy.

Schelling wrote that "all existence is spirit. Just as ice is water, so matter is also spirit. Mineral, vegetable, animal, or human—all are a condensed form of spirit." Instead of looking at the material realm as being at the bottom of reality, like the last waterfall tier, we should visualize our material realm like the layer of ice on top of a lake in winter.

If the world is less dense and rests over the otherworld, then we might be justified in calling the otherworld "infernal." Rather than being less dense, we should reimagine the subtle bodies and the Cosmos as less solid than the physical.

Questions to Consider

* Since Dark Paganism focuses on the Self, do you consider metaphysical ponderings about the Cosmos relevant? Or are such ponderings better left to the lightside/RHP?

* If you consider metaphysical concepts about subtle bodies and the Cosmos relevant, do you imagine these based on the classic models or some other?

* Do you consider the concept of frozen spirit accurate? If not, why?

XVIII
APPLIED DARK PAGANISM

After reading this book, some readers will have no problems applying the concepts to their daily lives. However, there will be those who struggle to apply them—even though they agree with what's written. Some want to change their lives and incorporate Dark Paganism into their spirituality but just can't bring themselves to do so. Something seems to hold them back. Then there are others who don't have such problems but simply aren't sure where to begin.

Set Point Theory

The set point theory was developed in the 1980s by Dr. William Bennett and Joel Gurin. Bennett and Gurin theorized that we each have a mechanism that places limits on how far we're willing to accept changes to our weight. Because of this set point, some individuals will not lose weight because their bodies will resist change. Bennett and Gurin called this limit a "set point."[531]

Sorcerer Jason Miller expands the set point theory to include different, primarily psychological, facets of our lives. For example, a person raised in a low-income family may subconsciously sabotage their efforts to move up into a better-paying field than the rest of their family. According to Miller, the set point can potentially impact nearly everything we wish to change about ourselves.[532]

The set point theory also applies to some individuals who struggle to apply Dark Pagan spirituality to their lives. Many people are taught to see the Self as

---

531. Brody, "New Dieting Theory's Delicate Balance."
532. Miller, *The Elements of Spellcrafting*, 161–67.

bad. This view of the Self isn't unique to Abrahamic religions; it appears in most religions, including some Pagan traditions. It is not limited to religion either. There were some classic philosophers of antiquity who viewed the Self as ugly. Some confused a healthy Self-centrism with unhealthy selfishness.

There are several steps that you can take if your set point is preventing you from adopting a Dark Pagan philosophy. Begin by reminding yourself that you're not obligated to follow the herd. Your life is your own. Also, work on your self-talk. We often sabotage ourselves through the statements we make to ourselves. Learn to be your best friend and your cheerleader.

This is not toxic positivity. The set point won't change overnight. Acceptance of the divinity of the Self for some will be an ongoing process. We have been conditioned to view the Self as a negative. Some have to give themselves booster shots, so to speak, to help themselves be comfortable with their divinity. For those individuals, the practice of perpetual dissent found among some members of Left-Hand Path traditions may be appropriate.

Dark Pagan Shadow Work

Carl Jung wrote that the unconsciousness in the form of the Shadow could hijack the consciousness and thereby sabotage the person's success in an endeavor. Therefore, in some cases, the Shadow will be why a person will struggle to adopt Dark Paganism. Thankfully, there are some excellent options available to the Dark Pagan for Shadow work.

If one has the financial resources and the time, one can visit an analytical therapist. Such a visit would not be a onetime thing but an ongoing therapeutic relationship. One doesn't have to be in a crisis or have a mental illness to visit a therapist. It's not uncommon for individuals today to have a therapist for no other reason than to maintain their mental health.

Continual therapy isn't a viable choice for most people. Most of us don't have the resources of time and money to be perpetually in therapy. However, that doesn't mean we can't incorporate Shadow work into our Dark Pagan practices.

In his book *Why Good People Do Bad Things: Understanding Our Darker Selves,* James Hollis explains that we need to develop an inner life that involves "becoming psychological." According to Hollis, becoming psychological demands that we continually ask ourselves the origins of our internal and external behavior. We should ask ourselves questions such as "Where does this come from within me?" and "What does this feel like?" Becoming psychological never ends but is a lifelong practice that we never fully complete.[533]

The Four Maxims

In *Transcendental Magic*, Éliphas Lévi wrote that there were "Four Words of the Magus." They were "To Know, To Dare, To Will, To Keep Silent."[534] A variety of Pagan traditions later picked up those four maxims. All of these traditions interpret the four maxims differently.

Lévi's four words are indispensable for anyone who wishes to walk a Dark Pagan path. Because of their importance, let's look at each maxim in more detail.

To Know

"Knowledge is power" is an aphorism that's truer today than ever. Those who lack knowledge are often the victims of those who have it. Knowledge today is so powerful that it's become a commodity. For example, entire industries exist to acquire and share knowledge about individuals. And knowledge has such value that criminal activity such as hacking and identity theft has become a significant problem.

Attributed to Francis Bacon, the aphorism "knowledge is power" very much applies to Dark Paganism and magick. Attempting magick without knowledge of correspondences and the various principles deduced over the years is a recipe for failure. Therefore, Dark Pagans need to educate themselves on a topic before attempting it.

A related aphorism is "know thyself." This aphorism is ancient Pagan wisdom given to us by the Oracle of Delphi and inscribed at the Temple of Apollo. With Dark Paganism's focus on the Self, this aphorism is central. A Dark Pagan must be bluntly honest with themselves about both their strengths and weaknesses. Hubris and false pride have no place in Dark Paganism, and both will result in failed magick.

---

533. Hollis, *Why Good People Do Bad Things*, 102.
534. Lévi, *Transcendental Magic*, 29.

To Dare

Carpe diem, or "seize the day," is an ancient Pagan aphorism that has been commodified and misused recently. One will find it plastered on everything from beer coozies to T-shirts. The result is that its punch is lost, and it has been relegated to the buzzword ash heap alongside "thinking outside the box" and "paradigm shift."

This aphorism first appeared in book one of the Roman poet Horace's *Odes* and dates to 23 BCE. Robin Williams, in the 1989 American film *Dead Poets Society*, popularized the phrase when his character said: "Carpe diem. Seize the day, boys. Make your lives extraordinary." Williams's character captured the spirit of Lévi's second maxim with this statement.

Dark Paganism requires one to take chances. Few of us are born within Pagan families, so coming out of the broom closet to one's family can be difficult for some. Even if one's family is supportive, not everyone will be accepting. A Dark Pagan has even more challenges than most Pagans, for some who are not Dark Pagans will fail to understand the Self-centrism that rests at the heart of Dark Paganism.

Also, magick requires taking risks. It's not always safe. The risky nature of magick is undoubtedly true to those of the Great Work. However, with great risks, there can be great rewards. Remember the Latin proverb "fortune favors the bold."

To Will

Friedrich Nietzsche's phrase "will to power" has a bad reputation. A major reason for this is that the Nazis and other fascists misappropriated the expression and used it as justification to oppress others. It doesn't help that Nietzsche himself was a complicated philosopher.

Nietzsche meant by this phrase that through the exertion of one's own will, one could affect ("power") oneself or another. As pointed out earlier, the will to power is neither good nor bad. It's how one uses one's own will and toward what ends that decides morality.

Not only does Lévi include "to will" as one of the four words of the magus, but it's also in Aleister Crowley's definition of magick. It's also one of the three components of magick listed by Christopher Penczak.[535] Without a doubt, the focus of will is essential in magick.

However, it goes far beyond magick. Nietzsche stressed the importance of "self-overcoming." By this, he meant striving for growth and self-improvement. Studies support that a successful venture depends on a person's will. The more a person wills the success, the greater the odds of achieving the goal.

To Keep Silent

Privacy is in danger in our interconnected age. People post online what they're watching on television. They post if they're at the gym. They even take images of their dinner plates and upload them for everyone to see. Privacy is in danger not because it's being taken from us by George Orwell's Big Brother but because we're willingly giving it up.

"To keep silent" caps the four maxims for several excellent reasons. Some magick practitioners say that discussing a recently cast spell will inhibit its effectiveness. Since so little is known about magick's working, we don't know how the discussion might impact it. Keeping silent about your spellwork doesn't hurt and may help your magick's efficacy.

Learning to keep silent about matters can also help build a healthy concept of Self. It creates boundaries and helps in individuation. With the Dark Pagan focus on the Self, it's essential to learn what to share and what not.

As mentioned, the world isn't always friendly to Pagans. It's certainly better than it's been for thousands of years here in the industrialized world. However, even if family and friends accept your beliefs, you will encounter those who will not. There are still news reports of Pagans, even in progressive countries, being persecuted for their beliefs. Keeping silent about your Paganism can become a matter of self-protection.

It's important to remember that keeping silent is a principle of self-discipline and must never be imposed upon you. Be careful if someone tells you that you must keep silent about anything they teach or have you do. Such a demand is the language of abusers. If someone tries to force silence upon you, flee and seek help.

---

535. Penczak, *Instant Magick*, 21.

Developing a Dark Pagan Lifestyle

John Beckett has an ongoing blog on Patheos.com titled *Under the Ancient Oaks*. On January 8, 2019, Beckett posted "8 Things to Make Your Paganism Stronger This Year." He recommends daily spiritual practice, weekly offerings, keeping a journal, learning a different magickal system, reading a foundational book of Paganism, new scholarship, leading a group ritual, and attending a Pagan conference.[536]

Beckett's recommendations are excellent for anyone, even the experienced Pagan who wants to revitalize their spiritual practice or for you to build a new Dark Pagan lifestyle. I, therefore, incorporated many of Beckett's recommendations into this chapter.

Meditation

Meditation is a great daily spiritual practice to cultivate. According to Miller, meditation is a process that cuts through mental distractions.[537] Meditation offers many benefits for the Dark Pagan. We spend a significant amount of time running on automatic. We sleepwalk through life until we're on our deathbeds. There we realize that we never fully lived, and then it's too late. Meditation helps us focus on the moment and truly live in this world in which we incarnate.

Meditation can also be helpful for breath control. In his book *The Sorcerer's Secrets: Strategies in Practical Magick*, Miller writes about the importance of breath control as a spiritual practice. He points out that the word *spirit* in Latin means "breath." Also, our breathing changes when we're under stress, and learning how to regulate one's breathing can help ease anxiety. Finally, breath control can be beneficial in magick.[538]

In his book *Apophis*, Michael Kelly includes a meditative practice he calls "the god," which doesn't require one to bend their legs up like a pretzel. "The god" pose involves sitting in a straight-backed chair. While sitting quietly, you breathe slowly and steadily. Don't think about your day or what you have planned. One doesn't have to sit long to gain benefits. Kelly recommends starting with ten-minute sessions.[539]

---

536. Beckett, "8 Things To Make Your Paganism Stronger This Year."
537. Miller, *The Sorcerer's Secrets*, 48.
538. Miller, *The Sorcerer's Secrets*, 32–37.
539. Kelly, *Apophis*, 75.

Prayer

Prayer is another practice that I recommend. If one wanted to boil Paganism's definition down to one word, it would be relationships. Paganism focuses on healing and building an individual's relationship with oneself, other people, ancestors, spirits, gods, the earth, and the Cosmos. As Joyce and River Higginbotham describe, the same is true for magick, which is a spiritual practice based on relationships within a conscious Cosmos.[540] I believe that prayer is one of the many methods to help heal and build such relationships.

What is prayer, and how does it work? Whether you're praying to your ancestors or a god, prayer is primarily communication. Just as having a conversation with a friend or loved one helps to build your relationship with them, prayer helps to build your otherworldly relationships as well.

Admittedly, such communication as a prayer might seem rather one-sided. Few of us are lucky (or, depending on your perspective, unlucky) enough to hear the voices of deities. Just because we don't hear a reply doesn't mean there isn't one. It's often hard to notice the subtle response of divinity over the cacophony of the world. However, with experience over time, some learn to see the subtle responses to prayers manifested in the world.

To whom should you pray? Readers who are new to Paganism may not know what deity or spirit they want to have a relationship with. That's okay. You can start by praying to a deceased loved one, such as an ancestor or someone who touched your life in a meaningful way. Or you can simply pray to the earth. Buddhist monk Thich Nhat Hanh wrote that because we each carry Mother Earth within us, one can have real communication with the earth, which he described as "the highest form of prayer."[541]

About what might one pray? Some say we should never make a request of gods and ancestors for something. I disagree. If I can help a friend or loved one, I want that person to ask me. Any deity who cares about you would like to hear your needs and concerns. However, while there isn't anything wrong with asking for something in prayer, I wouldn't start with a request. How would you feel if a stranger approached you out of the blue and made a significant request

---

540. Higginbotham and Higginbotham, *Paganism*, 164.
541. Phillips-Nania, *Unity*, 400.

of you? A friend who only asked favors from you but never showed any interest in you would probably lose your friendship.

The best place to start in prayer is with an expression of gratitude. As Meister Eckhart wrote, "If the only prayer you ever say in your entire life is thank you, it will be enough."[542]

Offerings

Making offerings to deities and ancestors is a good habit. While there is nothing that a god needs from us, it helps build relationships. Have you ever moved into a new residence and had a neighbor bring you a housewarming gift? Do you remember how good that felt? There is truth to the saying that one should practice random acts of kindness. Beyond being a nice thing to do, acts such as offering can lead to reciprocity on the part of deities.

What should you offer? If you're making an offering to an ancestor or loved one, consider an offering of their favorite item. My mother loved a specific soft drink brand, while my maternal grandfather had a preferred brand of cigarettes. Suppose you're making an offering to an otherworldly entity, such as a god or goddess. In that case, various helpful resources contain lists of favorite foods, herbs, incenses, or drinks. I highly recommend Judika Illes's *Encyclopedia of Spirits: The Ultimate Guide to the Magic of Fairies, Genies, Demons, Ghosts, Gods & Goddesses* as a resource.

How long should one leave an offering? There's no hard or fast rule for this. Listen to your instincts, and you will have an idea when it's time to remove the offering. Once you remove it, it needs to be disposed of respectfully. Most say that we shouldn't consume the offering. Nor should we just unceremoniously dump it in the trash or pour it down the drain. The best way to dispose of it is to respectfully return it to the earth with a prayer of gratitude for your temporary use of it.

One isn't limited to offering material goods. The gift of one's life force or energy is an excellent offering. To offer one's life force, stand or sit very still. Close your eyes, and rub the palms of your hands together. Not only does the friction give you the sensation of heat, but the hands have numerous acupuncture points by which the person's dark ether or life force moves. Once your

---

542. Borucki, *Managing the Motherload*, 90.

palms feel warm, turn them upward as though you're holding a large platter of food. Then speak the offering of your dark ether to the entity. Don't worry about the formality or informality of your wording. Speak from the heart.

Journaling

Journal keeping is a time-honored process that has fallen by the wayside for many. Over the years, many great people have kept journals. Mark Twain, Marie Curie, Ernest Hemingway, Emilie Davis, Benjamin Franklin, and Anaïs Nin all kept journals.

There are numerous benefits to writing a journal. For example, keeping a journal activates your brain's left side, which is responsible for analytical thought. Simultaneously, the right side of your brain, which is the creative and artistic side, is also activated. The result can be a positive increase in your mood and sense of well-being. It can also help with stress and improve your memory.

Journaling has a long tradition among esoterists and Pagans. Contemporary Pagans often compile their journal notes into magickal books that they call a Book of Shadows (BOS). Some keep an individual BOS while others maintain a group BOS. Gerald Gardner coined the title Book of Shadows. Gardner's early draft of the BOS was originally titled *Ye Bok of Ye Art Magical*.[543] Gardner liked Old English, and its use became a tradition that continues today among many Pagans.

Books

We are blessed that we live in a time when we have a cornucopia of books on Paganism. For example, my wife and I have multiple bookcases in every room of our house that are overflowing with Pagan and occult-related books. Even with all of these, we haven't scratched the surface of the available books on today's market.

With all of the new books on the market, we risk forgetting those who came before us—our trailblazing elders who were Pagan before Paganism was cool, much less legal. These trailblazers laid the foundation of what would become contemporary Paganism. Beckett recommends that we revisit these pioneers.

---

543. Bonewits, *Bonewits's Essential Guide to Witchcraft and Wicca*, 91.

Sit down and read the books of the Dark Pagan authors. Start with the foundational books. Read *Out of the Shadows: An Exploration of Dark Paganism* by John J. Coughlin, *Goth Craft: The Magickal Side of Dark Culture* by Raven Digitalis, and *Nocturnal Witchcraft: Magick After Dark* by Konstantinos. Go back and read Gardner's *Witchcraft Today*. Reread *Buckland's Complete Book of Witchcraft* by Raymond Buckland. These classics are full of wisdom that we dare not forget. Of course, when you've finished this book, go back and reread it (shameless self-promotion, I know).

Group Membership

Dark Pagans have a reputation as loners. The stereotype is that we tend to run with scissors and not play well with others. However, regardless of how much objectivists and Ayn Rand followers protest, we can't deny that we're social animals. The need for social interaction became apparent during the pandemic of 2020 when many were stuck at home.

Because of our social nature, it's good for us to engage others. Today, most metropolitan areas have several Pagan groups. Not all Pagan groups will be a good fit for a Dark Pagan. Therefore, it might take some effort to locate a coven or group that's a good fit.

One option is the Covenant of Unitarian Universalist Pagans (CUUPS), which is part of the Unitarian Universalists. Each CUUPS group is unique. I'm lucky to belong to the Denton CUUPS, which supports and encourages members of various traditions. There's likely a CUUPS in your area.

Became Politically Active

You can ignore politics, but politics will not ignore you. We Dark Pagans here in the Western world currently enjoy the right to practice our faith in peace (most of the time) because of our ancestors' sacrifices. In the United Kingdom, for example, Gardner could not practice his faith in public until the repeal of the Witchcraft Act in the early 1950s. In the 1980s, the United States had several court cases that recognized Wicca and other Pagan traditions as religions.[544]

However, discrimination isn't dead. While Christians can post religious artwork in most workplaces, Pagans know to keep a low profile. Occasionally,

---

544. "Excerpts from a US District Court Decision Recognizing Wicca as a Religion."

legislation is introduced to try to remove the recognition of Paganism as a religion. Just because this legislation has historically failed doesn't mean it always will.

This book certainly isn't about politics. It's about the development of positive, dark spirituality. However, I encourage each Dark Pagan to become politically engaged and active.

Building Your Magnum Opus

There are a plethora of resources available for improving the this-worldly Self. Self-improvement is a big business. As one reviews the vast number of self-improvement materials, it's essential for the Dark Pagan to remember Sturgeon's law and its belief that 90 percent of everything is crap. Therefore, the Dark Pagan must be skeptical of much self-improvement material and seek a few useful resources.

Apotheosis through magick, both theurgy and thaumaturgy, rests at the heart of the Dark Pagan magnum opus. While most of the other Pagan traditions, historical and contemporary, include magick in their systems, Dark Paganism differs in that the ultimate goal of magick is apotheosis. Because of magick's central role in apotheosis, let's review some of the Dark Pagan options.

There was a time when good books on magick were limited and hard to acquire. If one wanted knowledge about real magick and practical spells, it often required being initiated into a group, such as a Wiccan coven or magickal order, usually available only in large urban areas. Today, it's different. We're in a golden age of magickal books. Many publishing houses are now printing excellent material about Paganism and magick. Plus, most books are now available for purchase online, helping those who don't have access to brick-and-mortar bookstores.

There are several sound, practical magick systems available today. Chaos magick is a magickal system developed by Peter J. Carroll, who incorporated many of the occultist and artist Austin Osman Spare's concepts. Carroll laid out his initial ideas in his 1987 book *Liber Null & Psychonaut: An Introduction to Chaos Magic*, an occult classic. A central principle of chaos magick is a focus less on tradition and more on practical results. Another principle of chaos magick, possibly the most controversial, is that belief is simply a tool.

An excellent magickal system is strategic sorcery, developed by Miller. Miller is one of the rarities in the occult field in that he's the real deal that's succeeded at making a living as a full-time professional sorcerer. Miller advocates not only setting practical goals but also developing a plan with specific steps and following through by applying mundane and magickal efforts to each step until you reach your goal. His book *The Sorcerer's Secrets: Strategies in Practical Magick* is an excellent primer on his magickal system.

Earlier, I mentioned several Dark Pagan traditions that include achieving apotheosis as a goal. One is the Ordo Strigoi Vii, which involves acquiring energy and using it to transform with the ultimate goal of achieving apotheosis. Another system for achieving apotheosis is the Temple of Set with its Order of Leviathan and Order of Apep. There is also the Draconian Path, on which Asenath Mason wrote several books.

We have many great resources about thaumaturgy, but there's less information about Neoplatonism theurgy. Most of the Hellenistic theurgical rites, such as those advocated by Iamblichus, have been lost. The Neoplatonist theurgists held their rituals in secret and didn't write them down. Once they gained power in the Roman Empire, Christians' purges destroyed many Pagan documents. Before the Christian purge, many Roman laws forbid the ownership of books on magick.

While Greco-Roman theurgy rituals are lost, some theurgic tools are available from other cultures' existing wisdom traditions. Buddhism, for example, provides some excellent tools. One such Buddhist tool is deity yoga. Through deity yoga, one can merge with a deity while acknowledging oneself as a deity. Plus, deity yoga aids in understanding and accepting the fact that the Self is nothingness at its core.

Taoism is important because Coughlin considers it a dark path and in the same family as Dark Paganism.[545] As we saw, Taoism has a form of personal alchemy called *neidan*, or internal alchemy, that strives to achieve immortality. Also, since Taoism is a living wisdom tradition, practitioners have many opportunities to incorporate Taoism into their pursuit of apotheosis.

---

545. Coughlin, *Out of the Shadows*, 138–41.

Reviewing the Concepts

Many readers of this book will have no problems applying it to their daily lives. However, although they agree with what's written, there will be those who struggle to apply it.

There are several methods one can use to apply this book. Using set point theory, one can focus on resetting their mental base through repeated positive thoughts about oneself. Shadow work is something you can do on your own; you don't need a psychotherapist. A person can practice applying Lévi's four maxims: to know, to dare, to will, and to keep silent. There are various steps one can take to build a Dark Pagan lifestyle. Finally, the Great Work cannot be handed to you. An individual needs to create one's own magnum opus.

Questions to Consider

* Do you foresee challenges in applying Dark Paganism to your daily life? If so, what challenges might you encounter?

* In addition to the methods provided, what steps can you take to incorporate Dark Paganism into your life?

* What steps do you need to take to create your own magnum opus?

CONCLUSION

As I write this conclusion, it's the Summer Solstice in the Northern Hemisphere, or the first day of summer. The sun bakes the ground from a cloudless sky. The rains of spring have left the trees full of leaves and the grass green.

The Summer Solstice has always been a wondrous time, especially the night. It was a time of feasting and celebrating. As with Samhain, the veil between worlds is thin during Midsummer Eve, which aids in magick. Lovers would leap over bonfires, and maidens would practice folk magick in the hopes of finding their true love. Shakespeare immortalized the magick of the Summer Solstice in his play *A Midsummer Night's Dream*.

Midsummer Eve marks a festival day on the Wheel of the Year called Litha by some contemporary Pagans. Litha was the name of the Saxon grain goddess. Her festival involves going on picnics and blessing the plants and animals. Being that this is the longest day of the year, there's extra time for outdoor fun and the enjoyment of nature.

Despite the sun's dominance on the Summer Solstice, several Dark Pagan traditions celebrate this festival. The Strigoi Vii practices the Longest Day Mass, celebrating bodily existence and the five senses.[546] Nocturnal Witchcraft also celebrates this festival. Because it's the longest day, it's also the shortest night, making it easier for some to stay up for a nighttime vigil to recharge their nocturnal energies.[547]

---

546. Sebastiaan, *Vampyre Magick*, 49.
547. Konstantinos, *Nocturnal Witchcraft*, 27–28.

The contemporary Pagan Wheel of the Year and its festivals remind us that changes are constant in life. Like the festivals on the Wheel of the Year, this conclusion also marks an ending and a beginning.

While researching to write this book, I would sometimes become frustrated with the various Dark Pagan and Left-Hand Path writers because I never found one with which I fully agreed. I realized that it was an unconscious need arising from my Shadow. This characteristic of my Shadow was the product of the herd mentality indoctrinated in me from years of following the Right-Hand Path. I was looking for a tradition or belief system to follow rather than working to forge my way. Once I realized this, a whole new pathway opened up for my Dark Paganism and my book. I finally understood Toni Morrison, who wrote, "If there's a book that you want to read, but it hasn't been written yet, then you must write it."[548]

What does the future hold for Dark Paganism? We could turn to divination for a hint; however, divination has limits. At best, it can tell us probabilities. Ultimately, our fate is in our hands. As Shakespeare wrote, "The fault, dear Brutus, is not in our stars, but in ourselves that we are underlings."[549]

Much of this book has focused on presenting a view of the Divine Self. There's much more work needed in understanding all aspects of the Self, both its material and spiritual nature. While the study of the material Self is the purview of the social sciences, the study of the spiritual is the purview of philosophy and esoterica. Also, there is a need for much more work in developing original systems that aid in our self-cultivation during this postmodern era in which we live. Any new system needs to incorporate both magickal and mundane methods. These new methods will need to include ancient knowledge as well as modern revelations based on scientific study.

There's also a need to further flesh out the Dark Pagan values concerning socio-economic relations. The values presented here are the essentials and mark a jumping-off spot. In the meantime, as we work on such matters, we must not lose sight of what Dark Paganism is. Dark Paganism is and must always be a life-affirming Pagan spirituality focused on honoring and cultivating the Self. Changing society must always be considered secondary from the standpoint

---

548. Stephens, *Trademark 2.0*, 141.
549. Bartlett, *Bartlett's Favorite Quotations*, 215.

of Dark Paganism. Leo Tolstoy wrote, "Everyone thinks of changing the world, but no one thinks of changing himself."[550]

It's tempting to dream of vast numbers of individuals becoming Dark Pagans in the future. However, such dreams are exactly that—dreams. Humans are such social creatures that, by nature, we tend to be herd animals. Therefore, society will take our Self-centric focus and distort it into rugged individualism. Critics will confuse it with selfishness, creating social pressure against Dark Paganism.

While Dark Paganism will probably never be a massive movement, it's reasonable to expect that there will likely be some growth in numbers. Not only in those who explicitly wear the label "Dark Pagan" but also possibly the growth of like-minded individuals within lightside traditions. John Beckett explains that both Gardnerian and Alexandrian forms of Wicca were originally Self-centric.[551] We might expect, then, that Dark Paganism could help lead to a return to the elements of self-cultivation in Wicca and other lightside traditions.

One thing that isn't desired is a Dark Pagan institution that claims the power to decide what is and what's not Dark Paganism. We don't need a dark pope. This aversion to a dictatorial spiritual authority doesn't mean we don't need Dark Pagan traditions. As I wrote, there are several. We certainly want to see the growth of participants in these traditions. However, there's strength in diversity. What we need to see is other Dark Pagan traditions appearing.

Some say we've moved from a postmodern to a metamodern world, which alternates between elements of modernism and postmodernism. Whether or not this is true, there's far less face-to-face interaction than just a few years ago. For more people, their primary social contact is through social media. There's every reason to believe that this trend will be with us for the foreseeable future. The recent pandemic and the resulting lockdown accelerated this trend. Online social contact will likely grow, and face-to-face interactions will become less frequent.

Current technology creates a rise in tribalism. Rather than just three national networks, we have television entertainment available on-demand through numerous cable channels and apps. The same goes for the news. Instead of three

---

550. Brinkerhoff and Brinkerhoff, *Working for Change*, 51.
551. Beckett, *The Path of Paganism*, 45.

news sources that we all watch, viewers find their news from networks based on political orientation. Online news sources are even more personalized. We interact with like-minded people on social media and avoid those with different viewpoints.

Dark Paganism is well suited for this tribalism. Dark Pagans tend toward not only eclecticism but also being solitary practitioners. While this isn't unique to Dark Paganism, it's a growing trend within Paganism in general that we tend not to practice our faith in groups. Therefore, Dark Pagans should flourish within the independence that goes with the new tribalism.

In conclusion, I would like to encourage you as you begin the journey into Dark Paganism. Don't let the herd drag you down. Trust yourself. Have faith in your magick. Find the black flame within and turn it from a spark into a bonfire. You are at the beginning of a fantastic journey.

APPENDIX
FAMOUS MAGICIANS OF HISTORY

Magick is an ancient spiritual practice that stretches back into prehistory. Here's a short list of some of the most influential magick users that history records. My list stops around 1950. While it has ancient literary roots, contemporary Paganism as it exists today (except for Thelema and an occasional individual) most likely only dates back to approximately then. In addition to this list, I've included some brief biographies of a few of the most notable magick users. Whether or not all of those included here are historical isn't important. Nor is whether or not all of the magick users were Pagan. They are all part of a sacred tradition passed down that lives on in contemporary Paganism.

Note: Unfortunately, due to the toxic effects of patriarchy, the names of many women practitioners have been lost to history. Therefore, the list invariably has an inaccurate bias toward male magick users.

* Imhotep (?–circa 2600 BCE)

* Solomon (circa 1010–930 BCE)

* Pythagoras (circa 570–500 BCE)

* Jesus of Nazareth (circa 6 BCE–30 CE)

* Apollonius of Tyana (circa 15–100 CE)

* Simon Magus (circa 30–? CE)

* Mary the Prophetess (circa 200–? CE)

* Cleopatra the Alchemist (circa 200–300 CE)

* Merlin (circa 500–? CE)

* Morgan le Fay (circa 500–? CE)

* Abe no Seimei (921–1005 CE)

* Johann Georg Faust (1480–1540 CE)

* Heinrich Cornelius von Agrippa (September 14, 1486–February 18, 1535 CE)

* John Dee (July 13, 1527–1608 or 1609 CE)

* Isaac Newton (December 25, 1642–March 20, 1727 CE)

* Marie Laveau (circa 1801–June 15, 1881 CE)

* Éliphas Lévi (February 8, 1810–May 31, 1875 CE)

* George Pickingill (1816–April 10, 1909 CE)

* Paschal Beverly Randolph (October 8, 1825–July 29, 1875 CE)

* Helena Blavatsky (August 12, 1831–May 8, 1891 CE)

* A. E. Waite (October 2, 1857–May 19, 1942 CE)

* Grigori Rasputin (January 22, 1869–December 30, 1916 CE)

* Aleister Crowley (October 12, 1875–December 1, 1947 CE)

Imhotep

Imhotep was an Egyptian chancellor, architect, and high priest of the sun god Ra at Heliopolis who lived around 2600 BCE. It's believed that he designed the Step Pyramid of Djoser, although little else factual is known about his life. Over time Imhotep's reputation grew. Two thousand years after Imhotep's death, he was deified as a god of medicine and healing. His domain as a god later grew, and he eventually became equated with the god Thoth.[552]

---

552. Escolano-Poveda, "Imhotep."

Pythagoras

Pythagoras's place of birth was the Greek island of Samos. In 530 BCE, he migrated to the southern Greek city of Croton. There he established a commune with other mystics to study the Cosmos. Pythagoras determined that Earth was a sphere and calculated its rotation speed during his lifetime. He believed that the distances of planets were based on musical notes.[553] Pythagoras is also famous for his mathematical works and the Pythagorean theorem. He died around 495 BCE in either Croton or Metapontum.

Of the different beliefs held by Pythagoras, he's most identified with introducing reincarnation into the West. Termed *metempsychosis*, the Pythagorean concept of reincarnation holds that we reincarnate numerous times as either a human or some other life-form.[554] His belief may have influenced his choice to be a vegetarian.

Jesus of Nazareth

Mainstream scholars believe that Jesus was a Jewish rabbi living in Palestine around the turn of the first century CE. Jesus had a reputation for being a popular teacher, miracle worker, and social reformer. Like so many charismatic persons of his time, he most likely had a small group of close disciples during his life. Around 30 CE, Jesus ran afoul of the authorities and was executed by the Romans. After his death, Jesus became the focus of various new religious movements, some of which held that he returned to life and ascended to heaven.

Morton Smith was an acclaimed professor of ancient history at Columbia University and an authority on Jesus of Nazareth. According to Smith, Jesus most likely traveled to Egypt as a young man looking for work, typical for Jews in Palestine during the first century CE. Egypt was reputed to be a center for the study of magick, which Jesus studied during his time there.[555] Upon his return to Palestine, he held himself out to be a powerful magician who performed miracles and, through his power, claimed to have achieved apotheosis. Apotheosis by magick was the ordinary meaning of the phrase "son of God" rather than the Trinitarian doctrine of the church. The church distanced itself

---

553. Zell-Ravenheart, *Grimoire for the Apprentice Wizard*, 333.
554. Zell-Ravenheart, *Grimoire for the Apprentice Wizard*, 333.
555. Smith, *Jesus the Magician*, 110.

from the claim that Jesus was a magician and the importance of his magick work ("miracles").[556]

Apollonius of Tyana

Apollonius was born in Tyana. Tyana was in the south-central region of Anatolian, which is in modern Turkey. As a child, Apollonius was sent to the coastal town of Tarsus in Greece to study. While in Tarsus, Apollonius became a Pythagorean. He later traveled to Babylon and then to India to study with the Brahmans. He attracted a small group of disciples and became a wandering holy man and miracle worker upon returning. He was tried on charges of magick and sedition, as well as an accusation of sacrificing a young boy. The facts on how he escaped are murky. Apollonius died in 96 CE.[557]

There are numerous legends concerning Apollonius. One is that he escaped his trial by disappearing from the courtroom and magickally reappearing in Greece. Another is that he ascended to heaven, rather than dying, and appeared to a young man afterward. During his lifetime Apollonius had a reputation as a powerful miracle worker and was thought to be a son of god.[558]

Simon Magus

Simon Magus was a Samaritan magician living during the early part of the first century CE. Unfortunately, we know little authoritative information about him. Most of what's known about Simon comes from Christian sources. He was reputed to have formed a Gnostic sect called the Simonians, while some went so far as to credit him with Gnosticism's founding.

Simon was reputed to be a powerful magician even among his Christian critics. In one account, he made a brass serpent move and stone statues talk during a confrontation with the Apostle Peter. Christian texts claimed that Peter defeated him through prayer by causing him to fall while levitating.[559]

556. Smith, *Jesus the Magician*, 140–44.
557. Smith, *Jesus the Magician*, 116.
558. Smith, *Jesus the Magician*, 117.
559. Zell-Ravenheart, *Grimoire for the Apprentice Wizard*, 334.

Mary the Prophetess

Much of the life of Mary the Prophetess is a mystery. However, we know that she likely lived around the early third century CE and that she was also known as Mary the Jewess. Our primary source of information comes from Zosimus the Panopolitan, who lived around 300 CE and sometimes referred to her as the "divine Maria."[560]

Mary the Prophetess is famous for her invention of alchemical instruments and her work in alchemy. She invented a variety of ovens as well as various equipment from metal, clay, and glass. One of her inventions was a water bath, which consisted of a heated water container surrounding another container that held the substance to be heated. She also invented the still. Both inventions are in use today.[561]

Cleopatra the Alchemist

Cleopatra the Alchemist, not to be confused with Queen Cleopatra VII, was a Greek writer, philosopher, and pioneer in alchemy living in Alexandria during the third or fourth century CE. According to legend, she was one of four female alchemists who could change lead into gold. There are three books attributed to her. They are *On Weights and Measures*, *Chrysopoeia of Cleopatra*, and *Dialogue of the Philosophers and Cleopatra*. *Chrysopoeia of Cleopatra* (*chrysopoeia* translates as "gold-making") is her most famous work and was a single-page document with alchemical symbols.[562]

Merlin

Tradition holds that Merlin lived in Britain circa 500 CE. According to one legend, he was sired by a demon. When a tower under construction by King Vortigern repeatedly collapsed, the king was told that the blood of a fatherless boy would stabilize it. Knowing of Merlin's miraculous birth, Vortigern brought Merlin to the site to be sacrificed. Upon arrival, Merlin said that the cause of the tower's repeated collapse was an underground body of water. Merlin predicted

---

560. Patai, *The Jewish Alchemists*, 80.
561. Patai, *The Jewish Alchemists*, 81.
562. Klimczak, "The Forgotten Cleopatra."

that draining the pool would reveal two dragons fighting underneath. The men dug beneath the tower and found the pond and the dragons.[563]

Merlin is most famous for his central role in the legends of King Arthur. Uther Pendragon, King of Britain, fell in love with Igraine, the wife of Gorlois of Cornwall. At the request of Uther, Merlin used magick to transform Uther's appearance to resemble Gorlois so Uther could sleep with Igraine for one night. Later, Uther killed Gorlois and took Igraine as his wife. Igraine gave birth to a boy whom Merlin took away. The child would grow up to be King Arthur.[564]

There are different legends as to the fate of Merlin. One is that he dwells in an invisible glass house on an island off the coast of Wales. There's another legend that says he was imprisoned in a crystal cave by the fairy Nimue.[565]

Morgan le Fay

Some scholars believe that Morgan le Fay may have initially been a Celtic psychopomp, while others think she was more. Some scholars believe that she was worshiped as a goddess who ruled over the Celtic afterlife paradise known as Avalon.

Morgan first appears as a healer who leads the Nine Holy Women of Avalon in the Arthurian legends. After King Arthur was injured at the Battle of Camlann, Morgan and the Nine Holy Women tended to his wounds. Arthur decided to stay in Avalon after falling in love with Morgan. However, later legends written by Cistercian scribes with misogynist intentions turned Morgan into Arthur's half sister and chief antagonist. Through the use of magick and deceit, she destroyed Arthur, Merlin, Camelot, and the Knights of the Round Table.[566]

Abe no Seimei

Abe no Seimei lived in Japan from 921 to 1005 CE. During his life, he was recognized as a "preeminent practitioner of Onmyōdō." Onmyōdō is an ancient Japanese magickal practice. Because of his reputation, Seimei was the preferred sorcerer to the emperor and performed numerous cleansing rituals for him.

563. Lehane, *Wizards and Witches*, 35–36.
564. Lehane, *Wizards and Witches*, 36–37.
565. Lehane, *Wizards and Witches*, 38.
566. Illes, *Encyclopedia of Spirits*, 724.

Seimei was reputed to be able to see demons and control them. His talents included healing, prophesy, the lifting of curses, and many other occult talents.[567] Today the Japanese word for *pentagram* is *se-man* since it was the *mon*, or seal, of Seimei.[568] Seimei's reputation lives on today with a shrine dedicated to him in Kyoto and as a trendy character in literature and anime.

Johann Georg Faust

Johann Georg Faust was a German magician, alchemist, and astrologer. When it comes to Faust, it's difficult to separate the person from the myth. One of the earliest reliable records dates to 1506, in which a magician and astronomer named Faust appeared in Gelnhausen. Records exist for the next thirty years across Germany of a Faust who claimed to be an astrologer, physician, magician, and more. The one thing these records have in common are accusations that Faust was a fraud. Faust died around 1540 in an explosion thought to have been caused by his alchemical equipment.

Numerous grimoires exist attributed to Faust. However, none of these grimoires were published during his lifetime, and all are very likely fakes. Some of these grimoires date to before he was born. Faust is best known not for his actual life but as the inspiration to Johann Wolfgang von Goethe for his tragic play *Faust*. In it the protagonist sells his soul to a demon named Mephistopheles. It's from Goethe's play that we get the idiom of a "Faustian deal."[569]

Heinrich Cornelius von Agrippa

Heinrich Cornelius von Agrippa was a true Renaissance man. His areas of knowledge ranged from medicine to law. Agrippa received a master of arts from the University of Cologne when he was just sixteen. During his time at the university, he took an interest in the occult. As a professor, he promoted progressive ideas for his time, such as that women were superior to men. He also championed the cause of women accused of witchcraft. In addition, Agrippa publicly opposed the anti-Semitism that was ever-present at that time. He died in 1535.

---

567. Hayashi and Hayek, "Editors' Introduction," 1–18.
568. Cummins, *The Dark Side of Japan*, 52.
569. "Faust."

Agrippa is most famous for his trilogy titled *Three Books Concerning Occult Philosophy (De occulta philosophia libri tres)*. In these three books, Agrippa sought to reconcile natural magick with Neoplatonic thought and a dose of Christianity. Near his death, Agrippa distanced himself from his books. Nevertheless, one cannot overstate his work's impact on the esoteric writers that followed or upon modern magick.[570]

John Dee

John Dee was a Welshman and an advisor to Queen Elizabeth I. He was also an ardent imperialist and an advocate for British expansionism. Historians credit Dee with coining the term *British Empire*. He was also an astrologer, occultist, sorcerer, and scholar of Hermetic philosophy. Dee died at eighty-one in 1608 or 1609.

Of all of Dee's occult studies, and there were many, his "Enochian" language is possibly his most enduring work. Working with Edward Kelley, a known con man, Dee would receive messages from spirits that he believed were "angels." From these messages, Dee deduced what he thought was a divine language of angels, which he named after the Old Testament character Enoch. While many question the legitimacy of Dee and Kelly's work, it continues to be a significant source of inspiration for both Right-Hand Path and Left-Hand Path magick users today.[571]

Marie Laveau

There is a lot written about Marie Laveau, and much of it is bogus. We know for a fact that she was born in the French Quarter of New Orleans in 1801 CE. She married a French immigrant named Jacques Paris in 1819 and had two daughters, Felicite and Angele. Laveau died in 1881.

While Laveau's occupation was hairdresser, she's remembered as a powerful voodoo priestess or queen. Her reputation continues to this day, making her a popular figure in pop culture. Unfortunately, due to the vandalization of her tombstone in 2013, visitors can only visit her grave with tour guides.[572]

---

570. Zell-Ravenheart, *Grimoire for the Apprentice Wizard*, 336.
571. Zell-Ravenheart, *Grimoire for the Apprentice Wizard*, 337.
572. "Marie Laveau's Tomb."

Éliphas Lévi

Éliphas Lévi was born Alphonse Louis Constant. In 1832, he joined the seminary but left in 1836 because he had fallen in love. Shortly after, he became a strong advocate for socialism, believing it to be the "true Christianity," and was imprisoned several times for his beliefs. Lévi eventually adopted magick as his passion and wrote numerous books on the topic. Lévi died in 1875 at the age of sixty-five.

It's hard to overstate Lévi's role in the development of modern magick and occultism. One might go so far as to say that he's the most influential figure of all time in the field. His books, such as *Transcendental Magic: Its Doctrine and Ritual*, significantly influenced occultists such as Aleister Crowley, Helena Blavatsky, and Gerald Gardner. Much of what we consider modern occult thought traces back to the work of Lévi.[573]

George Pickingill

George Pickingill grew up in Hockley, England. Though his occupation was farm laborer, he was known as a cunning man or folk magick practitioner. He and his wife, Sarah Ann Bateman, had four children. In 1908, a newspaper reporter described Pickingill as "a tall, unkempt man, solitary and uncommunicative. He had very long fingernails and kept his money in a purse of sacking."[574]

Pickingill claimed a hereditary lineage back to eleventh-century witches. In some ways, he may be considered the first modern Pagan in that he wanted to establish what he termed the "Old Religion," which included worship of the Horned God. Pickingill was known to use his magick to both heal and curse. He established several covens that initiated famous magicians such as Crowley and Gardner. While most of his covens were open to men and women, at least one didn't accept men as members; women performed all rituals.[575]

Paschal Beverly Randolph

Paschal Beverly Randolph was an African American doctor, occultist, Spiritualist, and writer. Randolph was born a "free black" in New York City in 1825.

---

573. Zell-Ravenheart, *Grimoire for the Apprentice Wizard*, 338.
574. Maple, "The Witches of Canewdon," 241–50.
575. Zell-Ravenheart, *Grimoire for the Apprentice Wizard*, 338–39.

His father left his family while he was an infant and his mother died while he was a young child. As a teenager, Randolph became a sailor and traveled the world. During his travels, he became interested in the occult and studied under several different magick users across the globe.

Upon his return to America, Randolph was a public speaker, author, and Spiritualist. Randolph was a vocal abolitionist and taught literacy to freed slaves in New Orleans. In addition, he was an avid proponent of birth control. He was also trained as a doctor of medicine and published numerous books on health, sexuality, Spiritualism, occultism, and magick.

Randolph died in Toledo, Ohio, at the age of forty-nine, most likely by suicide.[576]

Helena Blavatsky

It's believed that Helena Blavatsky, also known as Madame Blavatsky, was born in the Ukrainian town of Yekaterinoslav. It's challenging to know the details of her early life because she often gave contradictory facts. We know that she was a daughter of aristocracy though she may have been of mixed heritage. It's thought that one lineage was of French Huguenots that had fled to Russia to escape persecution. Blavatsky traveled extensively worldwide, going to India, Asia, and Tibet. In 1877, she and others formed an organization called the Theosophical Society.

Blavatsky's influence on Paganism is extensive and profound. Her books, such as *Isis Unveiled* and *The Secret Doctrine,* still influence New Age and Pagan thought. She believed that there had once been a worldwide ancient wisdom tradition from which all modern religions are descended. Her cosmology and other beliefs, such as the various subtle bodies, still dominate contemporary occult and New Age thought.

Aleister Crowley

Aleister Crowley was born on October 12, 1875, which happened to be the same year that Lévi died. Crowley held that he was the reincarnation of Lévi and used this as one of the proofs. Of the different magicians, Crowley may be the most controversial since Faust. Known for his enormous appetite for magickal

---

576. West, *Sex Magicians*, 13–26.

knowledge (along with sex and mind-altering drugs), he traveled the world, studying as much esoterica as possible. Crowley was called the "Wickedest Man in the World" during his lifetime, although he preferred the title of "The Great Beast."

It's impossible to summarize the number of accomplishments by Crowley. He established the Pagan tradition of Thelema and founded the Ordo Templi Orientis. It's from Crowley that we have the ethical axiom of "Do what thou wilt shall be the whole of the law." His magickal principles still influence modern practices today. In the year of his death, he met Gardner, who incorporated much of Crowley's work into his own Book of Shadows.[577]

---

577. Zell-Ravenheart, *Grimoire for the Apprentice Wizard*, 339–40.

RECOMMENDED READING

Classic Paganism

Alchemy & Alchemists by Sean Martin

Heroes: Mortals and Monsters, Quests and Adventures by Stephen Fry

Inanna: Lady of the Largest Heart: Poems of the Sumerian High Priestess by Betty De Shong Meador

Mythos: The Greek Myths Reimagined by Stephen Fry

Secrets of the Druids: From Indo-European Origins to Modern Practices by Teresa Cross

The Secret Teachings of All Ages by Manly P. Hall

Contemporary Paganism (General)

Dealing with Deities: Practical Polytheistic Theology by Raven Kaldera

Ethics and the Craft: The History, Evolution, and Practice of Wiccan Ethics by John J. Coughlin

Paganism in Depth: A Polytheist Approach by John Beckett

Paganism: An Introduction to Earth-Centered Religions by Joyce and River Higginbotham

Pagan Spirituality: A Guide to Personal Transformation by Joyce and River Higginbotham

Pagan Theology: Paganism as a World Religion by Michael York

The Paths of Paganism: An Experience-Based Guide to Modern Pagan Practice by John Beckett

Seeking the Mystery: An Introduction to Pagan Theologies by Christine Hoff Kraemer

Dark Paganism

Apophis by Michael Kelly

Black Veils: The Vampire Lexicon by Father Sebastiaan

Embracing the Darkness: Understanding Dark Subcultures by Corvis Nocturnum

Goth Craft: The Magickal Side of Dark Culture by Raven Digitalis

Grimoire of Tiamat by Asenath Mason

Nocturnal Witchcraft: Magick After Dark by Konstantinos

Nocturnicon: Calling Dark Forces and Powers by Konstantinos

Out of the Shadows: An Exploration of Dark Paganism and Magick by John J. Coughlin

The Psychic Vampire Codex: A Manual of Magick and Energy Work by Michelle Belanger

The Vampire Ritual Book by Michelle Belanger

Vampyre Magick: The Grimoire of the Living Vampire by Father Sebastiaan

Vampyre Sanguinomicon: The Lexicon of the Living Vampire by Father Sebastiaan

Walking the Twilight Path: A Gothic Book of the Dead by Michelle Belanger

Goth

The Goth Bible: A Compendium for the Darkly Inclined by Nancy Kilpatrick

H. P. Lovecraft

H. P. Lovecraft and the Black Magickal Tradition: The Master of Horror's Influence on Modern Occultism by John L. Steadman

When the Stars Are Right: Towards an Authentic R'lyehian Spirituality by Scott R. Jones

Left-Hand Path

Infernal Geometry and the Left-Hand Path: The Magical System of the Nine Angles by Toby Chappell

Lords of the Left-Hand Path: Forbidden Practices and Spiritual Heresies by Stephen E. Flowers

Protection & Reversal Magick: A Witch's Defense Manual by Jason Miller

Uncle Setnakt's Essential Guide to the Left Hand Path by Don Webb

Magick

Beginning Mindfulness: Learning the Way of Awareness by Andrew Weiss

The Chaos Protocols: Magical Techniques for Navigating the New Economic Reality by Gordon White

The Elements of Spellcrafting: 21 Keys to Successful Sorcery by Jason Miller

Financial Sorcery: Magical Strategies to Create Real and Lasting Wealth by Jason Miller

Gothic Grimoire by Konstantinos

Grimoire for the Apprentice Wizard by Oberon Zell-Ravenheart

Instant Magick: An Ancient Wisdom, Modern Spellcraft by Christopher Penczak

Liber Null & Psychonaut: An Introduction to Chaos Magic by Peter J. Carroll

Real Energy: Systems, Spirits, and Substances to Heal, Change, and Grow by Phaedra and Isaac Bonewits

Real Magic: An Introductory Treatise on the Basic Principles of Yellow Magic by Isaac Bonewits

Ritual Magic: What It Is & How to Do It by Donald Tyson

Sex, Sorcery, and Spirit: The Secrets of Erotic Magic by Jason Miller

The Sorcerer's Secrets: Strategies in Practical Magick by Jason Miller

Summoning Spirits: The Art of Magical Evocation by Konstantinos

Tame Your Inner Critic: Find Peace & Contentment to Live Your Life on Purpose by Della Temple

Philosophy

Confucian Moral Self Cultivation by Philip J. Ivanhoe

Death by Todd May

A Decent Life: Morality for the Rest of Us by Todd May

Martial Virtues: Lessons in Wisdom, Courage, and Compassion from the World's Greatest Warriors by Charles Hackney

Neo-Confucian Self-Cultivation by Barry C. Keenan

Pursuits of Wisdom: Six Ways of Life in Ancient Philosophy from Socrates to Plotinus by John M. Cooper

A Significant Life: Human Meaning in a Silent Universe by Todd May

A Small Treatise on the Great Virtues: The Uses of Philosophy in Everyday Life by Andre Comte-Sponville

Theurgy and the Soul: The Neoplatonism of Iamblichus by Gregory Shaw

Psychology

Authentic: How to be Yourself and Why It Matters by Professor Stephen Joseph
The Self by Jonathon D. Brown
The Stories We Live By: Personal Myths and the Making of the Self by Dan P. McAdams

Shadow Work

Feeding Your Demons: Ancient Wisdom for Resolving Inner Conflict by Tsultrim Allione
Shadow Dance: Liberating the Power & Creativity of Your Dark Side by David Richo
Shadow Magick Compendium: Exploring Darker Aspects of Magical Spirituality by Raven Digitalis
Why Good People Do Bad Things: Understanding Our Darker Selves by James Hollis

Spirituality

After Buddhism: Rethinking the Dharma for a Secular Age by Stephen Batchelor
Buddhism Without Beliefs: A Contemporary Guide to Awakening by Stephen Batchelor
The Essence of Shinto: Japan's Spiritual Heart by Motohisa Yamakage
La Santa Muerte: Unearthing the Magic & Mysticism of Death by Tomás Prower
Lifecycles: Reincarnation and the Web of Life by Christopher M. Bache
The Modern Book of the Dead: A Revolutionary Perspective on Death, the Soul, and What Really Happens in the Life to Come by Ptolemy Tompkins
Naikan: Gratitude, Grace, and the Japanese Art of Self-Reflection by Gregg Krech
A New Buddhist Path: Enlightenment, Evolution, and Ethics in the Modern World by David R. Loy
The Shambhala Guide to Taoism by Eva Wong
Shinto: A Celebration of Life by Aidan Rankin
The Taoism of Inner Peace by Diane Dreher
Tao Te Ching by Lao Tzu

Tarot

Seventy-Eight Degrees of Wisdom: A Tarot Journey to Self-Awareness by Rachel Pollack

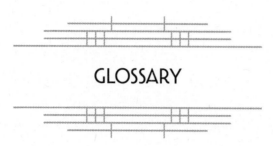

GLOSSARY

alchemy: An ancient field of study and practice focused on converting a substance from one type to another, such as converting lead into gold. It is also a spiritual practice to achieve godhood or transcendence. See *apotheosis* and *self-deification*.

animism: The belief that all things, not just humans, are infused with spirit or soul.

antinomian: A person who does not follow the laws of society or other institutions.

apotheosis: The act of achieving godhood. See *alchemy* and *self-deification*.

Asatru: A contemporary Pagan tradition focused on Norse or Scandinavian deities. See *Heathenry*.

astral: A term classically used to represent the heavenly realm. Synonymous with stellar.

astral body: The body of a god. It also means the Self in its transcended state. Many consider it synonymous with the spiritual body.

athame: A knife used for ritual magick.

azoth: An alchemical word for the fifth element. See *quintessence* and *mercury*.

Burning Times: A term for the historical period, primarily in Europe and North America, when individuals were accused of witchcraft and persecuted by religious and civil authorities.

Chi: A Chinese word for esoteric energy or life force thought to exist throughout the world. See *dark ether.*

chthonic: An underground or underworld realm.

cleanse: An act to remove unwelcome esoteric energies from a person or object.

corporeal: A term for the physical or material universe without considering any spiritual aspect.

correspondence: An esoteric belief that connections exist between all parts of the universe.

daemon (also spelled daimon): The Latin word for a Greek lesser deity or guiding spirit. Some daemons are benevolent, while others are dangerous. Because Abrahamic religions consider all Pagan spirits evil, the word became used exclusively to designate an evil spirit and was rewritten as demon.

dark aesthetics: A style of art, such as music, painting, and fashion, with dark themes. See *dark art.*

dark allure: The attraction that a person feels toward dark aesthetics.

dark art: An artistic presentation that often contains macabre or disturbing messages or elements. See *dark aesthetics.*

dark current: A Dark Pagan term for the flow of divine consciousness from the Source that travels with the emanations. The dark current is the organizing principle of the Cosmos. Various dark traditions use the term as a path to connect back to the Source. See *Demiurge.*

darke fluff: A derogatory term for the insistence by some on using only dark aesthetics.

dark ether: A Dark Pagan term for the divine consciousness carried by the dark current. See *Chi.*

Dark Pagan: One who follows a positive, spiritual Pagan path of honoring and cultivating the Self.

Dark Paganism: A positive, life-affirming spiritual philosophy centered on honoring and cultivating the Self.

darksider: One who focuses on the inner aspects of spirituality rather than the outer or light during their spiritual journey.

demigod: A mythological being that's half god and half human. Examples of demigods include Hercules and Jesus Christ.

Demiurge: A classic Greek word for the flow of divine consciousness from the Source that travels with the emanations. The Demiurge is the organizing principle of the Cosmos. See *dark current.*

divination: The practice of foretelling future events' probabilities, usually aided by materials such as cards or stones.

dualism: A belief that divides everything into ethical opposites. An example is good versus evil.

duality: A belief or representation of something in twos. Two sides to a coin, for example. Duality differs from dualism because it doesn't place an ethical value on either side.

duotheism: The belief that Divinity exists as two entities. Some duotheism models hold that the different gods and goddesses of the world religions are but masks of a singular god and a singular goddess.

eclectic Pagan: A Neopagan who doesn't follow an established tradition. Instead, this individual usually combines elements from different traditions and sources for their practice.

egregore: An occult term for an independently functioning spiritual entity created by one or more magick practitioners. Many egregores begin as thought-forms but then become capable of operating independently of the practitioners. See *thought-form.*

elements: Historically, elements are the building blocks of the corporeal universe. However, because of scientific revelations, elements are now generally understood as being spiritual essences of the Cosmos.

emanation: A metaphysical term for the Source's outer activity resulting in the dark current and the Cosmos's existence.

energy: An ill-defined term for an esoteric phenomenon characterized by its tendency to flow like a river or electricity. It can be healthy (positive) or unhealthy (negative).

etheric: An arcane term that is often synonymous with spirit.

fluffy bunny: A derogatory term for Pagan or New Age viewpoints deemed unrealistically optimistic or positive.

god/goddess: An immensely more powerful spirit than any other that has remarkable greatness. In addition, some believe that gods/goddesses are always virtuous.

grimoire: A term generally used for a European occult guidebook. Most of these were written during the Middle Ages and Renaissance.

Heathenry: A contemporary Pagan movement centered around pre-Christian deities of Northern Europe. See *Asatru.*

Hermeticism: An esoteric wisdom tradition based primarily on Hermes Trismegistus's writings.

infernal: From the Latin word *infernus,* meaning "below" or "lower regions." Its usage includes the lower parts or lowlands; flashes of lightning from the earth; the abdomen and lower parts of the body; the river Styx; and devoted or sacred to the infernal gods. Abrahamic traditions often use it as synonymous with hell as a place of torment.

kami: Divine beings of the Shinto religion of Japan. Unfortunately, translators often mistranslate the word *kami* into *gods.*

karma: A Sanskrit word for action, work, or deed. It's part of a belief that an individual's current actions will result in a future consequence for the same individual either in this life or the next.

Left-Hand Path (LHP): A term that covers a variety of topics. In Tantra, the Left-Hand Path involves a variety of taboo or ritual transgressions. The esoteric LHP is an esoteric spirituality that focuses on self-cultivation and incorporates distinctive aesthetics and techniques.

lightsiders: An individual whose primary focus is on the outer aspects of spirituality rather than the inner or dark during their spiritual journey.

liminal: A border between two sides or areas. In esoteric usage, *liminal* often represents a state of being or a physical place where the corporeal aspect and the spiritual aspect of existence interact.

logical positivism: A belief that only statements verifiable through systematic direct observation or logical proof are meaningful or real. Advocates of logical positivism are critical of anecdotal evidence and personal revelations. See *scientific materialism* and *scientism.*

macrocosm: An ancient term for the Cosmos.

magick: A spiritual practice and process to influence the probability of events.

magus: A person considered a master of magick. The term has historically been used in a misogynistic fashion and is limited to men.

Mercury/mercury: A god in the Roman pantheon. It is also an element and a planet nearest to the sun. The alchemists used the word *mercury* as a poetic term for the universal solvent.

microcosm: In classic thought, the microcosm refers to humans as a miniature of the Cosmos.

monotheism: The belief that divinity is one. This belief is most associated with the Abrahamic wisdom traditions of Judaism, Christianity, and Islam, although it is in some non-Abrahamic traditions.

mythopoeia: The process of creating new myths. J. R. R. Tolkien developed both the term and concept of mythopoeia.

Neopagan: A term coined by Isaac Bonewits to differentiate contemporary Pagans from the classic pre-Christian Pagans of history.

Neoplatonism: A school of Platonism developed during the first through fifth centuries CE in the Greco-Roman world.

netherworld: A term for the land of the dead commonly used in association with Mesopotamian beliefs.

nous: In Greek cosmology, the nous was a divine consciousness. From the nous arises emanations that spread out, creating the Cosmos.

occult: The word *occult* means hidden. The word is commonly used for a set of esoteric beliefs and practices.

Paganism: An umbrella term for various contemporary spiritual paths of Western esotericism inspired by pre-Abrahamic concepts, tropes, and mythology.

pantheism: The belief that the Divine is the total of all things.

pentagram: A five-pointed star. Although present in various religions, a pentagram is the most common symbol used by Right-Hand Path and Left-Hand Path Pagans.

poltergeist: A noisy or troublesome ghost.

polytheism: The belief that divinity exists in multiples of two or more.

postmodernism: A broad movement covering many disciplines from philosophy to the arts originating circa mid-twentieth CE. It's a common term for the trends and tropes that build on modernism currently in development.

Qabala: A Western esoteric tradition that draws heavily upon the Jewish Kabbalah.

quintessence: An alchemical term for the source of life. See *azoth* and *mercury*.

rebirth: The term *rebirth* is generally an alternate term for *reincarnation*. The word *rebirth* is a variant popular among Buddhists. See *reincarnation*.

reincarnation: The belief that the soul is reborn over multiple lifetimes. See *rebirth*.

Right-Hand Path (RHP): A philosophy and wisdom tradition that primarily focuses on the external approach to spirituality rather than the inner. The majority of world wisdom traditions and many traditions of Paganism are RHP. A common term used by members of the Left-Hand Path (LHP) and covers a variety of topics.

scientific materialism: A belief that nothing exists but the material world or that which the natural sciences can study. Not to be confused with science or the scientific method. See *logical positivism* and *scientism*.

scientism: A belief that the only trustworthy source of information about the universe is through established scientific methods; scientism is not the same as science or the scientific method themselves. See *logical positivism* and *scientific materialism*.

self-deification: The belief by someone that they are a god. It is also a process by which a person strives to elevate oneself to becoming a god. *Self-deification* is a term that's popular in many Left-Hand Path traditions. See *alchemy* and *apotheosis*.

solitary: In Paganism, *solitary* is a term used for someone who does not participate in a Pagan group.

sorcerer: A sorcerer is synonymous with a wizard. See *wizard*.

soul: A term usually associated with the non-corporeal aspect of a person. Souls are commonly considered eternal by nature.

spirits: Non-corporeal entities.

spiritualism: A religious movement of the late nineteenth and early twentieth centuries in which individuals believed they could communicate with the dead.

subtle bodies: Subtle bodies are various segments of the spiritual aspect of the Self. The number and nature of these segments vary among the different cultures and traditions.

Theosophy: A society created by Helena Blavatsky. Its doctrine includes reincarnation and a belief that there was once a worldwide ancient wisdom tradition from which all modern religions arose.

thought-form: An esoteric entity created by magick. See *egregore*.

warlock: An Old English word for "oath breaker." A warlock is stereotypically a male.

Wheel of the Year: A term used for the annual cycles of Pagan festivals. Pagans, especially Wiccans, use the Wheel of the Year in much the same fashion as Christians use the liturgical calendar.

Wiccan: A Pagan tradition founded by Gerald Gardner. The term is now used by various Pagan traditions not associated with Gardner.

witch: A term commonly used for a female magick user. *Witch* is now popular among many Pagans, especially Wiccans and those who practice Traditional Witchcraft.

wizard: From the Anglo-Saxon word *wysard*, which means "wise one." *Wizard* tends to be applied to men and is often representative of a magick user. See *sorcerer*.

BIBLIOGRAPHY

"About." Billelis. Accessed November 27, 2021. https://www.billelis.com/about.

"About OAO." Opus Aima Obscuræ. Accessed December 5, 2021. https://web .archive.org/web/20180326154018/http://www.opusaimaobscurae.org /about-oao/.

Achor, Shawn. *The Happiness Advantage: The Seven Principles of Positive Psychology That Fuel Success and Performance at Work*. New York: Crown, 2010.

Ahlquist, Diane. *Moon Spells: How to Use the Phases of the Moon to Get What You Want*. Avon, MA: Adams Media Corp., 2002.

Akṣapāda. *Walking with Albert Camus—950+ Concise Philosophical Disclosures*. Self-published, 2019.

"The Ancestors in the Asatru/Heathen Religion: Alfar (Alfs, Light Alfs, Dark Alfs)." Norse Gods Asatru. Accessed November 29, 2021. https://www .norsegodsasatru.net/alfar.

Axelrod, Robert. *The Evolution of Cooperation*. New York: Basic Books, 2009.

Bache, Christopher M. *Lifecycles: Reincarnation and the Web of Life*. New York: Paragon House, 1998.

Badhwar, Neera K., and Roderick T. Long. "Ayn Rand." *Stanford Encyclopedia of Philosophy*. Updated July 13, 2020. https://plato.stanford.edu/archives /fall2020/entries/ayn-rand.

Bargwanna, Nicole. "Religious Symbolism in Sumo Today." Australian National University. Accessed November 29, 2021. http://rubens.anu.edu.au/raid1/student_projects97/sumo/religion/symbols.html.

Barnum, Phineas Taylor. *The Life of P. T. Barnum*. New York: Redfield, 1855.

Barr, O. Sydney. *The Christian New Morality: A Biblical Study of Situation Ethics*. Oxford: Oxford University Press, 1969.

Barrabbas, Frater. *Magical Qabalah for Beginners: A Comprehensive Guide to Occult Knowledge*. Woodbury, MN: Llewellyn Publications, 2013.

Barth, John. *The Floating Opera and the End of the Road*. New York: Anchor Books, 1988.

Bartlett, John. *Bartlett's Familiar Quotations*. Edited by Geoffrey O'Brien. New York: Little, Brown, 2012.

Bartlett, Sarah. *The Afterlife Bible: The Complete Guide to Otherworldly Experience*. London: Godsfield Press, 2015.

Batchelor, Stephen. *Buddhism without Beliefs: A Contemporary Guide to Awakening*. New York: Penguin, 1998.

Becket-Griffith, Jasmine. *Gothic Art Now*. New York: Ilex Press, 2008.

Beckett, John. "6 Thoughts on Gods Claiming People." *Under the Ancient Oaks* (blog). *Patheos*, November 24, 2019. https://www.patheos.com/blogs/johnbeckett/2019/11/6-thoughts-on-gods-claiming-people.html.

———. "8 Things to Make Your Paganism Stronger This Year." *Under the Ancient Oaks* (blog). *Patheos*, January 8, 2019. https://www.patheos.com/blogs/johnbeckett/2019/01/8-things-to-make-your-paganism-stronger-this-year.html.

———. "A Conclave of Cats: Debating the Nature of the Gods." *Under the Ancient Oaks* (blog). *Patheos*, October 2, 2018. http://www.patheos.com/blogs/johnbeckett/2018/10/conclave-of-cats-nature-of-the-gods.html.

———. "Culture of Consent, Culture of Sovereignty: A Recipe from a Druid's Perspective." In *Pagan Consent Culture: Building Communities of Empathy and Autonomy*, edited by Christine Hoff Kraemer and Yvonne Aburrow. Hubbardston, MA: Asphodel Press, 2016.

———. *Paganism In Depth: A Polytheist Approach.* Woodbury, MN: Llewellyn Publications, 2019.

———. *The Path of Paganism: An Experience-Based Guide to Modern Pagan Practice.* Woodbury, MN: Llewellyn Publications, 2017.

Belanger, Michelle. *Walking the Twilight Path: A Gothic Book of the Dead.* Woodbury, MN: Llewellyn Publications, 2008.

Bell, Jeffrey A. *Philosophy at the Edge of Chaos: Gilles Deleuze and the Philosophy of Difference.* Toronto: University of Toronto Press, 2006.

Bem, D. J. "Feeling the Future: Experimental Evidence for Anomalous Retroactive Influences on Cognition and Affect." *Journal of Personality and Social Psychology* 100, no. 3 (2011): 407–25. https://doi.org/10.1037/a0021524.

Beresford, Peter. *Participatory Ideology: From Exclusion to Involvement.* Bristol, UK: Policy Press, 2021.

Betz, Hans Dieter, ed. *The Greek Magical Papyri in Translation, Including the Demotic Spells.* Chicago: University of Chicago Press, 1996.

Black, Jeremy, and Anthony Green. *Gods, Demons, and Symbols of Ancient Mesopotamia: An Illustrated Dictionary.* Austin: University of Texas Press, 1992.

Blackburn, Simon. *The Oxford Dictionary of Philosophy.* Oxford: Oxford University Press, 2016.

Bonewits, Isaac. "The Advanced Bonewits' Cult Danger Evaluation Frame (Version 2.7)." Religious Tolerance. Updated March 7, 2016. https://www .religioustolerance.org/bonewits-cult-danger-evaluation-frame.htm.

———. *Bonewits's Essential Guide to Witchcraft and Wicca.* New York: Citadel Press, 2006.

———. *Neopagan Rites: A Guide to Creating Public Rituals That Work.* Woodbury, MN: Llewellyn Publications, 2007.

———. *Real Magic: An Introductory Treatise on the Basic Principles of Yellow Magic.* Boston: Weiser Books, 1989.

Bonewits, Phaedra, and Isaac Bonewits. *Real Energy: Systems, Spirits, and Substances to Heal, Change, and Grow*. Franklin Lakes, NJ: New Page Books, 2007.

Borg, Marcus, ed. *Jesus and Buddha: The Parallel Sayings*. Berkeley, CA: Ulysses Press, 2020.

Borucki, Rebekah. *Managing the Motherload: A Guide to Creating More Ease, Space, and Grace in Motherhood*. Carlsbad, CA: Hay House, 2019.

Brinkerhoff, Derick W., and Jennifer M. Brinkerhoff. *Working for Change: Making a Career in International Public Service*. Bloomfield, CT: Kumarian Press, 2005.

Brody, Jane E. "New Dieting Theory's Delicate Balance." *New York Times*, May 19, 1982. https://www.nytimes.com/1982/05/19/garden/new-dieting -theory-s-delicate-balance.html.

Brooke, Roger. *Jung and Phenomenology*. London: Routledge, 2015.

Brown, Keah. *The Pretty One: One Life, Pop Culture, Disability, and Other Reasons to Fall in Love with Me*. New York: Simon and Schuster, 2019.

Brown, Lachlan. "Ego Death: 7 Stages to the Obliteration of the Self." Hack Spirit. Updated November 14, 2018. https://hackspirit.com /ego-death-7-stages-to-the-obliteration-of-the-self.

Bruce, Robert. *Astral Dynamics: A New Approach to Out-of-Body Experiences*. Charlottesville, VA: Hampton Roads, 2009.

———. *The Practical Psychic Self-Defense Handbook: A Survival Guide*. Charlottesville, VA: Hampton Roads, 2011.

Campbell, Joseph, and Bill Moyers. *The Power of Myth*. New York: Anchor Books, 2011.

Camus, Albert. *The Myth of Sisyphus and Other Essays*. Translated by Justin O'Brien. New York: Vintage International, 2012.

———. *The Rebel: An Essay on Man in Revolt*. Translated by Anthony Bower. New York: Vintage International, 2012.

Carey, Benedict. "Long-Awaited Medical Study Questions the Power of Prayer." *New York Times*, March 31, 2006. https://www.nytimes

.com/2006/03/31/health/longawaited-medical-study-questions-the
-power-of-prayer.html.

Carpenter, Dennis D. "Emergent Nature Spirituality: An Examination of the Major Spiritual Contours of the Contemporary Pagan Worldview." In *Magical Religion and Modern Witchcraft*, edited by James R. Lewis. Albany, NY: State University of New York Press, 1996.

Chappell, Toby. *Infernal Geometry and the Left-Hand Path: The Magical System of the Nine Angles*. New York: Simon and Schuster. 2019.

Christman, John. "Autonomy in Moral and Political Philosophy." *Stanford Encyclopedia of Philosophy*. Updated January 9, 2015. https://plato.stanford .edu/archives/spr2018/entries/autonomy-moral.

Cillizza, Chris. "What Barack Obama Gets Exactly Right about Our Toxic 'Cancel' Culture." *CNN*. Updated October 30, 2019. https://www.cnn .com/2019/10/30/politics/obama-cancel-culture/index.html.

Comte-Sponville, André. *A Small Treatise on the Great Virtues: The Uses of Philosophy in Everyday Life*. Translated by Catherine Temerson. New York: Macmillan, 2002.

Cooper, John M. *Pursuits of Wisdom: Six Ways of Life in Ancient Philosophy from Socrates to Plotinus*. Princeton, NJ: Princeton University Press, 2013.

Coughlin, John J. "About." John J. Coughlin. Accessed November 27, 2021. http://www.johncoughlin.com/.

———. *Ethics and the Craft: The History, Evolution, and Practice of Wiccan Ethics*. New York: Waning Moon Publications, 2009.

———. "An Exploration of Dark Paganism: The Asshole Effect." Waning Moon. Accessed November 27, 2021. https://www.waningmoon.com /darkpagan/lib/lib0047.html.

———. "An Exploration of Dark Paganism: What Is Dark Paganism?" Waning Moon. Accessed November 27, 2021. https://www.waningmoon.com /darkpagan/lib/lib0045.html.

———. *Out of the Shadows: An Exploration of Dark Paganism and Magick*. New York: Waning Moon Publications, 2009.

Cummins, Antony. *The Dark Side of Japan: Ancient Black Magic, Folklore, Ritual*. Gloucestershire, UK: Amberley Publishing, 2017.

"Dark Art Movement." Dark Art Movement. Accessed November 27, 2021. http://darkartmovement.com/dark-art-movement.

Darwin, Charles. *The Descent of Man, and Selection in Relation to Sex*. London: John Murray, Albemarle Street, 1871.

Davis, Fred. *Fashion, Culture, and Identity*. Chicago: University of Chicago Press, 2013.

de Biasi, Jean-Louis. *Rediscover the Magick of the Gods and Goddesses: Revealing the Mysteries of Theurgy*. Woodbury, MN: Llewellyn Publications, 2014.

DeCelles, K. A., D. S. DeRue, J. D. Margolis, and T. L. Ceranic. "Does Power Corrupt or Enable? When and Why Power Facilitates Self-Interested Behavior." *Journal of Applied Psychology* 97, no. 3 (2012): 681–89. https://doi.org/10.1037/a0026811.

de Jager, Peter. "The Tarde Challenge." *Municipal World*, July 2016.

de Tocqueville, Alexis. *Democracy in America*. Translated by George Lawrence. Edited by J. P. Mayer. New York: HarperCollins, 2000.

Dhammananda, K. Sri. *What Buddhists Believe*. Houston: Texas Buddhist Association, 2006.

Digitalis, Raven. *Goth Craft: The Magickal Side of Dark Culture*. Woodbury, MN: Llewellyn Publications, 2007.

———. *Shadow Magick Compendium: Exploring Darker Aspects of Magickal Spirituality*. Woodbury, MN: Llewellyn Publications, 2008.

Dillon, Steven. *The Case for Polytheism*. Winchester, UK: John Hunt Publishing, 2015.

Dougherty, Martin J. *Norse Myths: Viking Legends of Heroes and Gods*. London: Amber Books, 2016.

"Dragon's 'Radiation-Tolerant' Design." Aviation Week, November 20, 2012. https://aviationweek.com/dragons-radiation-tolerant-design.

Dworkin, Gerald. *The Theory and Practice of Autonomy*. Cambridge, UK: Cambridge University Press, 1988.

Ehrmann, Max. *Desiderata*. New York: Brooke House, 1972.

Escolano-Poveda, Marina. "Imhotep: A Sage between Fiction and Reality." American Research Center in Egypt. Accessed May 30, 2022. https://www.arce.org/resource/imhotep-sage-between-fiction-and-reality.

"Etymology of Sorcery." *Online Etymology Dictionary*. Accessed December 20, 2021. https://www.etymonline.com/word/sorcery.

"Excerpts from a US District Court Decision Recognizing Wicca as a Religion." Religious Tolerance. Accessed May 30, 2022. https://www.religioustolerance.org/witchcr3.htm.

Faivre, Antoine. *Access to Western Esotericism*. Albany, NY: SUNY Press, 1994.

Fatić, Aleksandar, and Lydia Amir, eds. *Practicing Philosophy*. Newcastle, UK: Cambridge Scholars Publishing, 2015.

Fitzgerald, F. Scott, "The Rich Boy," *All the Sad Young Men*. Leeds, UK: Kismet Press, 2018.

Flowers, Stephen E. *Lords of the Left-Hand Path: Forbidden Practices and Spiritual Heresies*. Rochester, VA: Inner Traditions, 2012.

Foley, John. *Albert Camus: From the Absurd to Revolt*. Kingston, ON: McGill-Queen's University Press, 2014.

Foster, Michael Dylan. *The Book of Yōkai: Mysterious Creatures of Japanese Folklore*. Oakland, CA: University of California Press, 2015.

Frankl, Viktor E. *Man's Search for Meaning*. New York: Pocket Books, 1985.

Freeman, Iam A. *Seeds of Revolution: A Collection of Axioms, Passages, and Proverbs*. Self-published, iUniverse, 2014.

Fry, Stephen. *Mythos: The Greek Myths Reimagined*. London: Penguin Books, 2018.

García, Héctor, and Francesc Miralles. *Ikigai: The Japanese Secret to a Long and Happy Life*. New York: Penguin, 2017.

George, W. L. *The Intelligence of Woman*. Self-published, Createspace, 2015. Originally published 1916.

Gifford, Terry. *Reconnecting with John Muir: Essays in Post-Pastoral Practice.* Athens: University of Georgia Press, 2010.

Gilchrist, Cherry. *Alchemy—The Great Work: A History and Evaluation of the Western Hermetic Tradition.* San Francisco: Weiser Books, 2015.

Gildenhuys, J. S. H. *Ethics and Professionalism: The Battle against Public Corruption.* Stellenbosch, South Africa: Sun Press, 2004.

Giversen, Søren, Tage Petersen, and Jørgen Podemann Sørensen, eds. *The Nag Hammadi Texts in the History of Religions.* Copenhagen, Denmark: Det Kongelige Danske Videnskabernes Selskab, 2002.

Goldstein, Jeffrey H., ed. *Why We Watch: The Attractions of Violent Entertainment.* New York: Oxford University Press, 1998.

Granholm, Kennet. "Dragon Rouge: Left-Hand Path Magic with a Neopagan Flavour." *Aries* 12, no. 1 (Jan. 2012): 131–56. https://doi.org/10.1163/147783512x614858.

———. "Embracing Others than Satan: The Multiple Princes of Darkness in the Left-Hand Path Milieu." In *Contemporary Religious Satanism: A Critical Anthology*, edited by Jesper Aagaard Petersen, 97–114. London: Routledge, 2009.

Grant, Richard. "Do Trees Talk to Each Other?" *Smithsonian Magazine*, March 2018.

Greer, John Michael. *A World Full of Gods: An Inquiry into Polytheism.* Tucson, AZ: ADF Publishing, 2005.

Griffiths, Mark D. "Why Do We Like Watching Scary Films?" *Psychology Today*, October 29, 2015. https://www.psychologytoday.com/us/blog/in-excess/201510/why-do-we-watching-scary-films.

Guran, Paula, ed. *The Mammoth Book of Cthulhu.* London: Robinson, 2016.

H. H. the Dalai Lama, Tsong-ka-pa, and Jeffrey Hopkins. *Deity Yoga: In Action and Performance Tantra.* Ithaca, NY: Snow Lion Publications, 1987.

Hall, Manly P. *The Secret Teachings of All Ages.* New York: Penguin Random House, 2003.

Hanegraaff, Wouter J. *Western Esotericism: A Guide for the Perplexed*. London: Bloomsbury Publishing, 2013.

Harris, Mathew A., Caroline E. Brett, Wendy Johnson, and Ian J. Deary. "Personality Stability from Age 14 to Age 77 Years." *Psychology and Aging* 31, no. 8 (2016): 862–74. https://doi.apa.org/fulltext/2016-59192-004.html.

Harvey, Graham, and Charlotte Hardman, eds. *Paganism Today: Wiccans, Druids, the Goddess and Ancient Earth Traditions for the Twenty-First Century*. London: Thorsons, 1995.

Harvey, John. *The Story of Black*. London: Reaktion Books, 2015.

Hayashi, Makoto, and Matthias Hayek. "Editors' Introduction: Onmyōdō in Japanese History." *Japanese Journal of Religious Studies* 40, no. 1 (2013): 1–18. https://doi.org/10.18874/jjrs.40.1.2013.1-18.

Hayden, Ben Y. "Science Confirms Astrology!" *Psychology Today*, July 30, 2011. https://www.psychologytoday.com/us/blog/the-decision-tree/201107/science-confirms-astrology.

Heath, Eugene, and Byron Kaldis, eds. *Wealth, Commerce, and Philosophy: Foundational Thinkers and Business Ethics*. Chicago: University of Chicago Press, 2017.

Heaven, Ross, and Simon Buxton. *Darkness Visible: Awakening Spiritual Light through Darkness Meditation*. Rochester, VA: Destiny Books, 2005.

Herrick, Robert, and Alfred W. Pollard. *The Hesperides & Noble Numbers: Vol. 1 and 2*. Project Gutenberg, 2007. https://www.gutenberg.org/ebooks/22421.

Higginbotham, Joyce, and River Higginbotham. *Paganism: An Introduction to Earth-Centered Religions*. Woodbury, MN: Llewellyn Publications, 2013.

———. *Pagan Spirituality: A Guide to Personal Transformation*. Woodbury, MN: Llewellyn Publications, 2012.

Ho, David Y. F. "Selfhood and Identity in Confucianism, Taoism, Buddhism, and Hinduism: Contrasts with the West." *Journal for the Theory of Social Behaviour* 25, no. 2 (June 1995): 115–39. https://doi.org/10.1111/j.1468-5914.1995.tb00269.x.

Hollis, James. *Why Good People Do Bad Things: Understanding Our Darker Selves*. New York: Gotham Books, 2008.

Ikuta, Jennie C. *Contesting Conformity: Democracy and the Paradox of Political Belonging*. New York: Oxford University Press, 2020.

Illes, Judika. *Encyclopedia of Spirits: The Ultimate Guide to the Magic of Fairies, Genies, Demons, Ghosts, Gods, & Goddesses*. New York: HarperCollins, 2010.

Ilya, ed. *The Mammoth Book of Skulls: Exploring the Icon—from Fashion to Street Art*. Philadelphia: Running Press, 2014.

Inoue, Katsuya. *Psychology of Aging*. Tokyo: Chuo Hoki Shuppan, 2000.

Ivanhoe, Phillip J. *Confucian Moral Self Cultivation*. Indianapolis, IN: Hackett, 2000.

James, William. *The Essential Writings*. Edited by Bruce W. Wilshire. Albany, NY: State University of New York Press, 1984.

Jefferson, Thomas. *Notes on the State of Virginia*. London: John Stockdale, 1787.

Johnny Cash Trail. "Why Did Johnny Cash Always Wear Black? 25 Facts about America's Outlaw." *Johnny Cash Trail* (blog), November 6, 2017. https://folsomcasharttrail.com/blog/articles/postid/50/why-did-johnny-cash-always-wear-black-25-facts-about-americas-outlaw.

Jones, Scott R. *When the Stars Are Right: Towards an Authentic R'lyehian Spirituality*. Victoria, BC: Martian Migraine Press, 2014.

Joseph, Stephen. *Authentic: How to Be Yourself and Why It Matters*. London: Piatkus, 2016.

Joshi, Mary Sissons, and Wakefield Carter. "Unrealistic Optimism: East and West?" Frontiers in Psychology 4, no. 6 (February 2013). https://doi.org/10.3389/fpsyg.2013.00006.

Kaldera, Raven. *Dealing with Deities: Practical Polytheistic Theology*. Hubbardston, MA: Asphodel Press, 2012.

Kastor, Frank S. "The Satanic Pattern," *Satan*. Edited by Harold Bloom. Philadelphia: Chelsea House, 2005.

Kaufman, Scott Barry. *Transcend: The New Science of Self-Actualization*. New York: Penguin Random House, 2021.

Keenan, Barry C. *Neo-Confucian Self-Cultivation*. Honolulu: University of Hawai'i Press, 2011.

Kelly, Michael. *Apophis*. The Order of Apep: Self-published, Createspace, 2009.

Kenny, Brian. *Ahead of the Curve: Inside the Baseball Revolution*. New York: Simon and Schuster, 2017.

Kilpatrick, Nancy. *The Goth Bible: A Compendium for the Darkly Inclined*. New York: St. Martin's Griffin, 2004.

King, Stephen. *The Shining*. New York: Anchor Books, 2008.

Klimczak, Natalia. "The Forgotten Cleopatra: Searching for Cleopatra the Alchemist and Her Golden Secret." Ancient Origins. Updated February 21, 2017. https://www.ancient-origins.net/history-famous-people /forgotten-cleopatra-searching-cleopatra-alchemist-and-her-golden -secret-007585.

Knowles, Elizabeth, ed. "Duchess of Windsor." *Oxford Dictionary of Quotations*. Oxford: Oxford University Press, 2009.

Konstantinos. *Gothic Grimoire*. St. Paul, MN: Llewellyn Publications, 2002.

———. *Nocturnal Witchcraft: Magick After Dark*. St. Paul, MN: Llewellyn Publications, 2002.

———. *Nocturnicon: Calling Dark Forces and Powers*. Woodbury, MN: Llewellyn Publications, 2005.

Kovel, Joel. *The Enemy of Nature: The End of Capitalism or the End of the World?* London: Zed Books, 2002.

Kraemer, Christine Hoff. *Seeking the Mystery: An Introduction to Pagan Theologies*. Englewood, CO: Patheos Press, 2012.

Krech, Gregg. *Naikan: Gratitude, Grace, and the Japanese Art of Self-Reflection*. Berkeley, CA: Stone Bridge Press, 2010.

LaFave, Sandra. "Psychological Egoism and Ethical Egoism." Accessed June 1, 2022. https://lafavephilosophy.x10host.com/Egoism.html.

LaVey, Anton Szandor. *The Satanic Bible*. New York: Avon, 2010.

Le Guin, Ursula K. "A Left-Handed Commencement Address." Humanity. http://www.humanity.org/voices/commencements/ursula-leguin-mills-college-speech-1983.

Lehane, Brendan. *Wizards and Witches*. The Enchanted World. Alexandria, VA: Time-Life Books, 1984.

LeRoy, Thomas. "The Sect of the Horned God." The Sect of the Horned God. Accessed November 29, 2021. https://www.thesectofthehornedgod.com/?page_id=3359.

Le Texier, Thibault. "Debunking the Stanford Prison Experiment." *American Psychologist* 74, no. 7 (2019): 823–39. https://doi.org/10.1037/amp0000401.

Lévi, Éliphas. *Transcendental Magic: Its Doctrine and Ritual*. Eastford, CT: Martino Fine Books, 2011.

Logan, Dave. "In Praise of Ego." *CBS News*, May 31, 2012. https://www.cbsnews.com/news/in-praise-of-ego/.

Lokke, Harvard. "Nichomachean Ethics: Ignorance and Relationships." *Kierkegaard and the Greek World: Volume 2, Tome II: Aristotle and Other Greek Authors*. Edited by Jon Stewart and Katalin Nun. Farnham, England: Ashgate, 2010.

Lovecraft, H. P. *The Annotated H. P. Lovecraft*. Edited by S. T. Joshi. New York: Dell Publishing, 1997.

———. *Bloodcurdling Tales of Horror and the Macabre: The Best of H. P. Lovecraft*. New York: Del Rey, 2002.

———. *Supernatural Horror in Literature*. New York: Dover Publications, 2000.

Lucarelli, Rita. "Gods, Spirits, Demons of the Book of the Dead." In *Book of the Dead: Becoming God in Ancient Egypt*, edited by Foy Scalf, 127–36. Chicago: Oriental Institute of the University of Chicago, 2017.

MacLellan, Lila. "Accepting Your Darkest Emotions Is the Key to Psychological Health." Pocket, July 23, 2017. https://getpocket.com/explore/item/accepting-your-darkest-emotions-is-the-key-to-psychological-health.

Mann, Mary. *Science and Spirituality*. Bloomington, IN: AuthorHouse, 2004.

Maple, Eric. "The Witches of Canewdon." *Folklore* 71, no. 4 (December 1960): 241–50. https://doi.org/10.1080/0015587X.1960.9717250.

"Marie Laveau's Tomb," Atlas Obscura. Accessed May 30, 2022. https://www .atlasobscura.com/places/marie-laveaus-tomb.

Marsak, Leonard M, ed. *French Philosophers from Descartes to Sartre*. New York: World, 1961.

Mason, Asenath. *Draconian Ritual Book*. Self-published, Createspace, 2016.

———. *Grimoire of Tiamat*. Timmonsville, SC: Nephilim Press, 2014.

Masterson, Kathleen. "From Grunting to Gabbing: Why Humans Can Talk." *NPR*, August 11, 2010. https://www.npr.org/2010/08/11/129083762 /from-grunting-to-gabbing-why-humans-can-talk.

Mavromataki, Maria. *Greek Mythology and Religion*. Athens: Chaitali, Aik., and Sia O. E., 2005.

May, Todd. *A Decent Life: Morality for the Rest of Us*. Chicago: University of Chicago Press, 2019.

McAdams, Dan P. *The Stories We Live By: Personal Myths and the Making of the Self*. New York: Guilford Press, 1993.

McDermott, Ray, and Jean Lave. "Estranged Labor Learning." In *Critical Perspectives on Activity: Explorations Across Education, Work, and Everyday Life*, edited by Peter Sawchuk, Newton Duarte, and Mohamed Elham-moumi, 89–122. Cambridge, UK: Cambridge University Press, 2009. https://doi.org/10.1017/CBO9780511509568.007.

McKay, Brett, and Kate McKay. "Practical Wisdom: The Master Virtue." The Art of Manliness. Updated June 3, 2021. https://www.artofmanliness.com /articles/practical-wisdom.

Melton, J. Gordon, *Vampire Gallery: A Who's Who of the Undead*. Detroit, MI: Visible Ink Press, 1998.

"Michael Egnor, Cartesian Dualism, David Chalmers, and the Hard (Non) Problem." *NeuroLogica Blog*, June 9, 2008. https://theness.com

/neurologicablog/index.php/michael-egnor-cartesian-dualism
-david-chalmers-and-the-hard-nonproblem.

Miles, Leroyce. *Introduction to the Study of Religion*. London: Ed-Tech Press, 2018.

Miller, Jason. *The Elements of Spellcrafting: 21 Keys to Successful Sorcery*. Wayne, NJ: New Page Books, 2018.

———. *Financial Sorcery: Magical Strategies to Create Real and Lasting Wealth*. Pompton Plains, NJ: New Page Books, 2012.

———. *Protection & Reversal Magick: A Witch's Defense Manual*. Pompton Plains, NJ: New Page Nooks, 2006.

———. *The Sorcerer's Secrets: Strategies in Practical Magick*. Franklin Lakes, NJ: New Page Books, 2009.

———. "Strategic Sorcery and the Left Hand Path." *Jason Miller's Strategic Sorcery* (blog). Accessed November 29, 2021. https://www.strategicsorcery .net/strategic-sorcery-and-the-left-hand-path.

Miyamoto, Musashi. *The Book of Five Rings*. Translated by William Scott Wilson. Boston: Shambhala, 2012.

Moore, Edward. "Neo-Platonism." *Internet Encyclopedia of Philosophy*. Accessed November 29, 2021. https://www.iep.utm.edu/neoplato.

———. "Plotinus (204–270 CE)." *Internet Encyclopedia of Philosophy*. Accessed November 29, 2021. http://www.iep.utm.edu/plotinus/.

Mukherjee, Hillol, and Nilanjana Sanyal. "The Status of Subjective Well-Being, Role Stress, Coping, and Ego-Functions of the Tribal and Non-Tribal People of Tripura." *Indian Journal of Health and Wellbeing* 5, no. 8 (2014). http://www.i-scholar.in/index.php/ijhw/article/view/92188.

Myers, Brendan. *The Earth, the Gods, and the Soul: A History of Pagan Philosophy, from the Iron Age to the 21st Century*. Winchester, UK: Moon Books, 2013.

Naifeh, Steven, and Gregory White Smith. *Van Gogh: The Life*. New York: Penguin Random House, 2012.

Nocturnum, Corvis. *Embracing the Darkness: Understanding Dark Subcultures*. Fort Wayne, IN: Dark Moon Press, 2005.

Numbers, Ronald L., ed. *Galileo Goes to Jail and Other Myths about Science and Religion*. Cambridge, MA: Harvard University Press, 2010.

O'Keefe, Tim. "Epicurus (341–271 BCE)." *Internet Encyclopedia of Philosophy*. Accessed November 29, 2021. https://www.iep.utm.edu/epicur.

Okun, Rich. *The Sun, the Moon, the Stars, and Maya: A Collection of Little Sayings about Enormous Things*. Bloomington, IN: Balboa Press, 2013.

Orpheus, Rodney. *Abrahadabra: Understanding Aleister Crowley's Thelemic Magick*. Boston: Weiser Books, 2005.

Ouis, Djamel. *Humorous Wit*. Self-published, 2020.

Ovid. *Metamorphoses*. Translated by A. D. Melville. New York: Oxford University Press, 1998.

"Parsing the Pew Numbers—Paganism." *The Wild Hunt*. Last modified February 26, 2008. Accessed December 30, 2021. https://web.archive .org/web/20090605012555/http://wildhunt.org/blog/2008/02 /parsing-pew-numbers.html.

Patai, Raphael. *The Jewish Alchemists: A History and Source Book*. Princeton, NJ: Princeton University Press, 2014.

Peck, M. Scott. *The Road Less Traveled: A New Psychology of Love, Traditional Values, and Spiritual Growth*. New York: Simon and Shuster, 1978.

Penczak, Christopher. *Instant Magick: Ancient Wisdom, Modern Spellcraft*. Woodbury, MN: Llewellyn Publications, 2006.

Phillips-Nania, Erik. *Unity: The Art and Science of Transformational Change*. Self-published, 2015.

Piff, Paul K., Daniel M. Stancato, Stéphane Côté, Rodolfo Mendoza-Denton, and Dacher Keltner. "Higher Social Class Predicts Increased Unethical Behavior." *Proceedings of the National Academy of Science of the United States of America* 109, no. 11 (February 27, 2012): 4086–91. https://www .pnas.org/content/109/11/4086.abstract.

Pojman, Louis P., and Peter Tramel, eds. *Moral Philosophy: A Reader*. Indianapolis, IN: Hackett, 2009.

Pollack, Rachel. *Seventy-Eight Degrees of Wisdom: A Tarot Journey to Self-Awareness*. Newburyport, MA: Weiser Books, 1997.

Preece, Rob. *The Psychology of Buddhist Tantra*. Ithaca, NY: Snow Lion Publications, 2006.

Prower, Tomás. *La Santa Muerte: Unearthing the Magic & Mysticism of Death*. Woodbury, MN: Llewellyn Publications, 2015.

Puett, Michael, and Christine Gross-Loh. *The Path: What Chinese Philosophers Can Teach Us about the Good Life*. New York: Simon and Schuster, 2017.

Rachels, James. "A Critique of Ethical Egoism." In *Moral Philosophy: A Reader*, edited by Louis P. Pojman and Peter Tramel. Indianapolis, IN: Hackett, 2009.

Ramage, Craufurd Tait. *Great Thoughts from Classic Authors*. New York: John B. Alden, 1891.

Rankin, Aidan. *Shinto: A Celebration of Life*. Winchester, UK: John Hunt Publishing, 2011.

Renou, Louis, ed. *Hinduism*. New York: George Braziller, 1962.

Riddle, Joseph Esmond, Karl Ernst Georges, and Thomas Kerchever Arnold. *A Copious and Critical English-Latin Lexicon: Founded on the German-Latin Dictionary of Dr. Charles Ernest Georges*. New York: Harper, 1849.

"Road Safety Facts." Association for Safe International Road Travel. Accessed November 29, 2021. https://www.asirt.org/safe-travel/road-safety-facts.

Roman, John. "The Truth Behind 10 Popular Crime Myths." Urban Institute, November 1, 2013. https://www.urban.org/urban-wire /truth-behind-10-popular-crime-myths.

Romo, Vanessa. "Why Marigolds, or Cempasúchil, Are the Iconic Flower of Día de los Muertos." *NPR*, October 30, 2021. https://www.npr .org/2021/10/30/1050726374/why-marigolds-or-cempasuchil-are-the -iconic-flower-of-dia-de-los-muertos.

Rooney, Anne. *The Story of Philosophy*. London: Arcturus Publishing, 2014.

Russell, Bertrand. *The Basic Writings of Bertrand Russell.* Edited by Robert E. Egner and Lester E. Denonn. New York: Routledge, 2009.

———. "What Desires Are Politically Important?" The Nobel Prize, December 11, 1950. https://www.nobelprize.org/prizes/literature/1950/russell/lecture.

Ryff, C. D. "Happiness Is Everything, or Is It? Explorations on the Meaning of Psychological Well-Being." *Journal of Personality and Social Psychology* 57, no. 6 (1989): 1069–81. https://doi.org/10.1037/0022-3514.57.6.1069.

———. "Psychological Well-Being Revisited: Advances in the Science and Practice of Eudaimonia." *Psychotherapy and Psychosomatics* 83, no. 1 (2014): 10–28. https://doi.org/10.1159/000353263.

Sams, Aaron. *I WANT TO BE A.L.I.V.E. PART II: Becoming Emotionally A.L.I.V.E.* Self-published, 2010.

"Sandra LaFave Retired from West Valley College Philosophy Department." LaFave Philosophy. Accessed November 28, 2021. https://lafavephilosophy.x10host.com/sandybio.html.

Scully, Stephen. *Hesiod's Theogony: From Near Eastern Creation Myths to Paradise Lost.* Oxford: Oxford University Press, 2016.

Sebastiaan, Father. *Black Veils: Master Vampyre Edition 888.* Self-published, 2021.

———. *Vampyre Magick: The Grimoire of the Living Vampire.* San Francisco, CA: Weiser Books, 2012.

———. *Vampyre Sanguinomicon: The Lexicon of the Living Vampire.* San Francisco, CA: Weiser Books, 2010.

Seneca. *Dialogues and Essays.* Translated by John Davie. New York: Oxford University Press, 2008.

Shantideva. *The Way of the Bodhisattva.* Translated by Padmakara Translation Group. Boston: Shambhala Publications, 2006.

Sharpe, Matthew. *Camus, Philosophe: To Return to Our Beginnings.* Leiden, Netherlands: Brill, 2015.

Shaw, Gregory. *Theurgy and the Soul: The Neoplatonism of Iamblichus.* Kettering, OH: Angelico Press/Sophia Perennis, 2014.

Sire, James W. *The Universe Next Door: A Basic Worldview Catalog.* Downers Grove, IL: InterVarsity Press, 1997.

Smith, Huston. *The World's Religions.* New York: HarperCollins, 2009.

Smith, Morton. *Jesus the Magician.* Newburyport, MA: Hampton Roads Press, 2014.

Stalter, Lisle A. "Becoming More Aware: A Few Tips on Keeping You and Your Family Safe." The Public Servant: Illinois State Bar Association, June 2013. https://www.isba.org/committees/governmentlawyers/newsletter/2013/06 /becomingmoreawareafewtipsonkeepingy.

Starhawk. *The Spiral Dance: A Rebirth of the Ancient Religion of the Goddess.* New York: HarperCollins, 2011.

Steiner, Rudolf. *True Knowledge of the Christ: Theosophy and Rosicrucianism.* Forest Row, UK: SteinerBooks, 2015.

Stephens, R. Todd. *Trademark 2.0: Defining Your Value in a Web 2.0 World.* Morris, NC: Lulu Publishers, 2007.

Strom, Dane. "Día de los Angelitos: Remembering Children on the Day of the Dead." Updated November 2, 2019. https://danestrom.com /dia-de-los-angelitos-remembering-children-day-dead/.

Sweeney, Jacqueline. *Incredible Quotations: 230 Thought-Provoking Quotes with Prompts to Spark Students' Writing, Thinking, and Discussion.* New York: Scholastic, 1997.

Thorne, Russ. *Vampires.* Gothic Dreams. London: Flame Tree Publishing, 2013.

Tipton, Harold F., and Micki Krause Nozaki, eds. *Information Security Management Handbook.* 6th ed. Boca Raton, FL: Auerbach Publications, 2012.

Tompkins, Ptolemy. *The Modern Book of the Dead: A Revolutionary Perspective on Death, the Soul, and What Really Happens in the Life to Come.* New York: Simon and Schuster, 2013.

Tzu, Lao. *Tao Te Ching: A Book about the Way and the Power of the Way.* Edited by Ursula K. Le Guin. Boulder, CO: Shambhala, 2019.

United Nations Office on Drugs and Crime. *Global Study on Homicide 2013: Trends, Contexts, Data.* New York: United Nations, 2014.

University of Washington. "Healthy vs. Unhealthy Relationships." Husky Health & Well-Being. Accessed November 29, 2021. https://wellbeing .uw.edu/resources/healthy-vs-unhealthy-relationships/.

Ustinova, Yulia. *Divine Mania: Alteration of Consciousness in Ancient Greece.* London: Routledge, 2017.

Waldrop, Mitchell M. *Complexity: The Emerging Science at the Edge of Order and Chaos.* New York: Simon and Schuster, 1993.

Webb, Don. *Energy Magick of the Vampyre: Secret Techniques for Personal Power and Manifestation.* Rochester, VA: Inner Traditions, 2021.

———. *Uncle Setnakt's Essential Guide to the Left Hand Path.* Bastrop, TX: Lodestar, 1999.

Weber, Courtney. "The Nightmare Before Christmas and Lessons on Cultural Appropriation." *Double, Toil and Resist* (blog). *Patheos,* October 16, 2019. https://www.patheos.com/blogs/doubletoilandresist/2019/10 /nightmare-before-christmas-cultural-appropriation/.

Weinstein, David. "Herbert Spencer." *Stanford Encyclopedia of Philosophy.* Updated August 27, 2019. https://plato.stanford.edu/archives/fall2019 /entries/spencer.

Wendell, Leilah. *Necromance: Intimate Portrayals of Death.* New Orleans: Westgate Press, 2003.

West, Michael William. *Sex Magicians: The Lives and Spiritual Practices of Paschal Beverly Randolph, Aleister Crowley, Jack Parsons, Marjorie Cameron, Anton Lavey, and Others.* Rochester, VA: Destiny Books, 2021.

White, Gordon. *The Chaos Protocols: Magical Techniques for Navigating the New Economic Reality.* Woodbury, MN: Llewellyn Worldwide, 2016.

Wildberg, Christian. "Neoplatonism." *Stanford Encyclopedia of Philosophy*, January 11, 2016. https://plato.stanford.edu/archives/spr2016/entries/neoplatonism.

Williams, Pat, Belinda Johnson-White, Suzie Debusk, Greg Kozera, Brian Johnson, Stan Levanduski, Susan West, et al. *The Advantage of Leadership*. Charleston, SC: Advantage Media Group, 2008.

Wolfe, Amber. *Personal Alchemy: A Handbook of Healing & Self-Transformation*. St. Paul, MN: Llewellyn Publications, 1995.

Wong, Eva. *Taoism: An Essential Guide*. Boston: Shambhala Publications, 2011.

Yamakage, Motohisa. *The Essence of Shinto: Japan's Spiritual Heart*. Translated by Mineko S. Gillespie, Gerald L. Gillespie, and Yoshitsugu Komuro. Tokyo: Kodansha International, 2010.

Yamamoto, Yukitaka. *Kami No Michi: The Way of the Kami: The Life and Thought of a Shinto Priest*. Granite Falls, WA: Tsubaki America Publications, 1987.

Yong, Ed. "A New Theory Linking Sleep and Creativity." *Atlantic*, May 15, 2018. https://www.theatlantic.com/science/archive/2018/05/sleep-creativity-theory/560399/.

York, Michael. *Pagan Theology: Paganism as a World Religion*. New York: New York University Press, 2005.

Zeitz, Joshua. *Flapper: A Madcap Story of Sex, Style, Celebrity, and the Women Who Made American Modern*. New York: Three Rivers Press, 2009.

Zell-Ravenheart, Oberon. *Grimoire for the Apprentice Wizard*. Franklin Lakes, NJ: New Page Books, 2004.

To Write to the Author

If you wish to contact the author or would like more information about this book, please write to the author in care of Llewellyn Worldwide Ltd. and we will forward your request. Both the author and publisher appreciate hearing from you and learning of your enjoyment of this book and how it has helped you. Llewellyn Worldwide Ltd. cannot guarantee that every letter written to the author can be answered, but all will be forwarded. Please write to:

Frater Tenebris
℅ Llewellyn Worldwide
2143 Wooddale Drive
Woodbury, MN 55125-2989

Please enclose a self-addressed stamped envelope for reply,
or $1.00 to cover costs. If outside the U.S.A., enclose
an international postal reply coupon.

Many of Llewellyn's authors have websites with additional information and resources. For more information, please visit our website at http://www.llewellyn.com.